GANGS

An Individual and Group Perspective

Kimberly Tobin, Ph.D.

Westfield State College

Upper Saddle River, New Jersey 07458

Library of Congress Cataloging-in-Publication Data

Tobin, Kimberly.
  Gangs : an individual and group perspective / Kimberly Tobin.
    p. cm.
  Includes bibliographical references and index.
  ISBN 0-13-172404-5
  1. Gangs—United States.   2. Gang members—United States.   I. Title.

  HV6439.U5T63 2008
  364.106'60973—dc22

                             2006100843

Editor-in-Chief: Vernon R. Anthony
Senior Acquisitions Editor: Tim Peyton
Associate Editor: Sarah Holle
Marketing Manager: Adam Kloza
Production Editor: Michael Shally-Jensen, Stratford / TexTech
Production Liaison: Barbara Marttine Cappuccio
Managing Editor: Mary Carnis
Manufacturing Manager: Ilene Sanford
Manufacturing Buyer: Cathleen Petersen
Senior Design Coordinator: Miguel Ortiz
Cover Design: Rob Aleman
Cover Image: Pictor Uniphoto, ImageState/International Stock Photography Ltd.
Composition: TexTech
Printer/Binder: R.R. Donnelley & Sons

10 9 8 7 6 5 4 3 2 1
ISBN 13: 978-0-13-172404-4
ISBN 10:   0-13-172404-5

*This book is dedicated to those youth who
mistakenly believe that gangs are their answer.*

Contents

Preface

This book has been written to introduce students to the topic of gangs. This knowledge is a critical component to courses that deal with gangs directly or indirectly, including juvenile delinquency, criminology, and social problems.

This book is written with a primary emphasis on the distinction between gangs and gang members, and it highlights the differences between the individual perspective and the group perspective. This focus aids in understanding and having an impact on the gang problem. By delineating individual members from the gang itself, we can gain a richer understanding of the gang phenomenon. This perspective can provide a true appreciation of gang variation.

This book is meant to introduce the reader to gang literature and summarize its key ideas and concepts. This summary will be enhanced by "A Closer Look" boxes to give the reader deeper insight into an issue discussed in the chapter. The reader will also be introduced to notable researchers in the field through "Focus on Research" boxes. Other ancillary items include chapter objectives, key terms, review questions, and discussion questions.

Chapter 1 will introduce the reader to foundation information about gangs. This chapter will present the time line of gangs within the United States from the 1800s to the current day. The chapter will explore the magnitude of the present-day gang problem and introduce the demographic characteristics of gangs. Chapter 2 will continue to provide the foundation of our modern gang understanding. Within this chapter, definitional issues that arise when discussing gangs and various definitions of gangs, gang membership, and gang crime will be explored.

Chapter 3 focuses on the reasons for gang formation. This group-level discussion will explain characteristics that are common in areas with gangs. These characteristics will be presented within a theoretical framework, including social disorganization, strain, and underclass theories. In contrast, Chapter 4 explores the individual perspective of gang joining. This chapter will focus on individual risk factors for joining a gang within a theoretical framework. Theoretical context will be provided, including social bonding, learning, and gang-specific theories.

As the differences between gangs and gang members are differentiated in Chapters 3 and 4, this same theme will carry forward in Chapters 5 and 6. The focus of Chapter 5 is the structure and dynamics of the gang as a group. This chapter will also explore different stages of gang development. The primary emphasis in Chapter 6 is on the experiences of gang members. This chapter will explore the levels of gang membership and the impact that gang joining has on the individual. A discussion of graffiti, tattooing, and gang signs will be discussed in this chapter within the context of group solidarity. With the groundwork established for gang members and gangs, the activities of gangs and their members will be explored in Chapter 7. The primary emphasis will be the criminal behavior of gangs and gang members. The relationship between gangs, drugs, guns, and behavior will also be explored.

The richness of gangs can be appreciated only after exploring diversity issues. Chapter 8 introduces the student to our understanding of race and ethnicity in gangs. This discussion includes greater insight into Hispanic, black, Asian, and American Indian gang experiences. Chapter 9 continues the development of diversity issues in a discussion of female gang members and their roles in gangs. Specific gender-based issues of gang dynamics will be explored. Chapter 10 brings insight into the prison gang–street gang connection for a more thorough comprehension of the gang phenomenon.

The knowledge base that is provided throughout the book is put to use in Chapter 11. This chapter introduces readers to issues related to prevention, intervention, and legal system responses to gangs. This discussion continues to emphasize the distinction between group and individual perspectives. The concluding chapter, Chapter 12, will anticipate the future of gangs based on the knowledge foundation provided in the book. It will also include a brief discussion of the potential political-social activist role of gangs.

Overall, this book is meant to provide students with academic, yet understandable, information on youth gangs. The distinction between the gang member and the gang gives students a greater understanding of the phenomenon.

Acknowledgments

This project actually began more than 10 years ago, while I was a graduate student at SUNY Albany and working as a research assistant for the Rochester Youth Development Study. This experience had such an impact on my professional career. I wish to thank Terry, Marv, Alan, Carolyn, and Pam for this life-altering opportunity.

This professional experience coincided with the birth of my daughter, Kailey. For the past decade, she has been my inspiration, and she has grounded me in an unforeseeable way. The world through Kailey's eyes is a different place. I know that this project was difficult on her at times, but her questions and my answers have enriched us both.

I wish to thank all of my family and dear friends for their constant love and support. Special thanks to John, my companion and best friend, who has taught me the value of slowing down and finding balance. He tempers my workaholic tendencies, and his presence makes my life complete. Thank you to my parents for helping me grow into the person I was meant to be and to my brothers, Phil and Detective Jay, for always challenging my perspective. Also, I need to express my gratitude to all of my dear friends. Your distractions were most welcome.

This writing project would not have been possible without the encouragement from Ed Weisman, Frank Mortimer, and Sarah Holle; thank you for believing in my ability. I greatly appreciate those who read through rough drafts of my work and to my reviewers—David Graff of Kent State University, Tuscarawas; Gwen Hunnicutt of University of North Carolina, Greensboro; and John Anderson of California State University, Fullerton—for their valuable feedback.

CHAPTER 1

INTRODUCTION

CHAPTER OBJECTIVES

- Become aware of the history of street gangs in the United States.
- Recognize the common theme among the four gang eras.
- Understand the scope of the present-day street gang phenomenon.

THE PROBLEM

> Society has always had a love/hate reaction to the ghetto. Getting rid of the ghetto and economic inequality is never going to happen in this particular society. . . . We'll always have people who haven't gotten their foot up. Back in the day, it was Irish people and Jewish people. Now the Black and Mexicans fill the ghettos. (Ice T, 2005, p. xviii)

The word *gang* in and of itself is not a negative term. It has been used in the past to describe groups of youngsters, including Charlie Brown and his Peanuts pals and Fat Albert and his friends. However, as you begin to read this book, you already know that this is not the topic that will be discussed. Take a moment and think about what *gang* means to you. If someone says, "There are gangs in this area," what vision comes to mind? In the past 20 or so years, the term *gang* has been re-created for the general public. This re-creation is the result of attention from politicians, the criminal justice system, and the media. The more recent picture that has been painted is a group of young gun-toting minority males who wear colors, sell drugs, randomly kill, and create massive problems for their communities. Others envision neo-Nazi skinheads with shaven heads and steel-tipped boots who listen to Oi! and ska music.

This modern image of street gangs as painted for the American public is sometimes accurate, but most of the time it is not. There are many different kinds of gangs and many different types of gang members. However, most people identify gangs and their members with an exaggerated, sensationalized image. Spergel (1995, p. vii) states, "Media reporting has also not adequately reflected the character of the problem." McCorkle and Meithe (2002), in their study of the social construction of street gangs, more obviously explain, "There seems little question that gang members have been portrayed as modern day 'folk devils' in order to sell papers, attract viewers, increase police payrolls, secure federal funds, and win elections" (p. 217). Not only is the portrayal of gangs and membership inaccurate but also it generates fear of and bias toward gangs in American society (Dukes and Valentine, 1998; Jankowski, 1991; Katz, Webb, and Armstrong, 2003; Lane and Meeker, 2000, 2004; Moore, 1991).

There are gangs that are creating problems in their communities, and there are gang members who are involved in extensive criminal behavior. However, they are by no means all gangs or all gang members. As Thrasher (1963/1927) states, "No two gangs are just alike" (p. 36). There is variation in the gang world that is not presented in the movies, on TV, or in the newspaper. Most research shows diversity and variation among gangs (Cloward and Ohlin, 1960; Decker, Bynum, and Weisel, 1998; Klein, 1995; Knox, 1994; Moore, 1991; Short and Strodtbeck, 1965; Thrasher, 1927/1963). There are gangs that are minimally organized and do not engage in organized criminal behavior (Decker and Van Winkle, 1996; Fagan, 1989; Hagedorn, 1988; Thrasher, 1963/1927), and there are other gangs that are involved in more organized criminal behavior (Jankowski, 1991; Padilla, 1992; Sullivan, 1989; Taylor, 1990). There are also members who are only minimally involved in gang life and others who are hard-core members (Curtis, 2003; Klein, 1995; Spergel, 1995). Therefore, the knowledge of street gangs presented to the general public is not completely accurate. At the same time, it is important to state that some gang members in most gangs will engage in serious violent behavior. This is the reason we are concerned.

Klein (1995) states, "Where we continue to fall down is in educating the interested lay public in these matters. Here we err in leaving it to the media, and what a mistake it has turned out to be" (p. 55). This book educates the "interested lay public" with accurate and detailed information regarding gangs in America. Many gang-related concepts that are introduced throughout the book are consistently reinforced. At times, concepts are briefly introduced and then explained in more detail in subsequent chapters. After reading this book, you should have an understanding of research, theory, and policy related to gangs, and you should have a greater appreciation of the phenomena in the United States.

HISTORY AND PRESENT DAY

To understand the present-day street gang, we need to explore the historical roots of gangs in American history. Academics, practitioners, and media alike have been intrigued with gangs throughout history, dating back to more than a century ago. Their work allows us to understand the similarities and differences in gangs over time. These changes help us identify common causes of gangs and appreciate the new challenges that face us with changing gang structure. There are four distinct periods of time when attention was given to gang growth and activity (Decker and Van Winkle, 1996). These periods—the late 1800s, the 1920s, the 1960s, and the late 1980s and beyond—coincide with "rapid changes in the composition of city populations and economies" (Decker and Van Winkle, p. 2). The rapid changes took place as a result of immigration, urbanization, ethnicity, and poverty.

The First Era

The late 1800s was a time of mass immigration and urbanization in the United States. These factors coincided with gang development. Early gangs were most prominent in urban centers with rapid population growth and a relatively unstable social climate. Gangs in the United States, during this period, trace to immigrant groups of European descent, primarily Irish and German. Between 1881 and 1890, immigrants from Germany doubled to 1.45 million from the decade prior; Irish immigration was consistently high throughout the mid- to late 1800s, ranging from a decade high of 914,119 between 1851 and 1860, to 655,482 between 1881 and 1890 (U.S. Dept. of Homeland Security, n.d.b.). Gangs at this time were documented in New York, Boston, Chicago, St. Louis, Philadelphia, and Pittsburgh (Curry and Decker, 2003, p. 14). Limited academic attention was given to gangs during this period, but there was a journalistic focus on these groups (Decker and Van Winkle, 1996, p. 3). Herbert Asbury's (1928) *The Gangs of New York*, although written several decades later, historically documents gangs of this era. In 2002, his work was turned into a movie that was a box office hit. Urban centers, such as New York City, became havens for newly arriving immigrants in pursuit of a new life. However, immigrants faced difficulty in obtaining work because of discrimination from native-born Americans and had an overall tough time fitting into conventional society. The result was poverty, crime, the formation of gangs, and a host of other social problems. The activities of gangs were primarily fighting and thievery (Asbury, 1928).

As cities developed in the early 1900s, new immigrant groups continued to arrive in the United States. Overall U.S. legal immigration rates reached their highest ever between 1901 and 1910, with about 8.8 million immigrants entering into the country. Italian immigration began to rapidly increase in the late 1800s[1] and was more than 2 million between 1901 and 1910. This number was surpassed by immigrants from Austria-Hungary,[2] who totaled 2.1 million in the same decade. Newer groups of immigrants were perceived as a threat and were discriminated against because of their differences. Urbanization, population growth, and political influence opened up doors for unskilled labor and government-based employment, such as police officers and firefighters (see Abadinsky, 2003). As a result, immigrants were able to find jobs, assimilate, and become part of mainstream culture. Although organized crime is not the focus of this book, at this point in history there is a definitive split in the criminal world that is worthy of discussion. With employment opportunities flourishing, many immigrants were able to transition into conventional lifestyles. However, new and old immigrants who were more criminally inclined transitioned their way into the emerging world of organized crime (see Abadinsky, 2003).

BOX 1–1: A Closer Look

Herbert Asbury's (1928) *The Gangs of New York* presents a historical account of gangs in the Five Points District of New York City in the nineteenth century. His work "makes no pretense of offering solutions for the social, economic, or criminological problems presented by the gangs" (p. xiii). Asbury's statements have an interesting ring of familiarity that should be considered. He clearly identifies the pockets of poor immigrants in Five Points and specifies the intersections of the social world, poverty, and crime that resulted. Other detailed accounts of the dilapidation and squalor of Five Points are given by Charles Dickens in *American Notes* and more recently by Anbinder (2002) in *Five Points*. Asbury's gangs were violent, feuding groups who were aligned along ethnic lines, similar to today's gangs. However, Asbury states that gangs in the nineteenth century were protected by the corrupt political machine of the time, which is different than the situation today. Asbury also states that, by the time of his writing, "there are no gangs in New York, and no gangsters in the sense that the word has come into common use" (p. xiii). This is a theme that is also present throughout history. Despite denial of gang problems, gangs have never completely disappeared. What has changed is the common use of the word *gang*. This will be discussed in the next chapter. Consider for a moment how we might learn from Asbury's work. What would our society be like today if we recognized that gang history repeats itself like a broken record?

The Second Era

The focus on gangs subsided until the second gang era of the 1920s. It was the work of Frederic Thrasher (1927/1963) that drew the academic world's first notable attention to gangs. His study of 1,313 gangs in Chicago made its mark in gang research history and is considered a classic in the field. Thrasher's study presents the role of immigrants in gangs; 87.4% of his gangs were of "foreign extraction" (p. 132). The primary immigrant populations represented in Thrasher's gangs were Polish, Irish, and Italian. He discusses immigration within the context of community change, population mobility, economics, poverty, and disorganization. Thrasher's significant contribution to our knowledge of gangs will be discussed throughout the book. This early era also included Whyte's (1943/1981) *Street Corner Society*, which detailed the nonviolent gambling activities of a group of boys in Depression-era Boston.

There was a lull in academic gang interest through the next generation that was due in part to the war that preoccupied the American public. In 1924, Congress passed the Johnson-Reed Act, also known as the National Origins Act, in an attempt to restrict immigration from Southern and Eastern Europe. This act limited the number of immigrants who could come to the United States to 2% of the number of residents from that country who were living in the United States in 1890. However, this act did

---

BOX 1–2: Focus on Research

Frederic M. Thrasher's (1927/1963) groundbreaking work documents seven years of research with 1,313 gangs and "a conservative estimate of 25,000 members" in Chicago (p. 5). Thrasher's research methodology is weakly discussed but is "a wide variety of data collection techniques . . . including utilization of census and court records, personal observation, and personal documents collected from gang boys and from persons who had observed gangs in many contexts" (p. xviii). Despite this limitation, Thrasher presents a rich snapshot of gangs during the 1920s in Chicago. A link that can be made to the content of this chapter is his description of "Gangland" and its "three great domains." It is in this description that Thrasher introduces the influence of immigration and ethnicity in gang life. He describes "The North Side Jungle," with "a community of southern Italians." This area has been "invaded" by many "negro families." The North Side Jungle is also home to Polish gangs. In fact, "the majority of gangs in Chicago are of Polish stock" (p. 9). Polish, Italian, and Negro gangs are also found in "The Westside Wilderness." Other nationalities represented include Irish, Jewish, and Lithuanian gangs. The same ethnic patterns of gang activity are found in "The South Side Badlands" (p. 13). Thrasher's gangs were involved in deviant behavior: "Our gang used to go robbing stores almost every day" (p. 77). Gangs involved themselves in warfare: "[I]f one boy crosses into enemy territory he does it at some peril. Armed invasions are not infrequent" (p. 117).

---

not apply to immigrants from the Western Hemisphere (U.S. Dept. of Homeland Security, August 15, 2006). This led to an all-time immigration low between 1931 and 1940, when only 528,431 immigrants came into the United States (U.S. Dept. of Homeland Security, n.d.b.). This period of reduced immigration coincided with a lull in gang attention.

Despite this lack of academic and public interest in gangs, several notable changes occurred that lay the foundation for modern street gangs. With immigration from Latino countries, this group became the new outgroup—the group that faced discrimination and difficulty in transitioning into mainstream culture. The Sleepy Lagoon murder and the Zoot Suit Riots in Los Angeles in the early 1940s exemplify the rift between the Latino community and mainstream society. The origins of modern street gangs are rooted in this period and will be discussed in greater detail in Chapter 8. The emergence and activity of Latino gangs lead into the next era of gangs.

The Third Era

The third era of gangs, in the 1950s and 1960s, brought heightened media and increased public interest. *West Side Story*, a movie released in 1961 and based on a 1957 Broadway musical, portrayed a romanticized version of gangs in Latino communities.

This era brought more gang intervention policies and a proliferation of gang research (see Bloch and Niederhoffer, 1958; Cloward and Ohlin, 1960; Cohen, 1955; Miller, 1958; Short and Strodtbeck, 1965; Yablonsky, 1962). This surge was due to a mid-century gang explosion in large urban centers, including Los Angeles, Chicago, and New York. The gangs of this period differed from the earlier generations of gangs, as their ethnic origin was primarily Latino and black. The Civil Rights Movement was in full swing, and minority populations were migrating from the South to the urban centers in the North. "Between 1940 and 1970 continued migration transformed the country's African-American population from a predominately southern, rural group to a northern, urban one" (Library of Congress, 2005). There was also immigration from Mexico, the Caribbean, and South America during this time. Immigration from Mexico steadily increased from 60,589 in the 1940s, to almost 300,000 in the 1950s, to more than 450,000 in the 1960s. Similar trends are seen with Caribbean, Central American, and South American immigration.[3] Despite the ethnic difference, the current immigrant and migrant populations experienced similar issues of prejudice, discrimination, and poverty. However, the social dynamic of the current group of minority youth differed from generations past. These issues were confounded and accentuated by the heightened interaction with mainstream culture as a result of desegregation in *Brown v. Board of Education* (1954).

The gangs of the 1950s and 60s were seen as more violent than generations past (Yablonsky, 1962). The difference in the gang dynamics is best illustrated in an example given by Yablonsky (p. 6). He describes a violent encounter of one of his gang members and one of Whyte's (1943/1981) gang members. The primary differences in the two encounters are regret and use of weapons. The earlier gang member felt regret for beating up a rival, but Yablonsky's gang member stabbed a rival and felt little regret. Yablonsky states, "The element of friendship and camaraderie" of the past "is almost entirely absent from the violent gang of today" (p. 7). Research during this time was focused on data specific to those large cities that were experiencing a gang problem (Klein, 1995). Much attention was given to the cultural experiences and economic difficulties of minority youth.

Very little public and media attention was paid toward gangs in the 1970s, perhaps because of a focus on the Vietnam War and continued social change. While media and political attention toward gangs waned, the gangs of the prior era did not disappear as they had in generations past, as evidenced by sporadic academic research in the 1970s (Klein, 1971; Moore, 1978). However, during this lull the urban landscape was rapidly changing, and this change is especially important to understanding gangs today. Public assistance programs, put in place after World War II, were the breeding ground for a generation of segregated youth, more isolated from mainstream society than any groups in the past. An example is large-scale high-rise public housing, which clustered urban poor and young minorities. Interestingly, the future of this housing plan has been recently reexamined and is evident in the destruction of high-rise housing projects across the country, including Chicago's largest housing project, the Robert Taylor Homes (see Venkatesh, 2002).[4] These youth were made more acutely aware of their plight through forced busing, which reduced racially segregated schools. This also led to the presence of gangs in areas that were previously immune. In addition to the impact of prior public policy decisions, the urban poor were also affected by changes yet to come. Changes that began in the 1970s that ushered in the next era of gangs included computerization, deindustrialization, and the movement toward a global economy.

The Current Era

The final era of gang attention began in the 1980s and continues through today. The change that was documented by Yablonsky in the 1960s is similarly echoed in this new era of gangs. Moore (1991) compares Chicano gangs of the prior era with those that emerged in the 1970s and 1980s. She details more lethal violence in modern-day gangs, with the increased use of guns and the initiation of drive-by shootings. Moore states, "Older gang members were also disturbed by the impersonality with which guns were used," "aggression among 'noncombatants,'" and "the virtual disappearance of 'fair fights'" (pp. 59–60). Another difference between present-day gangs and gangs of past periods is the connectedness to a prior generation. Stable gangs, which are present at this time, have their roots in the mid-century movement. These gangs are found in **chronic gang cities**, such as Chicago and Los Angeles (Maxson, 1998). Gangs in chronic gang cities became an institution, and they engaged in serious and violent crime. They had difficulty in transitioning out of the criminal environment and integrating into mainstream America. During this era, gangs also emerged in smaller cities and suburban areas throughout the United States (Klein, 1995, p. 32).

Present-day gangs represent a continued struggle in chronic gang cities, while **emerging gang cities** have developed from the economic plight that is the result of deindustrialization. In addition, immigrant groups continue to come to the United States. Rapid increases continue to be documented in immigrants from Mexico, Central and South America, and the Caribbean. There is also increasing immigration from the former Soviet Union and Asian countries (U.S. Homeland Security, 2005).[5] Thus, the new struggles of the modern-day gangs are compounded by the same processes of immigration that have faced groups coming into the United States since the 1800s.

Our reaction to gangs changed dramatically in the 1980s and beyond. Gang units were created throughout the legal system, including law enforcement, prosecution, and corrections. The media began to pay more attention to the gang phenomenon. Since the 1980s, people have had more exposure to more news, more of the time, because of technological changes and widespread access to PCs, the Internet, cell phones, and cable television (Fang and Ross, 1996). Copycatting and brainstorming, as a result of increased exposure to media, has brought gangs from Los Angeles and Chicago to all areas of the country. This idea is reinforced in Decker and Van Winkle's (1996) study of St. Louis gangs, whose members identify the movie *Colors* as their origination point (p. 88).

To state the obvious, academic gang research has been prolific during this latest gang era. Field research has continued (see Moore, 1991; Vigil, 1988; Sullivan, 1989; Taylor, 1990; Jankowski, 1991; Hagedorn, 1988). Research continues in chronic gang cities and is now conducted in emerging gang cities (see Thornberry et al., 2003; Hill,

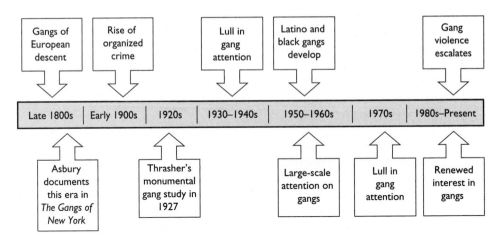

Figure 1–1   Gang Presence throughout History (time line).

Howell, Hawkins, and Battin-Pearson, 1999). The academic world has also seen the application of more elaborate data-gathering techniques that enhance our understanding of gang phenomena. Longitudinal research allows us to examine gang behavior over time (Hill, Howell, Hawkins, and Battin-Pearson, 1999; National Youth Gang Center, 2000; Thornberry et al., 2003), and cross-city comparisons have been conducted (Battin-Pearson, Thornberry, Hawkins, and Krohn, 1998; Decker, Bynum, and Weisel, 1998; Esbensen, Winfree, He, and Taylor, 2001; Jankowski, 1991; Huff, 1998). This later gang era also brought attention to female gangs and gang members (see Chesney-Lind and Hagedorn, 1999).

The themes of immigration, ethnicity, poverty, and changing urban centers are apparent throughout gang history. The stability in social conditions is essential to understanding gangs today. At the same time, the gang world is evolving. There are changes in the economic structure that present unique challenges for today's gangs. Some gangs have more elaborate organization structures because of their longevity, and areas that were immune to gangs have now seen their emergence. Gangs are also no longer the exclusive problem of the urban poor.

THE SCOPE OF TODAY'S PROBLEM

Official Data

Official data are regularly gathered from criminal justice agencies, including law enforcement and corrections. The highlights from the most recent **National Youth Gang Survey (NYGS)** state that there are "approximately 731,500 gang members and

21,500 gangs active in the United States in 2002" (Egley and Major, 2004, p. 2). This is a 14% decrease in the number of gang members and a 32% decrease in the number of gangs since the survey began in 1996. The average number of gangs per jurisdiction is 14, and the average number of gang members is 559 (National Youth Gang Center, 2000, p. 14).

The NYGS is one of the few sources we have to track trends in gangs, gang membership, and gang crime. This information is collected through an annual survey of law enforcement agencies across the country (see National Youth Gang Center, 2000, for methodology). However, as with any other official data source, there may be issues of validity. Definitional inconsistencies often lead to variation in the reporting of youth gangs (Hughes and Short, 2005). This issue will be discussed further in the next chapter. Official data are also sensitive to the bias of political agendas and funding requests, leading to underreporting and overreporting of gang behavior. Numbers represented in official data can be distorted under certain circumstances. For example, in the 1980s and 1990s, government monies to combat gangs were given to agencies with documented gang problems. An agency that is able to show a "gang problem" may receive monies. Adolescent groups hanging out can easily be identified as a gang in official data. There is also the situation of underreporting in gang areas that do not want to publicly acknowledge that they have a gang problem (Huff, 1990).

Official data are also used in W. Miller's (2001) study of trends in gang proliferation from 1970 to 1995. Miller's results paint a very different picture from that of the NYGS. He finds that the number of cities reporting gang membership in the 1990s increased about 640% over the 1970s (p. 15). Most of this change was experienced in South Atlantic, Southern, and Midwestern cities (p. 17). There were also cities that reported a gang problem in the 1970s that no longer report a problem. Four of these cities are in California, three in Massachusetts, four in Pennsylvania, and one each in Illinois and South Carolina (p. 18).

Self-Report Data

Other information we have about gangs, its members, and gang crime comes from **self-report studies**. These studies rely on information reported by gang members. Self-report information of gang membership is considered valid (see Thornberry et al., 2003, pp. 22–23 for a discussion). However, self-report data are also sensitive to definitional differences and varying sampling frames (Hughes and Short, 2005). This leads to variation in the reporting of gang membership across different cities. Research based in Seattle finds that 15% of the sample report gang membership before the age of 18 (Hill, Howell, Hawkins, and Battin-Pearson, 1999). This compares with 30.9% of the sample from Rochester, New York (Thornberry et al., 2003). These percentages are city specific, but other research examines gang membership in wider geographical areas. Esbensen, Winfree, He, and Taylor's (2001) sample includes about 6,000 eighth-grade students from 11 cities throughout the United States, who were sampled in 1995. Approximately 17% of their sample report ever belonging to a gang.

Geographic Area

Research shows that "gangs, gang members, and gang-related homicides are predominantly concentrated in larger cities" (Egley, 2005, p. 2). At the same time, small cities reported greater changes in their gangs from 1970 to 1995 (W. Miller, 2001, p. 39). California and Illinois represent the top two gang-city states. This is not surprising, given they are chronic gang areas. Other notable states include Texas, Florida, and New Jersey (W. Miller, 2001). The largest increases in gang cities were reported by Florida and Washington between 1970 and 1995 (W. Miller, 2001). One view of gang proliferation is that gangs are expanding their business into other cities, like a corporation. Contrary to popular belief, the increased presence of gangs throughout the United States is not due to gang migration (Maxson, 1998). "Local, indigenous gangs usually exist prior to gang migration," although "indirect migration" might exist, whereby one gang is influenced by other gangs (Maxson, 1998, p. 57).

Rural and Suburban Areas. Gangs have been reported in rural and suburban areas (W. Miller, 2001). However, the percentage of jurisdictions reporting a problem has been consistently decreasing in recent years (Egley, Howell, and Major, 2006). Nonurban areas have less persistent gang problems, with only about 4 to 10% reporting chronic problems (Howell and Egley, 2005, p. 2). Their short-lived nature is attributed to their inability to recruit new members because they "do not have the necessary population base to sustain" the gang (Howell and Egley, 2005, p. 1). Nonurban gangs are similar to urban gangs in that social and demographic factors contribute to the presence of gangs in both areas. However, they are different in that nonurban gangs are less likely to be associated with economic factors (Wells and Weisheit, 2001). Rural gang members are also less likely than urban gang members to report feeling threatened by gangs and violence (Evans, Fitzgerald, Weigel, and Chvilicek, 1999). Nonurban gangs are also more ethnically diverse than their urban counterparts (Starbuck, Howell, and Lindquist, 2001).

Gender

Today's gangs "are principally but not exclusively male" (Klein, 1995, p. 75). Virtually all research shows a higher percentage of male gang members than female gang members. Law enforcement respondents report that about 90% of gang members were male (Egley, Howell, and Major, 2006, p. vi). However, some research shows a smaller gender gap. Esbensen, Deschenes, and Winfree (1999) find in their survey of eighth graders that females are 38% of gang members, and a significant amount of research suggests fairly high percentages of female gang membership (see Esbensen and Huizinga, 1993; Esbensen and Winfree, 1998; Moore and Hagedorn, 2001; Thornberry et al., 2003). This discrepancy may be due to a number of reasons. First, females generally join and leave gangs earlier than males (see Esbensen and Huizinga, 1993; Thornberry et al., 2003). Therefore, research that utilizes an older sample would report a lower number of female gang members. It is also the case that officially reported membership differs from self-reported membership. Historically, perceptions of female gang membership have affected the enumeration of female gang members (see Curry, 1999). This issue will be further discussed in Chapter 9.

Race/Ethnicity

Gangs are also "principally but not exclusively minority in ethnicity or race" (Klein, 1995, p. 75). While there are obvious racial/ethnic patterns found in gangs, gangs do not always exclude members based on race/ethnicity. Approximately 36% of all gangs in the United States were reported as **mixed race gangs** (NYGC, 2000, p. 23). The NYGS finds most gangs reported are Hispanic (46%), followed by African American (34%), Caucasian (12%), Asian (6%), and 2% other. Hispanic gangs were more likely to be found in large cities (47%), whereas African American gangs were more prominent in rural counties (36%). Interestingly, Caucasian gangs were 30% of gangs present in small cities and 27% of gangs present in rural counties (NYGC, 2000, pp. 20–21). These race/ethnicity compositions are consistent across time (see Egley, Howell, and Major, 2006). More recently, the NYGS collected data from Indian communities and found a startling number of gangs present (Major et al., 2004).[6] About 23% of respondents "reported having active youth gangs" (p. 4). The number of gangs in a community ranged from 1 to 5 to more than 10, and the number of gang members ranged from 25 or fewer to more than 50 (pp. 5–6). Self-report studies find race/ethnicity breakdowns that differ from the NYGS. In the Esbensen and associates (2001) sample, 30% were black, 30% were Hispanic, 25% were white, and 15% other.

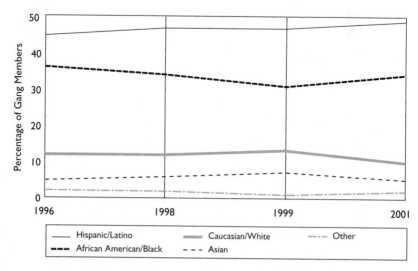

Figure 1–2   Race/Ethnicity of Gang Members (selected years).
National Youth Gang Survey (2006).

Age

Gang members are on average 17 or 18 years of age (Curry and Decker, 2003). "The typical age range is 12 to 24" (Howell, 1998a, p. 2), but the average age has been consistently increasing (Egley, Howell, and Major, 2006), primarily because chronic gang cities experience members staying in gangs longer. This is evident in larger cities reporting a greater percentage of older members, with about 70% age 18 and older, compared with other sizes of jurisdictions (Egley, Howell, and Major, 2006, p. 18). The majority of members from smaller cities (47%) and rural counties (46%) are between the ages of 15 and 17 (NYGC, 2000). Both smaller cities and rural areas also have healthy percentages (20%) of members below the age of 15 (NYGC, 2000). The age range of gang membership has important implications for the dynamics of the gang, which will be explored in later chapters.

The variation in the enumeration of gangs and gang members may come as a surprise to those who have never been academically introduced to gangs. The variation spoken about at the beginning of the chapter is best reflected in the preceding statistics. Research design becomes incredibly sensitive to this variation. An older sample from a small city may have vastly different results than a younger sample from a large city, just as officially reported results might differ significantly from self-reported results. Part of the inconsistency is also due to the fact that academics and practitioners have a difficult time developing a common definition.

CHAPTER SUMMARY

> Cornerville people appear as social work clients, as defendants in criminal cases, or as undifferentiated members of "the masses." There is one thing wrong with such a picture; no human beings are in it. Those who are concerned with Cornerville seek through a general survey to answer questions that require the most intimate knowledge of local life. (Whyte, 1943/1981, p. xv)

Gang is just a term with a popular meaning that has changed throughout history. This history of gang phenomena in the United States is rooted in the late 1800s amid the nation's massive changes due to immigration, urbanization, and industrialization. Newly arriving immigrant groups in every generation experienced poverty, discrimination, and related social ills. It was and still is today these groups that form gangs. Academic attention to gangs has come and gone throughout the 1900s but has remained a steady force from the 1980s into the twenty-first century, primarily because of the changing nature of gangs and their increased criminal tendencies.

Today, gangs are usually comprised of young black or Hispanic males who come from backgrounds of urban poverty. However, we have seen recent increases in the age range of gang members, female gang membership, rural and suburban gangs, and gang membership increases in other ethnic groups. Some stable gang cities have had a chronic gang problem for several generations, and some emerging gang cities have only more recently experienced a problem. The fact is that gangs are considered a social problem for many communities. Only through understanding gang dynamics and the experiences of individual gang members will we be able to develop informed and effective policies and programs.

KEY TERMS

chronic gang city   mixed race gangs
emerging gang city   official data
National Youth Gang Survey (NYGS)   self-report studies

QUESTIONS FOR REVIEW

1. What are the four primary periods of gang activity and attention?

2. What common themes of gang development are prevalent throughout history?

3. What are the general demographic trends in modern gangs in regard to age, gender, and race?

DISCUSSION QUESTIONS

1. We know that throughout history immigration, discrimination, and poverty have been underlying features of gang activity. Given your knowledge of this recurring history, why do you think we still have a gang problem?

2. Much gang research is based on official and self-report data, each with their own advantages and weaknesses. Which data do you feel are most beneficial to our understanding of gangs?

NOTES

1. Immigration from Italy rose to 307,309 between 1881 and 1890, up from 55,759 a decade earlier.

2. Until 1919, Austria-Hungry data included immigrants from lands that became Czechoslovakia, Poland, and Yugoslavia after World War I.

3. Between the 1940s and the 1960s, immigration from the Caribbean rose from about 50,000 to 470,000, from Central America from 21,665 to just over 100,000, and from South America from 21,831 to over 250,000.

CHAPTER OB

• Recognize the v:

• Understand mul

• Become familiar behavior.

DEFINITIO

It's more
They ain
to them.

One of many
gang, gang me
toward widesp
believe that e:
"lack of consis
ity to compare
(Decker and V
common defir
means for stu
1993, p. 581)
basis of reliab
multiple defin

A lack of a uniform definition leads to problems in determining the true extent of the nation's gang problem. It is difficult to develop standard definitions because of the variation that exists in gangs (Maxson, 1998). There is also the added complexity of what the purpose of the definition is: "Some researchers prefer a broad definition that includes group criminal and noncriminal activities, whereas law enforcement agencies tend to use definitions that expedite the cataloging of groups for purposes of statistical analysis or prosecution" (Maxson, 1998, p. 2). The gang "problem" becomes dependent on the definition that is used. The definition used establishes "whether we have a large, small, or even no problem; whether more or fewer gangs and gang members exist; and which agencies will receive most of the funds to address the problem" (Spergel, 1995, p. 17). Differing definitions can lead to a different picture of the problem. A jurisdiction can use a broader definition of gangs to demonstrate a "problem" that is not so, in order to secure government funding. Varying definitions can also lead a jurisdiction to ignore an emerging gang problem, when indeed one exists.

Historically, the term **gang** is more often applied to youth groups in low socio-economic areas (Spergel, 1995, p. 59; Bloch and Niederhoffer, 1958, p. 7). "Rarely in sociological literature are middle class adolescent groups referred to as gangs, irrespective of their similarity to their lower economic-class counterparts" (Bloch and Niederhoffer, 1958, p. 7). Definitions are often constructed within a social and cultural context that changes over time. Definitions will be based "on those aspects of the phenomena in question that were most visible and most salient at the time" (Ball and Curry, 1995, p. 239). Many acceptable definitions have been developed over time, but often new definitions are needed "either because of changes in the phenomenon itself or changes in the purposes for which definition is required" (Decker and Van Winkle, 1996, p. 3). This idea is also discussed by Goldstein (1991, p. 7).

The shift in definitional emphasis alters our notion of what a gang is. Groups that were identified by Asbury and Thrasher as gangs might not be considered gangs by today's standards. This definitional adaptation is also evidenced by shifts in the term used to identify gangs in literature. The common term for gangs in the 1950s and 1960s was "juvenile" or "delinquent" gang, indicating the prominent adolescent age component of the group. However, the age structure of gangs changed and began to include older adolescents and young adults. This shift in age structure brought a change to the commonly used terms for a "youth" gang. Our understanding of gangs continues to improve, and the commonly used term in the twenty-first century is "street" gangs, representing the current focus on dynamics within the group (Klein, 1995, p. 21).

It is also possible that groups that we identify as gangs today never sought the label. Oddly, many early "clubs" did not identify themselves as gangs when others around them were giving them the title. This is evidenced in a documentation of the emergence of the Los Angeles Crips. Stanley "Tookie" Williams states, "I envisioned our being not a gang in the customary sense, but an unstoppable force that no gang in Los Angeles or the world could defeat" (Williams, 2004 , p. 77). In fact, Williams believed that his group could serve a positive function: "For us, the alliance would commence an urban cleaning of the gang element, or so we thought" (p. 79).

BOX 2-1: A Closer Look

This chapter involves much discussion of definitional differences in academic literature. To better understand where your definitional loyalties lie, consider the following examples:

- What makes a gang? A cohesive group of adolescent males, named "AQX," have been accused of gang rape. This accusation comes as no surprise to the community, as they are known for their public substance use and verbal harassment of passersby. New community members are warned about the group and told to stay away from their "turf," benches along the street where they lived. Would you consider this group a gang? Is there anything else you would want to know?

- What makes someone a gang member? "G-dog" hangs out with gang members and has strong emotional bonds with them. "G-dog" is present when the "Dukes" let off shots at the "Clarence Street Locos." He drives into "Dukes" territory yelling, "Did you want to f-in' kill me?" "G-dog" is aware of the criminal behavior of his friends but does not report the behavior to legal authorities because he does not want to break any trust. Would you consider "G-dog" a gang member? Is there anything else you would want to know?

The "gang" in the first example is a fraternity described by Peggy Sanday (1990) in her book on fraternity gang rape. This particular fraternity, located at a prestigious university in Philadelphia, was involved in a gang rape in 1983. Her description is often used as an example of the confusion over what a gang is. It exemplifies the social usage of the term and the hesitation to apply the term to something other than low-income minorities.

The "gang member" in the second example is Father Gregory Boyle, a Jesuit priest in East Los Angeles. A priest in the projects, he became committed to making a difference in the lives of gang members. As a result, he is respected by the youth he serves, earning him the nickname "G-dog" (Fremon, 1995). Father Boyle is currently the director of Jobs for a Future and Homeboy Industries, an organization aimed at ensuring job opportunities for gang and at-risk youth.

DEFINITIONS OF *GANG*

In spite of this debate, there are notable, varying definitions in the literature that we will explore. The presentation of these definitions is meant to help you gain an understanding of the variability and complexity of the gang phenomenon. As you read through the prominent definitions of *gang* that have been put forth, the common themes and striking differences should become apparent. Definitions take several

TABLE 2–1

Gang definitions

There are two prominent yet conflicting types of definitional classifications used for youth gangs. Each has its supporters and critics. The following summarizes their primary views.

Positive or Neutral Definitions

- Emphasize group process, without including criminal behavior
- Believe that use of criminal behavior is tautological and focuses on only one gang trait
- Notable positive or neutral definitions have been developed by Thrasher (1927/1963) and Short (1990)

Negative Definitions

- Suggest that crime is a necessary component of the definition
- Exclusion of crime creates little distinction between gangs and nongang groups
- Notable negative definitions have been developed by Klein (1995) and Spergel (1995)

forms. Some of the common themes in definitions are the collective behavior of the group, permanence, communication, territory, and criminal behavior (Curry and Decker, 2003). Some definitions are **"positive"** or **"neutral"** and emphasize the group nature and processes of the gang. Other definitions emphasize the **"negative,"** more violent and criminal qualities of the group (Spergel, 1995).

Group Process Definitions

One group of prominent definitions emphasizing group process, without including criminal behavior, is preferred by some researchers (see Ball and Curry, 1995; DiChiara and Chabot, 2003; Jankowski, 1991; Moore, 1991; Padilla, 1992). The first academic definition, put forth by Thrasher (1927/1963), is an example of a group process definition:

> The gang is an interstitial group originally formed spontaneously, and then integrated through conflict. It is characterized by the following types of behavior: meeting face to face, milling, movement through space as a unit, conflict, and planning. The result of this collective behavior is the development of tradition, unreflective internal structure, esprit de corps, solidarity, morale, group awareness, and attachment to a local territory. (p. 46)

Thrasher's definition emphasizes group structure and collective behavior and captures some of the fundamental features of gangs that have remained stable over time. For instance, "integrated through conflict" is a characteristic of gangs that will be further explored, as will the roles of territory and group awareness. His definition would be characterized as positive or neutral, because it does not contain reference to criminal behavior.

Short's (1990) definition is another example of a neutral process definition. He states that a gang is "a group whose members meet together with some regularity, over time, on the basis of group-defined criteria of membership and group-determined organizational structure, usually with (but not always; see Hagedorn, 1988) some sense of territoriality" (p. 239). In this definition, Short excludes behaviors as defining characteristics and identifying characteristics such as dress and names. He recognizes that these features are part of the phenomenon gang researchers are trying to explain.

Other definitions, usually put forth by gang members, stress the gang in a positive light and focus on the family and friendship network of the group (Curry and Decker, 2003; Spergel, 1995). Curry and Spergel (1988) recognize the difference between youth groups and gangs in terms of organization. They see youth groups as "ephemeral, i.e. loosely organized with shifting leadership," whereas youth gangs are "complexly organized although sometimes diffuse, sometimes cohesive with established leadership and membership rules" (p. 382).

There are several advantages to focusing on group process while limiting the role of criminal behavior. Some researchers suggest that the inclusion of crime creates a tautology, meaning that we are defining something based on a behavior we are trying to explain (Bursik and Grasmick, 1993; Hagedorn, 1988; Moore, 1991). Another reason not to include crime as part of the definition is that it perpetuates the notion that gangs exist simply to be deviant and that criminal behavior is their primary focus (Peterson, 2000a). Although we focus on gangs because of their criminal behavior, much of the gang member's time is spent doing a whole lot of nothing (Klein, 1995; Moore, 1991; Vigil, 1988). More organized groups, such as the Gangster Disciples and Latin Kings in Chicago, do not like being called a gang and believe that it unfairly depicts a negative view of their group (Curry and Decker, 2003). At the same time, the "essence of the gang lies in the weakening of conventional norms" (Ball and Curry, 1995, p. 241). As a result, criminal behavior occurs within this group context. According to Ball and Curry, "it is preferable that illegal activity not be part of the definition unless clearly specified as a correlate rather than a property" (p. 240).

Crime-Based Definitions

Another camp of gang researchers insists that crime is a necessary component of the definition (Klein, 1995; Spergel, 1995), and others recognize crime as a major definitional component (Bursik and Grasmick, 1993; Howell, 1998). Without the inclusion of crime, there is no distinction between a gang and other groups. For example, police agencies could easily be classified as a gang in many positive or neutral definitions. The use of crime as a definitional component is also suggested by gang members themselves (Curry and Decker, 2003; Klein, 1995; Peterson, 2000a).

Malcolm Klein is undoubtedly one of the most well-known and well-versed gang researchers to date, partly because he has been in the game for over 35 years. He began his research in the 1960s and he continues to write today.[1] He put forth a "negative" definition that included deviant behavior in 1971:

> For our purposes, we shall use the term gang to refer to any denotable adolescent group of youngsters who (a) are generally perceived as a distinct aggregation by

others in their neighborhood, (b) recognize themselves as a denotable group (almost invariably with a group name) and (c) have been involved in a sufficient number of delinquent incidents to call forth a consistent negative response from neighborhood residents and/or enforcement agencies. (p. 13)

Klein's definition is particularly useful because it specifies the necessity for the group to see itself as a gang. The group is also "reacted to as a distinctly antisocial group of genuine concern" (p. 14). The community has to see the group as a problem as a result of deviant behavior. More recently, Klein (2005) has utilized a "consensus Eurogang definition" in defining a street gang. According to this definition, "[a] street gang is any durable, street-oriented youth group whose own identity includes involvement in illegal activity" (p. 136).

Klein and others recognize the need to distinguish between a gang and other deviant organizations, such as skinheads, biker gangs, and drug gangs (Curry and Decker, 2003; Howell, 1998a; Klein, 1995, 2005). The primary distinction between street gangs and these other groups is the purpose of the groups. However, Knox (1994), in defining a street gang, broadens the approach to include extremist groups such as the Ku Klux Klan and the Aryan Brotherhood.[2] Knox states that "a group is a gang when it exists for or benefits substantially from the continuing criminal activity of its members" (p. 7) and that the group must be aware of and approve of the behavior.

Miller (1980) presents a crime-based definition that stresses the group process of the gang but also includes the element of crime. His definition is based on responses by criminal justice agencies in 26 localities:

A youth gang is a self-formed association of peers, bound together by mutual interests, with identifiable leadership, well-developed lines of authority, and other organizational features, who act in concert to achieve a specific purpose or purposes which generally include the conduct of illegal activity and control of a particular territory, facility, or type of enterprise. (p. 121)

Other crime-inclusive definitions have been used in research. Decker and Van Winkle (1996) state that a gang is "[a]n age-graded peer group that exhibits some permanence, engages in criminal activity, and has some symbolic representation of membership" (p. 31). The National Youth Gang Center states that a "youth gang is commonly thought of as a self-formed association of peers having the following characteristics: three or more members, generally ages 12 to 24; a name and some sense of identity, generally indicated by such symbols as style of clothing, graffiti, and hand signs; some degree of permanence and organization; and an elevated level of involvement in delinquent or criminal activity" (Howell and Egley, n.d.).

Another category of definitions that emphasize the criminal nature of gangs is that used by the criminal justice system. Definitions of gangs can be found in some legal codes and police policy statements, which sometimes help to take the guesswork out of identification for local agencies. For example, Arizona statutes define a "criminal street gang" as "an ongoing formal or informal association of persons whose members or associates individually or collectively engage in the commission, attempted commission, facilitation or solicitation of any felony act and who has at least one individual who is a criminal street gang member" (Institute for Intergovernmental Research, 2000, Arizona 13-105). The Massachusetts legal code prohibits gang recruitment and establishes the group as "a criminal street gang or other organization of three or more persons which has a common name, identifying sign or symbol and whose members individually or collectively engage in criminal behavior" (Institute for Intergovernmental Research, 2000, Massachusetts 265.44).

A more systematic overview of definitions by law enforcement is found in the National Youth Gang Survey (NYGS), which has been collecting information on gangs since 1995. In the survey, a sample of law enforcement agencies throughout the country report gang problems in their jurisdiction. The survey defines a youth gang as "a group of youths or young adults in [the respondent's] jurisdiction that [the respondent] or other responsible persons in [the respondent's] agency or community are willing to identify as a 'gang.'" Respondents were asked to exclude "motorcycle gangs, hate or ideology groups, prison gangs, and exclusively adult gangs" (p. 6). This leaves a broad interpretation for agencies that are completing the survey. The survey further asked the agency to rank six characteristics that are used to define gangs. The two most important characteristics identified were committing crime together (50%) and having a name (19%). Other important characteristics identified were hanging out together (10%), claiming a turf or territory (9%), colors or other insignia (8%), and leadership (7%).

The NYGS (2000) conducted a more in-depth examination of the definition. The 1998 survey asked jurisdictions to report their gang problem with the original definition and with an alternate definition, developed by Klein. The alternate definition had less discretion and asked the respondent to identify a gang as "a group of youths or young adults in your jurisdiction whose involvement in illegal activities over months or years marks in their own view and in the view of the community and police as different from most other youthful groups" (p. 42). They were also instructed to exclude motorcycle gangs, hate or ideology groups, prison gangs, and exclusively adult gangs, as in the original definition. About 79% of the original reporting was also reported in the alternate definition. This suggests that, for the most part, agencies are accurately reporting gangs. However, the difference of 21% in the two definitions suggests that one in every five gangs reported may not be "street gangs" in the traditional sense.

The Gang versus Peer Groups.   Perhaps the most compelling argument for the use of crime in defining street gangs is in the comparison of gangs with other peer groups. As one researcher states, gang members are "hyperadolescents" (Goldstein, 1991), indicating a difference between gang members and their nongang peers in terms of personality and behavior. As we delve into the world of gangs, it becomes imperative that we distinguish between a gang and a deviant peer group and between a gang member and a highly deviant individual.[3] This distinction begins with establishing a

---

BOX 2–2: Focus on Research

The National Youth Gang Center (NYGC) has used the National Youth Gang Survey to collect annual data from law enforcement agencies throughout the United States. The survey is a part of a federal initiative sponsored by the Office of Juvenile Justice and Delinquency Prevention and the Institute for Intergovernmental Research (NYGC, 2000, p. 1). Although NYGC conducted previous surveys, it was in 1996 that a representative sample was created, allowing for "a more complete national picture of youth gang activity" (p. 1). The sample consisted of all police departments in large cities (25,000 or more residents), randomly selected small cities (2,500 to 24,999 residents), all suburban police and sheriff departments, and randomly selected rural county police and sheriff departments. A response rate of 88% yielded a final 1998 representative sample of 3,018 jurisdictions (pp. 2–3). The sampling design allowed the NYGC to generalize to the larger population. The information gathered from the survey includes the number of gangs and members, the types of gangs, the year of onset and patterns of migration, gang and gang member demographics, and gang crime. This annual survey allows us to consistently monitor national and regional trends in gang and gang member activity. Trends are best summarized in two full reports published in 2000 and 2006.

---

definition that highlights these primary differences so that we can more easily differentiate between these groups. By nature, juvenile delinquency is a group phenomenon (Bloch and Niederhoffer, 1958; Shaw and McKay, 1942; Short and Strodtbeck, 1965; Thrasher, 1927/1963), and "group influences, in particular associating with delinquent peers, are among the strongest and most consistent predictors of delinquent behavior" (Thornberry et al., 2003, p. 140). Therefore, if delinquency is a group phenomenon, is delinquency that takes place in peer groups different than a gang? The answer to this question may capture the fundamental nature of gangs.

Moore (1991) connects Fine's theory of normal deviance to gangs. Fine's theory presents an argument for deviant behavior as a normal stage in adolescent development. This behavior eventually leads to definitions of normal and deviant behavior within the group setting. The values that are established vary along a continuum that "runs from what Fine calls 'goody-goody' to 'rowdy'" (p. 41). Moore applies these ideas to gang behavior and concludes that gang value systems and behavior may be considered rowdy behavior on the end of Fine's continuum. In essence, gangs are adolescent groups that are on the extreme end of a continuum that contains all peer groups. This is similar in nature to Klein's (1995) explanation that gangs are peer groups that have reached a **"tipping point"** (p. 29). This tipping point is reached when the group becomes committed to a criminal orientation and self-recognizes their group status. As a result of this tipping point and associated characteristics, "street gangs are something special, something qualitatively different from other groups and from other categories of law breakers" (p. 197).

Thornberry and colleagues (2003) also make the case for the difference between the gang and other adolescent peer groups. The gang, by nature of its solidified group status, will exert more influence over an individual than other deviant peer groups. They predict that an individual who joins a gang will be more delinquent than an individual who hangs out with a highly deviant peer group that is not a gang. In their study, they find support for this prediction. Gang members "generally exhibit higher rates of delinquency and drug involvement" (p. 162) than nongang youth with similar numbers of deviant friends and compared to nongang youth in a matched group.

Peterson's (2000a) research qualitatively explores the differences between gangs and other peer groups. She conducted in-depth interviews with 34 incarcerated young gang and nongang females and asked them to identify differences between a gang and a group of people getting into trouble. Some of the women did not think there was much difference; others focused on the criminal activity of the group: "Not all gangs have to participate in crimes and drugs, but most of them do." "[A gang] does three, four times over what a bunch of normal kids would do, like speeding, getting high, causing trouble" (p. 29). Some explain that gangs are "more protective of their members and more protective of their territory than groups of youth causing trouble" (p. 29).

There is general consensus in academic literature that gangs are different than other adolescent peer groups. As discussed in later chapters, the gang serves goals other than criminal behavior. At the same time, the group supports a deviant value system that helps to perpetuate and exacerbate criminal behavior. Research consistently shows that gangs are involved in significantly more deviant behavior than nongang groups (Battin-Pearson, Thornberry, Hawkins, and Krohn, 1998; Huff, 1998; Thomas, Holzer, and Wall, 2003; Thornberry, Krohn, Lizotte, and Chard-Wierschem, 1993; Thornberry et al., 2003). The reasons for this difference will be explored in Chapter 7.

DEFINITION OF GANG MEMBER

This issue of debate about defining a gang member is less obvious and seen as not as "difficult as defining a gang" (Curry and Decker, 2003, p. 6). This ease is primarily due to the reliance of self-identification in research, by simply asking, "Are you a member of a gang?" Most of what we know about gang members comes from their life stories and self-reporting. The gang member's definition of membership takes it out of the hands of academics or practitioners. This could be seen as a weak standard of definition (Spergel, 1995). One obstacle of self-identification is that gang member definitions often fail to pick up on variations in gang membership. This, in turn, makes it difficult to understand rationales and develop theories and policies that address the individual gang member. Different levels of membership will be further discussed in Chapter 5. However, it is important now to make the point of distinguishing what a gang member is.

The level of commitment to the gang is usually identified by terms, such as "wannabe," "core," "fringe," "associate," "hardcore," and "O.G." (original gangster)

(Maxson, 1998). This arbitrary system of identification relies little on consensus among researchers and practitioners. However, it does represent qualitative differences among those connected to gang life. The membership levels remind us that "any one individual affiliated with the group may have different reasons for investing time and energy" (Venkatesh, 2003, p. 4). However, little gang research is sensitive to these distinctions. The importance of identifying varying levels of membership is evident in Esbensen, Winfree, He, and Taylor's (2001) analysis of self-designation by gang membership. They allowed self-identification of members based on varying degrees, from the less restrictive "Have you ever been in a gang?" to a more restrictive "Are you a current gang member? Belonging to a delinquent gang? That has organizational aspects? and Identify yourself as a core member?" (p. 125). They found that the more restrictive the definition, the lower the reported membership (2%), and the less restrictive the definition, the greater the reported membership (17%).

Law enforcement agencies rely on self-identification and external indicators of gang membership in their definition. In discussing legal classification systems, Klein (1995, p. 191) states, "There remains considerable ambiguity in this definitional system, as indeed must be the case. Street gangs themselves seldom have rosters, dues, clear membership classes, and other accoutrements of social clubs or professional associations. Membership is ephemeral; turnover is relatively high; and group versus individual behaviors are difficult to classify." Some jurisdictions place individuals in their gang database if they meet just one of the following criteria: "self admission; tattoos indicating gang membership; clothing indicating gang members; the statement of a reliable informer with the gang; or association with other gang members along with commission of gang-related crimes" (Siegel, 2003, p. 224). This is exemplified in Texas's statutes, which state that two of the following need to be met for classification as a gang member:

(A) a self-admission by the individual of criminal street gang membership;

(B) an identification of the individual as a criminal street gang member by a reliable informant or other individual;

(C) a corroborated identification of the individual as a criminal street gang member by an informant or other individual of unknown reliability;

(D) evidence that the individual frequents a documented area of a criminal street gang, associates with known criminal street gang members, and uses criminal street gang dress, hand signals, tattoos, or symbols; or

(E) evidence that the individual has been arrested or taken into custody with known criminal street gang members for an offense or conduct consistent with criminal street gang activity. (Institute for Intergovernmental Research, 2000, Texas Art. 61.02)

It is also acceptable practice for "gang associates" to become part of gang databases, just for having a close association with known gang members (Klein, 1995; Siegel,

2003). This method paints membership with an incredibly broad stroke. Later chapters have further discussion of criminal legislation related to gangs and the implications of this identification system.

DEFINITION OF GANG CRIME

The issue of membership becomes most apparent when we discuss what a gang crime is. Gang crimes also bring to the forefront the importance of distinguishing a gang and its members. A plethora of issues arise in discussing gang crime. What if a member isn't self-identifying? Or what if there is an overidentification of membership (see Huff, 1990)? Does the crime have to be gang sanctioned? This is the "gang-related" or "member-based" versus "gang-motivated" dichotomy (Maxson and Klein, 1990). Many times gang members engage in crime on their own without the behavior being connected in any way to the gang (Jankowski, 1991). Research finds that active gang membership increases criminal behavior. However, some individuals are criminally active before joining the gang and after leaving the gang (Thornberry et al., 2003). Consider the fact that the behavior would be considered gang crime only during active membership. This view of gang crime is sometimes accurate, but many times it is not. The gang-motivated definition requires that the motivation for the crime be based within the gang, such as retaliation, profit making, or defense of territory (Maxson and Klein, 1990).

Maxson and Klein (1990) compared gang homicides in two cities that utilized the two different methods of classification, Chicago and Los Angeles. Los Angeles used **gang-related crime** definitions for homicide classification, which counts any homicide that was committed by a gang member as a gang homicide. Chicago used the more conservative, **gang-motivated crime** definition. To be cataloged as a gang homicide, the motive for the homicide had to be based within the gang. When Los Angeles homicides were reclassified according to Chicago's definition, there was a significant reduction in the number of gang homicides. It is also the case that if Chicago's homicides were tallied according to the Los Angeles definition, there would be an increase in gang homicides. Regardless, Klein (1995) reports that there was no substantive difference between the cases included in each of the definitions: "Both the participant and the situation variables looked much the same" in the two jurisdictions (p. 15). The gang-related method used by Los Angeles is not uncommon. In fact, 58% of jurisdictions used member-based definitions of crime, and 32% used motive-based definitions (NYGS, 2000).[4]

CHAPTER SUMMARY

The word "gang" generally appears in a pejorative context, though within "the gang" itself members may adopt the phrase in proud identity or defiance. (Wikipedia, n.d.)[5]

The interesting debate around the issue of definitions further challenges academics and practitioners alike to develop sound theory and policy rooted in high-quality knowledge. Despite the inconsistencies and controversies, there are facts that we know about gangs. A gang is a group of individual young people who are bound together by common backgrounds and experiences. The group supports individual deviant value systems and collectively acts out these common values. It is through these deviant values and collective behavior that they distinguish themselves as a group that is different than other peer groups.

KEY TERMS

gang (youth gang, street gang)
gang-motivated crime
gang-related crime

negative gang definition
positive or neutral gang definition
tipping point

QUESTIONS FOR REVIEW

1. How do positive or neutral definitions of gangs differ from negative definitions of gangs?

2. What is the difference between gang-related crime and gang-motivated crime?

3. How do gangs differ from other adolescent peer groups?

4. What are the strengths and weaknesses of self-reported and officially identified gang membership?

DISCUSSION QUESTIONS

1. How important do you think it is to agree on a definition of gangs and gang crime? What problems do you see with the lack of a common definition?

2. Is it important to distinguish between different types of gang members? Why or why not?

3. Should we rely on official or self-reported identification of gangs and gang members? Why?

NOTES

1. For a background on Malcolm Klein, see Klein, 1995.

2. Anderson, Mangels, and Dyson (2001) also make the case for including hate crime as part of the gang definition.

3. Sullivan (2005) believes that this distinction should be minimized because moral panics have led to the labeling of collective youth behaviors as gangs.

4. 11% of jurisdictions used some other form of classification.

5. The author recognizes the questionable academic integrity of Wikipedia. However, this quote best reflects the conflicting understanding of what a gang is.

CHAPTER 3

EXPLANATIONS OF GANGS

CHAPTER OBJECTIVES

- Become familiar with macro-level risk factors for gang presence.

- Understand different theoretical perspectives of gang existence.

- Identify key differences between the prominent theoretical paradigms explaining gang formation.

THE ENVIRONMENTAL EFFECT

I was a normal child in an abnormal environment. (Williams, 2004, p. 39)

There are multiple dimensions that create an environment that is primed for gang activity, as there are multiple reasons why an individual would be inclined to participate in gang activities. This creates a complex picture in our understanding of gangs and gang membership. This chapter introduces prominent theories in the field that help to explain gang formation and continuation. These are known as macro-level, ecological, or environmental theories. These explanations were developed to explain the presence of gangs, not necessarily why an individual joins a gang. Individual-level explanations will be presented in the next chapter. Ecological theories have been a consistent force in gang literature throughout the 1900s. The first such theory was developed in the 1920s, and theoretical development continues today.

Researchers regularly recognize the multiple factors that are related to gang formation. Environmental factors have been specified as one of several areas that contribute to the gang phenomenon (Brotherton and Salazar-Atias, 2003; Hill et al., 1999; Howell, 1998a ; Thornberry et al., 2003). Gangs have always been more prevalent in urban areas with high concentrations of poor immigrants or migrants. Therefore, explanations of gang formation must account for this pattern. The prominent environmental theories of gang formation focus on many of the themes that were discussed in Chapter 1. Historical themes of gang formation include the role of the

---

TABLE 3–1

Summary of major environmental theories

Social Disorganization Theory

- Rapid change leads to weak community institutions that cannot control the behavior of adolescence. This lack of control may lead to gang formation.
- An early prominent gang researcher is Frederic Thrasher.
- Reformulated as collective efficacy in the 1980s by Bursik and Grasmick (1993) and Sampson, Raudenbush, and Earls (1997).

Strain Theory

- Society and communities have similar values. However, some adapt to society inequity by developing deviant value systems. This value system may lead to gang formation.
- Prominent gang researchers include Merton, Cohen, Cloward, and Ohlin.

Subcultural Theory

- Lower class culture, as a whole, adapts to social inequity through development of an alternate value system. This value system may lead to gang formation.
- A prominent gang researcher is W. Miller.

Underclass Theory

- Society (i.e., economy and institutions) is ineffective. As a result, gangs may form to replace what society cannot provide. This can also lead to community tolerance for gangs.
- Prominent gang researchers include Moore and Hagedorn.

Integrated Theory

- Theories that link macro- and micro-level causal factors.
- Prominent gang researchers include Klein and Vigil.

---

economy, poverty, and the effects of immigration, urbanization, and industrialization. Therefore, each of the theories is conceptually linked, sometimes making it difficult to understand the differences between them. One of the easier ways to distinguish between the theories is to recognize the links between conventional society, the community or local institutions, and the gang.

SOCIAL DISORGANIZATION THEORY

Thrasher and the Chicago School

Thrasher (1927/1963) published the first significant study of gangs in 1927. His research, based in the Chicago School tradition, relied on patterns of urbanization in explaining gang formation in urban slum areas. The Chicago School tradition was put in motion by Park and Burgess (1925/1984), who recognized that urban areas were established in a predictable pattern. New immigrants, upon arriving in cities, would settle in areas of low-cost, dilapidated housing. These areas became known as **zones of transition** and portrayed extreme poverty, high population turnover, deteriorated living conditions, and overall social decay. Shaw and McKay (1942) advanced the understanding of the dynamics of the zones of transition in their **social disorganization** theory. The social disorganization theory is based in the assumption that there is a set value structure in conventional society and that local institutions help to constrain individuals and reinforce this value system. However, rapid social change leads to weakened institutions that are ineffective social control agents. Family, schools, churches, and other institutions cannot effectively instill a common value system. These areas of disorganization are typically found in low-income urban areas that are home to newly arriving immigrant groups. Once immigrant groups have achieved a certain level of success, they move out of urban slum areas and are replaced by a new wave of immigrants. High levels of population mobility, as a result of these immigrant patterns, are the root cause of rapid social change. Urban areas are constantly in a state of transition. They are unable to develop strong institutions that would effectively control community members; therefore, competing value systems develop.

It is within this school of thought that Thrasher studied gangs in Chicago. Thrasher believed that natural adolescent development requires peer group interaction. This peer group interaction leads to the formation of playgroups. In disorganized areas, normal playgroups would be left unsupervised, engage in more delinquent behavior, and "make possible the freedom which leads to ganging" (p. 339). According to Thrasher, the gang is a natural consequence of disorganized areas. He states:

> The most important agency in directing the spare-time activities of the boy is the family. In the underprivileged classes, family life in a large number of cases—either through neglect, misdirection, or suppression—fails to provide for or control the leisure-time behavior of the adolescent. School, church, and the recognized agencies of recreation, which might supplement this lack, are woefully inadequate to the need in gang areas. The boy with time on his hands, especially in a crowded or slum environment, is almost predestined to the life of the gang, which is simply a substitute, although a most satisfactory one from the boy's point of view, for the activities and controls not otherwise provided. (p. 65)

Thrasher's contribution of social disorganization to the study of gangs is still a foundation of gang research, and research supports its principles (Curry and Spergel, 1988). Social disorganization is still evident in some communities that face high levels of immigrant settling, resulting in violent gang formation. Spergel (1984) discusses this path as an integrated route of gang formation. This route occurs in areas that have institutions that are not meeting the needs of the population. Despite the strength and longevity of Thrasher's theory, there are some inherent problems associated with applying his work today. The criticisms assert that immigration and mobility cannot explain disorganization in many communities today, and in fact, there are many communities with gang problems that are actually organized. Thrasher's theory is unable to account for these variations, but this may be due to the fact that his study relied on areas with European immigrants and not concentrations of racial minorities.

Collective Efficacy

More recently, social disorganization theory has been revitalized through the work of notable researchers such as Bursik and Grasmick (1993) and Sampson, Raudenbush, and Earls (1997). This newer work fills in some of the gaps left behind by traditional social disorganization theories. Rather than think of communities as disorganized, Sampson and colleagues (1997) see variations in **collective efficacy,** or the cohesion of the community. Their research links collective efficacy to lower levels of community violence. Bursik and Grasmick's (1993) elaboration of social disorganization recognizes different levels of community or network organization. These levels include private networks, which include family and friends; parochial networks, which are informal and casual acquaintances found in local clubs and organizations; and public networks, which enable community residents to secure resources from outside agencies. If any of these network levels is weakened, a community will be less effective at social control. For example, Venkatesh (2003) states that social disorganization misses the mark and does not account for access to resources to control problems of crime and disorder. This would be considered a malfunction at the public level, and it can have devastating effects on organized communities.

STRAIN THEORY

Anomie Theory

Alternative theoretical paradigms have been established since Thrasher's original formulation. The next era of macro-level explanations originate from **strain** theory principles developed by Robert Merton, a prominent sociologist. Merton (1938) emphasizes a common value system that establishes the goals that individuals strive for. He focused primarily on the American goal of material success. However, for some, it can be difficult to reach this goal because the institutionalized means of achievement, such as access to jobs or education, are limited or not available. Merton states, "On the one hand, they are asked to orient their conduct toward the prospect of accumulating wealth and on the other, they are largely denied effective opportunities to do so institutionally" (p. 679). **Anomie** is strain that develops when an individual is unable to achieve societal goals though sanctioned, institutionalized means. This strain requires adaptation that may be criminal in nature. "The pressure of prestige-bearing success tends to eliminate the effective social constraint over means employed to this end" (p. 681), resulting in "the-end-justifies-the-means" doctrine. It is from this theoretical foundation that Cohen and Cloward and Ohlin address gang formation.

Status Frustration Theory

Cohen's 1955 book, *Delinquent Boys*, specifies what became known as status frustration theory.[1] Staying true to a strain theory paradigm, Cohen believed that delinquent subcultures are the result of strain experienced by lower class males, which requires an adaptation. In Cohen's theory, the primary goal is status and not money. He believed that youth begin to experience strain before they understand the value of money and that schools are the primary institution for status attainment. The status frustration theory explains that lower class youth have difficulties when compared with middle-class standards. This difficulty is due to differences in socialization. Middle-class youth are raised to be ambitious, delay gratification, exhibit self-control, and pursue conventional success, and these values are less emphasized in working and lower class households. This disparity becomes apparent as youth enter schools, which are middle-class institutions. Teachers, who primarily come from middle-class backgrounds, do not lower class norms. Therefore, lower class youth have difficulty achieving success and status when compared with this "middle-class measuring rod." Lower class youth who are faced with this strain in status attainment will adapt by associating with others who face similar stress. The group engages in "reaction formation" and rejects the system that does not accept them. Ice T (1995) remarks about gang life, "If you can't be special by being the smartest person in school, you're going to be special by being really different or really tough" (p. 150). The collective group rejects middle-class values, and it leads to an alternative value structure that is characterized by nonutilitarianism, maliciousness, negativism, short-run hedonism, and group autonomy. The gang becomes the new reference group for the youth who does not fit in, and in this environment youth are able to achieve the desired status. This theory is supported by Padilla's (1992) research. He states that the school experiences were "associated with much pain as teachers and staff refused to understand and respect their cultural and socioeconomic status background" (p. 69). As a result of this rejection, "youngsters adopted different forms of oppositional behavior" (p. 69).

Differential Opportunity Theory

Cloward and Ohlin (1960), in *Delinquency and Opportunity*, utilize strain theory assumptions in their differential opportunity theory. They concur with much of Merton's core assumptions. They agree that we strive for material success, not all have access to means of achieving success, and this strain requires an adaptation. There was a deeper question for Cloward and Ohlin. Why were there people who experienced strain who were not criminal? To answer this question, Cloward and Ohlin took a closer look at opportunity structures. They believed that just as individuals have access to legitimate opportunity structures, they have access to illegitimate opportunity structures. Illegitimate opportunity structures develop criminal values and the means to engage in illegal behavior. This differential opportunity structure determines what type of adaptation to economic strain will result. It is through this opportunity structure that Cloward and Ohlin explain three different types of subculture formation. The **criminal subculture,** which engages in money-making adaptations, develops in relatively stable communities with access to illegitimate opportunities through adult criminal role models and deviant value socialization. The **conflict subculture,** characterized by violent behavior, is more likely to develop in disorganized areas where there is limited access to illegitimate opportunities. Groups in this area gain status and reputation through fighting, because economic success is not available. The **retreatist subculture,** which primarily engages in drug use, develops in areas that may have access to both illegitimate and legitimate opportunities. However, these youth cannot achieve in either of the opportunity structures.

BOX 3-1: A Closer Look

Alex Kotlowitz (1991) presents a startling look at growing up in poor America in *There Are No Children Here*. His work demonstrates many of the environmental theories discussed in this chapter. Kotlowitz, a journalist, documents the lives of two brothers, Lafeyette and Pharaoh, growing up in the Henry Horner Homes in Chicago. The project housed more than 60,000 people, mostly black and almost half below poverty level. The housing project was riddled with problems of poverty, gangs, crime, drugs, and overall deteriorated conditions. There are details of Lafeyette, almost 12, and his cousin caught in gunfire: "Suddenly, gunfire erupted. The frightened children fell to the ground. 'Hold your head down!' Lafeyette snapped. . . . The two lay pressed to the beaten grass for half a minute until the shooting subsided" (p. 9). The residents of Henry Horner are isolated from the city around them and from each other. "There was little sense of community at Horner, and there was even little trust. Some residents who didn't have a phone, for instance, didn't know any others in their building who would let them use theirs" (p. 13). The project itself was in a state of decay. Rotting animal carcasses in the basement caused foul odors to seep up through the toilet piping (p. 241).

Poverty in America is a real problem. The federal poverty level for 2006 was $20,000 for a family of four. However, it is estimated that in most cities a family of four needs $40,000. Some cities, such as Boston, have higher estimates (National Center for Children in Poverty, 2006). In 2004, approximately 12.7% of people were officially poor. Children were most affected by poverty levels, as 17.8% of children under the age of 18 (about 13 million) were poor. It should be noted that black and Hispanic poverty rates are significantly higher (U.S. Census, 2004). In 1998, 3.2 million families with children were living in "extreme poverty," which is half of the federal poverty guideline. This measure of poverty includes the value of food stamps (Zedlewski, Giannerelli, Morton, and Wheaton, 2002). What do you think it would be like to grow up in poverty conditions? How do you think your life would be different? Do you think you would be more likely to view gangs as a "natural" alternative to a conventional lifestyle?

Summary of Strain Theory

Strain theories contribute important pieces of gang knowledge to our understanding. Both strain theories embrace the idea that the community generally holds the same value system as the larger society. The gang is an adaptation that is at odds with this dominant value system. Cohen recognizes the early development of gang culture, and he points to status, which is a consistent theme in current research and from the gang member's perspective. Cloward and Ohlin bring to the table variations in gang behavior. They do not assume that all gangs are equal, and they recognize that not all individuals who live in limited opportunity structures will be deviant. However, there are numerous criticisms of strain theories. Strain theories are rooted in the assumption that gangs are a lower class male phenomenon. Although this may have been prevalent in the days of early strain theory writing, it is certainly not the case now. As previously discussed, gangs are now prevalent in suburban and rural areas that do not have limited opportunity structures to achieve money or status. Traditional strain theories also assumed that gangs were a male phenomenon. Therefore, as originally stated, they are unable to explain the emergence and growth of female gangs.

SUBCULTURAL THEORY

Subcultural theories take on a similar tone to strain theories. Both schools recognize that crime is the result of an adaptation to one's environment. They also both recognize that alternative value systems play a role in deviant behavior. The primary difference between subcultural theory and strain theories lies in the development of value systems. Subcultural theories believe that lower class culture *as a whole* has a different value structure than conventional society. Therefore, there is a disparity in the value system of the community and the value system of society. This alternative value structure is generations old and based on the cultural experiences of the lower class. According to Short and Strodtbeck (1965), the subculture "serves to insulate their adherents from experiences which might make possible achievement of many 'respectable' goals by 'respectable' steps toward their achievement, and to evolve values which compensate, in some measure, for failure or the likelihood of failure" (p. 271).

Lower Class Focal Concerns

Miller (1958), within a subcultural paradigm, develops a theory that emphasizes poverty. He suggests that lower class culture has a distinct set of values called **focal concerns.** These focal concerns are values that other classes may hold, but they are emphasized and persistent in lower class subcultures. Miller identifies six focal concerns:

1. Trouble is the preoccupation with getting into or staying out of trouble.
2. Toughness is physical prowess, masculinity, and bravery.

3. Smartness refers to street smarts and not allowing someone to get one over on you.
4. Excitement is thrill seeking and risk taking.
5. Fate is the notion that one's future is beyond control.
6. Autonomy is resisting control by others and striving for independence.[2]

Similar to theories of this era, Miller explains male gang behavior in his application of focal concerns. He believes that gangs are the result of lower class focal concerns, combined with predominantly female-headed households. In accordance with focal concerns, masculinity, trouble, and street smarts are valued. This is exemplified by a gang member in Vigil's (1988) study who states, "The first robbery I did was for kicks. In fact, all of the robberies I did were for kicks, not for the money or to hurt anybody" (Vigil, 1988, p. 74). Males, in adolescence, will seek identity within this normative structure. Due to female-headed households, they are unable to find male role models within the family structure and must develop role models and these valued traits outside the home. These peer groups, acting in accordance with focal concerns, engage in deviant "gang" behavior. The gang serves a socialization function and is not always seen as negative by the community. The gang in this theory embraces values that are consistent with the local community.

The same criticisms that were raised about the social disorganization theory and strain theories apply to subcultural theory. Miller's focal concerns can only explain the search for masculinity within a male-based peer group. Therefore, the explanation of female gangs is unmet. Miller is also solely focused on gangs as a lower class phenomenon, and his theory would do little to explain gangs in other areas. Substantial criticisms have also been raised toward subcultural theories generally. There are looming questions as to whether the lower class has distinctly different value systems than other classes and if it emphasizes certain values that other classes do not. Empirical evidence of subcultural theories is also difficult to come by. That being said, these four theories established the foundation for gang research until the 1970s. Thrasher, Cohen, Cloward and Ohlin, and Miller are notable theorists and revered in gang literature. As we will see, today's macro-level theories are still heavily influenced by their work.

UNDERCLASS THEORY

In the 1980s, there were theoretical holes that had to be filled. According to Bursik and Grasmick (1993), "Some aspects of these traditional theories are grounded in assumptions that are no longer relevant" (p. 144). The prior theories that we have discussed were written when new immigrant groups could get ahead. Poverty and lower class status was a temporary path in pursuing the American dream. There were opportunities available for economic success. This is no longer the case. We now have gangs that are multigenerational and experience persistent poverty. They are unable to mature out of gangs or take steps up the ladder to success. New theoretical developments focus their attention on contemporary economic conditions and the notion of underclass.

Wilson's Truly Disadvantaged

Wilson (1987) discussed the notion of the black underclass in *The Truly Disadvantaged*. Wilson presents a general theory, and his ideas are the basis for this newer breed of gang-specific theory. He sees **"underclass"** individuals as different than those who experienced poverty or were lower class in the past (p. 8). Underclass individuals are the product of recent changes in the structure of urban areas. These environmental changes led to "increasing rates of social dislocation" (p. 3). **Social dislocation** refers to "rates of inner-city joblessness, teenage pregnancy, out-of-wedlock births, female-headed families, welfare dependency, and serious crime" (p. 3). Wilson identified several reasons for greater levels of social dislocation.

Wilson begins establishing his theory by discussing the role of historic discrimination and immigration. He recognizes that many social ills of the inner city today are rooted in early 1900s reactions to black migration. As we have already discussed, immigration has always been a source of threat and social problems in America. Throughout the 1900s, blacks constituted a dominant migrant group and experienced the same social ills. They have historically experienced more severe forms of discrimination than European immigrants as a result of skin color.[3] Much of the difficulty blacks had in succeeding in America is the result of urban dynamics. The flow of migration brought blacks to the North, and continued movement to urban centers made it difficult for blacks to find their occupational niche. In the past, when the population of European groups stabilized, economic success resulted. It was not until the 1970s that black populations stabilized in urban areas. Historically, it would be during this time that improvements should occur in migrant lifestyle, but there were other factors that would interfere with progress on the economic ladder.

By the 1970s, urban centers were affected by the constant migration pattern, skewing the age dynamics of urban centers. The black population in urban centers was younger than society as a whole, which, in and of itself, leads to greater rates of social dislocation. This dynamic was worsened by public housing projects, such as Cabrini-Green and Robert Taylor Homes. Youth in these high-density living environments were relatively unsupervised by adults. The housing projects became poster children for social disorganization. The perfect storm was created by changes in the American economy. The occupational structure in the United States was changing from a manufacturing market to a service-based market. The service industry provided less money, fewer benefits, and generally worse jobs than the goods-producing sector. These were the jobs for the less educated. Higher paying jobs were reserved for those with more education or were located in nonmetropolitan areas. Basically, there was limited access for unskilled urban residents.

Another piece to the underclass puzzle is the exodus of middle- and working-class blacks out of urban areas into suburban areas. Minorities who were able to climb the ladder to success quickly left poverty-stricken urban centers and left a major void in the urban landscape. Middle- and working-class families provided stability and role models for urban youth in their communities, and their absence had profound impacts on the community. It removed "an important 'social buffer' that could deflect the full impact of the kind of prolonged and increasing joblessness that plagued inner-city neighborhoods in the 1970's and 1980's" (p. 56). It also led to increased segregation from the labor market. Wilson states, "Thus, in a neighborhood with a paucity of reg-ularly employed families and with the overwhelming majority of families having spells of long-term joblessness, people experience a social isolation that excludes them from the job network system that permeates other neighborhoods and that is so important in learning about or being recommended for jobs that become available in various parts of the city" (p. 57).

   Equally important to Wilson's theory is the impact of such bleak economic prospects. According to Wilson, the economy leads to chronic unemployment and high crime and incarceration rates. Ultimately, the pool of "marriageable" or economically secure males is limited, leading to a high occurrence of mother-only households and the increased strain of single-parent households, out-of-wedlock births, and dependency on public assistance. The cumulative effect of these dynamics is a high concentration of extremely poor residents who have difficulty seeing their way out of this environment.

Segmented Labor Market Theory.   Wilson's underclass notion and the related economic structure have been used to explain the development and continua-tion of gang behavior into the 1980s. This is referred to by Spergel (1984) as the seg-mented route to gangs and refers to gangs that arise in potentially organized but segregated areas with high rates of family instability and extreme poverty. In these areas, gangs primarily provide economic opportunities to youth. The economic foun-dation of gang life is very well documented in academic literature (see Hagedorn, 1988; Jankowski, 1991; Moore, 1991; Padilla, 1992; Sullivan, 1989).

   Sullivan (1989) discusses labor market theory and distinguishes between the primary and secondary labor markets. The **primary labor market** is one of steady employment with decent wages that can support a family. As previously stated in Wilson's theory, this is the market that has quickly been closing for the underclass. These job opportunities are in decline in urban areas. The change from manufacturing industries to service industries has led to a void in the lower class economy. Moore (1991) notes that "good factory jobs have disappeared and been replaced by poor-paying service jobs" (p. 43) and that "compared with gang men and women a generation earlier, these people were facing much stiffer competition (from large numbers of exploitable and highly motivated immigrants) for jobs that were less and less attractive" (p. 22). It is difficult to raise a family on such jobs. Hagedorn's (1988) research makes us aware that the underclass issue and resulting gang problem is not just a big city phenomenon. His research in Milwaukee points to deindus-trialization as creating the economic dynamics for smaller emerging gang cities.

   The lack of access to the primary labor market gives way to a reliance on the secondary labor market, which helps to fill in the financial holes that are left in our new economy. The **secondary labor market** is one of low-paying jobs, welfare, unemployment, training programs, and crime. These avenues are often alternated and combined, because any one of these activities alone can rarely support a family. "Welfare, bartering, informal economic arrangements, and illegal economies become substitutes—simply because people must find a way to live" (Moore, 1991, p. 43). The gang naturally fits into this picture. As discussed in strain theories, gangs can provide illegal economic opportunities.

The secondary labor market is reinforced by the lack of middle- and working-class role models in urban areas. Hagan (1993) describes this dynamic in his presentation of **social embeddedness.** According to Hagan, to become regularly employed, you need more than skills and education; you need to be socially embedded in the labor market. This embeddedness is a network of contacts and development of a work ethic. In middle-class areas, this starts with babysitting, delivering newspapers, and mowing lawns. However, this network is difficult to establish in underclass areas. Hagan also points out that just as some become embedded in the conventional labor market, there are those who become embedded in the criminal labor market. There is a snowball effect in poverty-ridden urban centers where parental crime and deviant peers further isolate youth from the labor market.

Based on these theoretical arguments, gangs can exist in organized communities. According to Jankowski (1991), "Gangs emerge not as a result of disorganization and/or the desire to find order and safety, but as a consequence of a particular type of social order associated with low-income neighborhoods in American society. Low-income areas in American cities are, in fact, organized, but they are organized around an intense competition for, and conflict over, the scarce resources that exist in these areas. They comprise an alternate social order" (p. 22). In some communities, Jankowski finds a symbiotic relationship between communities and their gangs. The gang becomes a quasi-institution and fills "gaps in the existing institutional structure" (Moore, 1991, p. 137). The gang's role as an institution is to "restore order and structure in what had become a chaotic situation" (Curtis, 2003, p. 56). Spergel (1995) writes:

> Gangs are created when established institutional and organizational arrangements in a community are weak or break down. Gangs are collectives, quasi-institutions, and are somewhat tribal or clanlike, with long-term viability, to the extent that normal communal and economic arrangements for the social and job development of youths are unsatisfactory or unavailable. Gang organization, it can be argued, substitutes in distinctive ways for a particular pattern of inadequacy of existing community institutions and organizational interrelationships. (p. 70)

This institutional replacement by gangs can also occur in disorganized areas. As previously discussed, high-rise housing projects created an environment that placed together large numbers of poor minority youth without proper community-level guardianship. The result was that these areas "witnessed the evaporation of institutional and neighborhood-level controls, a vacuum that enabled corporate-style drug distribution organizations to emerge and operate with impunity" (Curtis, 2003, p. 45). Gangs also become institutions in organized areas (Jankowski, 1991; Spergel, 1984).

Gangs are a quasi-institutional way to get paid in a system that restricts opportunities. "Any hope for careers for this generation of young men and women had been drastically curtailed by the disappearance of decent jobs and job ladders" (Moore, 1991, p. 6). Restricted opportunity in the legitimate world makes gang life more appealing. In generations past, gang members matured out of the gang. However, in modern gangs, maturing out becomes a less viable option (Hagedorn, 1988; Moore, 1991; Sullivan, 1989). Bloch and Niederhoffer (1958) also recognized that gang behavior is more likely in environments where entry into adulthood is prolonged. Moore believes that transitioning out of the gang will be more of a problem for those members who would otherwise be on the periphery of conventional adaptation. She notes that there will always be gang members who will adapt to conventional lifestyles in adulthood, and there will also be gang members who will be committed to a life of crime, no matter what opportunities are presented to them. However, the marginal group will face a more difficult choice in conformity.

Summary of Underclass Theory

There are themes in current underclass theory that are reminiscent of past theories. There is still a focus on the economy, institutional effectiveness, and ethnicity, so the primary factors are similar. However, the relationship between society, the community, and the gang is different. Ineffectiveness and disorganization is seen from the perspective of lower class society. As the urban environment shifts, the gap between poor, urban America and the rest of the country grows greater. Rather than placing the blame on disorganized communities, the underclass theories see ineffectiveness in

---

BOX 3-2: Focus on Research

Joan W. Moore (1978, 1991) and James Diego Vigil (1988) study barrio gangs in East Los Angeles. Their research provides "insights into the histories and dynamic qualities of two traditional urban gangs, El Hoyo Maravilla and White Fence" (Vigil, 1988, p. 13). These two gangs represent the intergenerational gang. The cliques of El Hoyo Maravilla and White Fence trace back to the 1940s, and they still exist today. Moore's research began in the 1970s through her work on the Chicano Pinto Research Project, which is presented in *Homeboys* (1978). Her follow-up research, presented in *Going Down in the Barrio* (1991), documents the changing dynamics of these two gangs. Vigil's gang education began in his youth. His research, presented in *Barrio Gangs* (1988), is based on "informal and formal" knowledge of Hispanic communities in Los Angeles. Vigil's knowledge of gangs began with close ties to street life in his youth; as he entered adulthood, his connections became professional, as a teacher. His first formal study of gangs was conducted between 1976 and 1981. His research relies primarily on ethnographic fieldwork, including life histories, interviews, and participant observation research.

society at large. This leaves room for organized communities to experience a gang problem, but it also allows for local disorganization. Another difference apparent in underclass theories is the community's relationship to their gangs. The gangs become a replacement for what society is unable to offer. Therefore, in some communities there is a tolerance for the gang.

The theoretical paradigm is in its infancy in comparison with alternative theoretical arguments. Therefore, it is met with optimism. It gives gang research a boost and adds currency to a field that had been theoretically stagnant. There is considerable support for the connection between economic problems and gang formation (see Decker and Van Winkle, 1996; Hagedorn, 1988; Jankowski, 1991; Moore, 1991; Padilla, 1992; Sullivan, 1989).

INTEGRATED THEORY

Other theories are more integrated and difficult to neatly characterize. These theories go beyond the macro level and include the influence of more proximate factors, such as family and psychological concepts, the two specifications that have made their greatest mark on our macro-level understanding of gang formation.

Multiple Marginality

Vigil (1988) conducted research on Chicano gang members in barrios in southern Los Angeles in the 1980s. A barrio is "a neighborhood in a Chicano community, a district in a Mexican colony" (p. 177). Vigil's research led to an interdisciplinary approach to the explanation of gangs that creates a comprehensive framework for understanding area differentiation in gangs. Interestingly, Vigil originally specified, "The multiple marginality construct offers an integrative interpretation, a way to build theory rather than a theory itself" (p. 172). Vigil's "theory" has become dominant in the field and continues to influence research and help us understand gangs.

Multiple marginality is a response to the interaction of stresses and pressures that barrio youth experience. These unique experiences are part of "a web of ecological, socioeconomic, cultural, and psychological factors" (p. 9). Ecological and socioeconomic stresses result from barrio life and the experience of Mexican youth. The environment fits the profile of social disorganization, where social institutions are weak. These are also environments that can be characterized as underclass, with limited good-paying job opportunities. These issues are enhanced by social and racial discrimination. Ultimately, area characteristics and economic strains may cause family stress. Mexican youth growing up in the barrio are consistently reminded that they are on the periphery of American society, that they do not fit in economically, culturally, socially, and racially. When these youth try to fit into American culture, it creates further difficulties at home because the value structure of the Chicano family unit is at odds with the mainstream. This leads to one more layer of marginality. This constant conflict creates an atmosphere where marginalized youth have "more of a need to associate and identify with other marginal street youths like themselves" (p. 63). The gang is where youth feel accepted and find a place to fit in and acquire identity without assimilating into mainstream culture. Vigil discusses finer elements of the psychological process associated with multiple marginality, which will be discussed in more detail in Chapter 4.

Klein's Integrated Model

Another integrated perspective of gang formation is put forth by Klein (1995). It may be more beneficial to consider Klein's specification as a review of prior theoretical arguments. He asks the question "What is it about the growth of the urban underclass that might exacerbate the coming together of lower-class, male, minority youth in urban settings that would result in the formation of street gangs?" (p. 199). As stated in his question, Klein recognizes that the underlying factor of gang formation is the underclass notion developed by Wilson (1987), which has been previously discussed. He also sees the urban, ethnic, male nature of gang activity. These underclass variables essentially cause more proximate onset variables that include "sufficient numbers of lower-class minority males, aged 10–30, hard-to-employ, in an area featured by high crime, absence of social control, and absence of alternative activities" (p. 198). This combination of structural and community difficulties can lead to the onset of gangs (see Figure 3–1). Additionally, Klein's review explores maintenance factors that lead to the longevity of gangs, including oppositional institutions such as the police, gang rivalries, perceived barriers to improvement, and gang intervention programs. It should be noted that Klein's specification also includes psychological variables that lend an individual-level explanation of gang membership. This aspect of Klein's theory will be discussed in more detail in the next chapter.

CHAPTER SUMMARY

> Gangs flourish when there's a lack of social recreation, decent education or employment. Today, many young people will never know what it is to work. They can only satisfy their needs through collective strength—against the police, who hold the power of life and death, against poverty, against idleness, against their impotence in society. (Rodriquez, 1993, p. 250)

Macro-level theories have been a consistent theme in gang literature since Thrasher's work in 1927. Each contributes to our understanding in unique ways and suggests different things about the relationship between society, communities, and gangs. Thrasher's theory recognizes the community as the weak link in the gang phenomenon and its role in not supervising normal adolescent playgroups. Strain theories, such as those of Cohen and Cloward and Ohlin, see society and the community in agreement on value systems, but the gang as a deviant adaptation. In contrast, Miller recognizes a conflict between society's values and the local community's values. In this theory, the gang is a manifestation of this

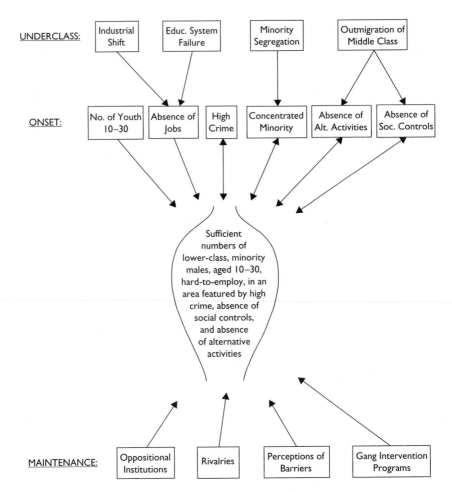

Figure 3–1   Klein's Structural Model of the Emergence of Gangs.
(From *The American Street Gang: Its Nature, Prevalence, and Control* by Malcolm W. Klein;
copyright © 1995 by Oxford University Press, Inc. Used by permission.)

local value system. The underclass theories, on the other hand, see society as the greatest contributor to gang behavior, closely followed by the community. Community problems that exist are in large part due to societal neglect. The gang thrives in this environment.

There has been more focus on area characteristics and community-level explanations of gangs than on individual-level explanations. The focus on macro-level factors over the individual-level factors of early theorists is a common pattern in gang research (Jankowski, 1991; Spergel, 1995; Venkatesh, 2003). Portions of gang theories have been largely ignored, primarily the focus on the individual. For example, Thrasher's work details individual-level experiences within the gang. However, researchers have overlooked this contribution in favor of his definition and playgroup-transition explanation. Vigil's psychological processes also fall into this category.

KEY TERMS

anomie
collective efficacy
conflict subculture
criminal subculture
focal concerns
multiple marginality
primary labor market
retreatist subculture

secondary labor market
social dislocation
social disorganization
social embeddedness
strain
underclass
zones of transition

QUESTIONS FOR REVIEW

1. What are the primary differences between social disorganization, strain, and subcultural theories?

2. What dynamics in the zone of transition help to create gangs?

3. What is the difference between criminal, conflict, and retreatist gangs?

4. How do underclass environments lead to gang formation?

5. What do integrated theories add to our understanding of gang development?

DISCUSSION QUESTIONS

1. In your opinion, which of the theories in this chapter best explains gang formation? Why?

2. What policies could be put in place in underclass areas to reduce gangs?

NOTES

1. Cohen's theory is sometimes characterized as a subcultural theory because of his emphasis on alternative value system development.

2. Although autonomy is valued, much lower class behavior contradicts this. They seek out controlling situations, including gang life.

3. This idea is also applied to Hispanics in Vigil's (1995) work.

CHAPTER 4

EXPLANATIONS OF GANG MEMBERSHIP

CHAPTER OBJECTIVES

- Become familiar with individual-level explanations of gang membership.
- Know major risk factors for gang involvement.
- Understand traditional criminological theories that are applied to gang membership.
- Comprehend theories that specifically explain gang membership.

THE INDIVIDUAL EFFECT

> My relationship with my mother soured continuously as I was drawn deeper and deeper into the streets and further away from home and school. . . . My homeboys became my family—the older ones were father figures. (Shakur, 1993, p. 25)

There is little theoretical development specific to individual gang membership. The academic activity has revolved around three areas: risk factors, traditional delinquency theory, and gang-specific theory. Much research that focuses on risk factors for joining fits in with traditional criminological theory. However, one has to ask if traditional crime theories offer an adequate explanation of why youth join gangs. The literature shows that in the most gang-infested areas, at most about 25% of youth join gangs and "the majority select themselves out" (Klein, 1995, p. 76). There are more youth in high-crime areas who engage in deviant behavior but do not pledge gang membership (Klein, 1995; Vigil, 1988). There is also the fact that the behavior patterns of gang members are very different than those of members of other peer groups.

Gang-specific theories, on the other hand, have been primarily ecological. Those theories that have emphasized the psychological processes of gang members have been largely ignored, or the portion of the theory that emphasizes gang member identity has fallen by the wayside (Venkatesh, 2003). According to Spergel (1995), "Social scientists have tended to view the gang problem in aggregate group, subcultural, or community terms with little attention to distinctions by types and variations of gangs or delinquent groups, or of the individuals within them, within or across communities" (p. 14). Therefore, "[l]ittle attention has been paid to different gang social psychological or individual gang member psychological perspectives" (p. 14).

The issue may be that the theories that are specific to gang members are psychological in nature (see Goldstein, 1991; Jankowski, 1991; Yablonsky, 1962). These are not easily researchable in a field that is predominantly sociological. These factors are recognized in the literature (e.g., Klein's deficient aggressive factor) and are exemplified in the qualitative research that asks youth why they join gangs. However, the connection between these works is relatively weak. There is little research that tests whether gang members are different from nongang members on their self-reported reasons for joining, that is, their desire for money, needing to belong, or protection. (An exception is Maxson and Whitlock, 2002.) Other theories that highlight individual and social psychological factors often do so within a structural paradigm (see Klein, 1995; Thornberry et al., 2003; Vigil, 1988). These integrated theories are valuable, but often theoretical tests and applications do not capture the psychological features. This limits our theoretical understanding of gang members and, more important, our ability to create effective social programs that address individual gang members' needs.

RISK FACTORS

Many researchers recognize the multiple layers of gang membership (see Brotherton and Salazar-Atias, 2003; Hill, Howell, Hawkins, and Battin-Pearson, 1999; Howell, 1998a; Klein, 1995; Spergel, 1995; Thornberry et al., 2003). No one factor can sufficiently explain why an individual chooses to join a gang. In fact, the individual gang member usually has multiple disadvantages and multiple risk factors. Any one risk factor alone is usually not enough for someone to join a gang, but the cumulative effect of risk across several life areas increases the chances of gang membership (Hill, Howell, Hawkins, and Battin-Pearson, 1999; Thornberry et al., 2003). Some risk factors are macro level, as explained in the previous chapter. There are also more proximate risk factors, such as family, school, and other institutions, and micro-level factors, such as psychological features, identity, and status. Curry and Decker (2003) explain risk factors as pushes and pulls into gang membership:

> No single path exists that can capture the reasons or the processes by which individuals come to join a gang. But a key issue to understand in this context is whether individuals are *pulled* or *pushed* into gang membership. Young people who are pulled into membership join their gang because of the attractions it offers to make money, or the ability to provide something for the neighborhood. Being pushed into the

gang conveys a very different motivation for joining the gang. Individuals who see themselves as pushed into gang membership join their gangs out of fear for physical consequences if they do not do so, or because they see themselves as powerless to resist the temptations of gang life. (p. 68)

Pushes and pulls represent the multiple conditions that surround gang membership. Other researchers have broadened this pull-push approach to gang membership beyond what Curry and Decker (2003) and Decker and Van Winkle (1996) identify. Brotherton and Salzar-Atias (2003) conceptualize push factors as "a combination of socioeconomic, political, psychological, and cultural determinants" (p. 185) and pull factors as narrower instrumental and social features of the gang.

Push Risk Factors

There is general agreement that each of these areas is important to understanding gang membership. **Push risk factors** are usually put into categories of community, family, school, peers, and individual.[1] These factors are prominent in gang research and are often tested by comparing gang members with nongang members. Generally, push risk factors are more salient in male gang members than in female gang members (Maxson and Whitlock, 2002; Thornberry et al., 2003).

Community Risk.   Community risk factors for gang joining include gang presence in the neighborhood, drug use, and area poverty rate. Research finds that these factors increase the risk of gang joining (Curry and Spergel, 1992; Hill, Howell, Hawkins, and Battin-Pearson, 1999; Moore, 1991; Padilla, 1992; Thornberry et al., 2003; Wang, 1999).

Family Risk.   The role of family is extensively discussed in gang literature. Gangs act as a surrogate family for some gang members (Decker and Van Winkle, 1996; Vigil, 1988). Moore (1991) concludes that "gang members come from troubled families" (p. 103). The troubled environment includes family stress (Moore, 1991; Vigil, 1988), family gang membership or involvement in criminal activity (Decker and VanWinkle, 1996; Jankowski, 1991; Maxson and Whitlock, 2002; Moore, 1991; Vigil, 1988), family disadvantage (Bowker and Klein, 1983; Hill, Howell, Hawkins, and Battin-Pearson, 1999; Moore, 1991; Thornberry et al., 2003), and single-parent households (Bowker and Klein, 1983; Hill, Howell, Hawkins, and Battin-Pearson, 1999; Thornberry et al., 2003; Vigil, 1988). Poor family management skills, as measured by discipline, monitoring and control, and weak parent-child affectionate ties, are also risk factors for gang membership (Bowker and Klein, 1983; Hill, Howell, Hawkins, and Battin-Pearson, 1999; LeBlanc and Lanctot, 1998; Moore, 1991; Thornberry et al., 2003; Wang, 1999). Family background characteristics, such as parent education and family income, also predict stability of gang membership (Thornberry et al., 2003). Those gang members who stay in gangs longer have more deficient family backgrounds than gang members who are in a gang for only a year or so.

> ### BOX 4–1: A Closer Look
>
> Kids have individual backgrounds that may predispose them to gang joining. However, many times these backgrounds are so different that we are left to wonder if we can ever pinpoint the exact factors. This is why so many theories are appealing. Consider the contrasting child-hoods of "Tookie" Williams (see Williams, 2004) and "Lil' C" (see Simpson, 2005). Both were members of the Los Angeles Crips, albeit Tookie's membership precedes Lil' C's. Although life histories of serious gang members are difficult to generalize to all gang members, the brief descriptions of these two Crips allow us to compare their early childhood experiences and recognize that their differences add to the complexity of understanding gang members.
>
> Tookie discusses his upbringing and his relationship with his mother. She was "hard-working, serious, tough, soft-spoken" (p. 4). He states, "My mother tried to instill in me the fundamentals of right and wrong" (p. 5). "[S]he is not responsible for my actions. Any of them. My mother exhausted every possible effort to raise me properly, but she could not stand guard over me 24/7. She was in thrall to some handed down Black rendition of a Euro-American parenting philosophy which was in total conflict with the environment I saw around me and its stringent requirements for survival. Clearly, not even my mother's intentions and religious guidance could have compelled or prayed me into conforming to society's double standards" (p. 13).
>
> Lil' C chronicles a different childhood, with a substance-using mother who is victim and perpetrator of family violence. Lil' C recounts, "I smell her marijuana. She enters the kitchen and pours a glass of wine and rinses dishes. I listen to predict her mood. . . . I know what's coming next. I sense it when she starts her search, sense it in her restless movements, how she scatters from place to place . . . searching with angry hisses. . . . She whacks me on my back, my legs . . . Mom grabs the plastic bat, Oh, no. I remember how it hurts, the welts it leaves" (p. 5). His mother blames her kids for her situation and states, "That's why I can't keep no man, It's because of you fuckin' kids" (p. 10). She even blindfolded her pajama-clad children with "blue beanies over [their] face and dropped [them] off in a Blood neighborhood."

School Risk.   School risk factors, such as commitment to school, educational achievement, and educational expectations, are important in understanding gang join-ing. Gangs are attractive to youth who are not committed or connected to teachers or the school environment (Hill, Howell, Hawkins, and Battin-Pearson, 1999; Esbensen, Huizinga, and Weiher, 1993; Padilla, 1992; Thornberry et al., 2003; Wang, 1995, 1999). There is mixed support for involvement in extracurricular activities. Some research finds that gang members are not involved in these activities (Decker and Van Winkle, 1996), and other research finds no significant differences in the extracurricular activities of gang members, nongang deviants, and nonoffenders (Esbensen, Huizinga, and Wei-her, 1993). Gang members often turn off from school before they drop out (Vigil, 1988, p. 81). Gang members are more likely than nongang youth to be lower achievers in school (Hill, Howell, Hawkins, and Battin-Pearson, 1999; Thornberry et al., 2003) and have low expectations for educational success (Bjerregaard and Smith, 1993; Bowker and Klein, 1983; Hill, Howell, Hawkins, and Battin-Pearson, 1999; Thornberry et al., 2003). Educational frustrations have a profound impact on some gang members and increase their risk for joining (Bowker and Klein, 1983; Curry and Spergel, 1992). School experiences seem to have a greater impact on Hispanics (Curry and Spergel, 1992) and females (Bjerregaard and Smith, 1993; Maxson and Whitlock, 2002; Thornberry et al., 2003).

Peer Group Risk.   Peer associations are perhaps the most consistent risk factor discussed in gang literature. Many gang members hang out with other deviant peers and/or gang members before joining the gang (Bjerregaard and Smith, 1993; Bowker and Klein, 1983; Esbensen, Huizinga, and Weiher, 1993; Hill, Howell, Hawkins, and Battin-Pearson, 1999; Lahey et al., 1999; LeBlanc and Lanctot, 1998; Maxson and Whitlock, 2002; Thornberry et al., 2003; Vigil, 1988; Winfree, Backstrom, and Mays, 1994). Deviant peer groups were the predominant risk factor for African American gang members in Curry and Spergel's (1992) research. Gang membership is also related to early dating and early sexual activity (Bjerregaard and Smith, 1993; Bowker and Klein, 1983; LeBlanc and Lanctot, 1998; Thornberry et al., 2003).

Individual Risk.   Individual risk factors include deviant values, prior delinquency, self-esteem/identity, and stressful life events. Deviant value systems consistently predict gang membership (Hill, Howell, Hawkins, and Battin-Pearson, 1999; Esbensen, Huizinga, and Weiher, 1993; LeBlanc and Lanctot, 1998; Thornberry et al., 2003). Esbensen, Winfree, He, and Taylor (2001) found that "gang members reported substantially more antisocial attitudes and behaviors than nongang youths" (p. 123). Values were more deviant as commitment to the gang increased, "with the relatively small sample of core members manifesting the most extreme responses" (p. 123). Prior deviant behavior is also a risk factor for gang membership (Bjerregaard and Smith, 1993; Curry and Spergel, 1992; Decker and Van Winkle, 1996; Esbensen and Huizinga, 1993; Hill, Howell, Hawkins, and Battin-Pearson, 1999; LeBlanc and Lanctot, 1998; Thornberry et al., 2003).

Self-esteem and identity issues of the gang member are prominently discussed in literature (see Cohen, 1990). However, research results are less consistent than the literature suggests. Some find that gang members experience lower levels of self-esteem than others (Dukes, Martinez, and Stein, 1997; Wang, 1995), but there is more evidence that rejects the direct link between self-esteem and gang membership (Bjerregaard and Smith, 1993; Bowker and Klein, 1983; Esbensen, Huizinga, and Weiher, 1993; Thornberry et al., 2003). Some research shows a link between depression (Thornberry et al., 2003) and stressful life events (Maxson and Whitlock, 2002; Thornberry et al., 2003).

Pull Risk Factors

Pull risk factors are more apparent in research that asks gang members to explain why they join gangs. Gang members consistently report similar reasons for joining gangs.

Some of these reasons are directly related to the risk factors discussed, such as the influence of family and friends, or the desire for money and reputation. However, other reasons for gang joining are not as obviously apparent in the academic literature, such as protection and excitement. Maxson and Whitlock (2002) compared reasons for group joining in their sample of gang members and nongang youth. They found that gang members report joining groups because friends and family were involved, to get a reputation, and for belonging and excitement. Nongang youth report joining groups to make friends, fill empty time, and keep out of trouble. These results are consistent with other research that explores reasons for gang joining. Many members report that they join gangs because family or friends were involved (Esbensen, Deschenes, and Winfree, 1999; Taylor, 1989; Thornberry et al., 2003; Wang, 1999); others report they join because of a sense of commitment to their neighborhood (Decker and Van Winkle, 1996; Jankowski, 1991). Gang members also report they join for money (Decker and Van Winkle, 1996; Esbensen, Deschenes, and Winfree, 1999; Jankowski, 1991; Stone, 1999; Taylor, 1989; Wang, 1999), protection (Decker and Van Winkle, 1996; Esbensen, Deschenes, and Winfree, 1999; Jankowski, 1991; Stone, 1999; Taylor, 1989; Thornberry et al., 2003; Wang, 1999), image/reputation (Esbensen, Deschenes, and Winfree, 1999; Taylor, 1989), and fun or excitement (Esbensen, Deschenes, and Winfree, 1999; Jankowski, 1991; Taylor, 1989; Stone, 1999; Thornberry et al., 2003).

Risk factors are the primary elements in theories of delinquency and gang membership. As we explore individual-level theory, there will be risk factors that fit into many different theoretical ideas. The easiest way to distinguish the theoretical ideas is to focus on how the link between the risk factor and gang membership is explained.

TRADITIONAL DELINQUENCY THEORY

Several criminological theories that were originally developed to explain general deviant behavior have been used in gang research. They offer an explanation of the decision to become involved in a gang. Traditional theories nicely accommodate the intermediate factors associated with gang membership, such as family, peers, and school. Some of the theories also leave room for psychological explanations.

Learning Theory

Risk factors and self-reported reasons for gang joining suggest that family, peers, value systems, money, and other rewards are a fundamental part of the process. These ideas are consistent with social learning theory (Akers, 1973). The basic tenet of learning theory is that we learn to be deviant by our interactions with our environment. Sociological learning theory is rooted in the work of Sutherland's differential association theory (1947). Sutherland identified, in a series of nine propositions, that we learn deviant behavior from our primary social groups, those that we interact with most often and who are important to us. We learn methods and motives of criminal behavior and definitions about the legal code. If we learn more law-violating definitions than law-abiding ones,

TABLE 4-1

Summary of traditional delinquency theories

Learning Theory

- Operates under the assumption that youth learn deviant behavior from the environment.
- Social learning theory, by Akers, specifies that learning take place through imitation and a system of punishments and rewards.

Control Theory

- Youth not connected to conventional society will be free to engage in deviant behavior.
- Social bonding theory, by Hirschi, specifies four elements that make up the social bond.
- A general theory of crime, by Gottfredson and Hirschi, specifies that self-control and opportunity foster deviant behavior.

The Classical School

- People will engage in behavior that brings the most pleasure with minimal pain.
- Rational choice theory, by Cornish and Clarke, specifies that this process involves rationality and calculation that is based on prior experience.

Interactional Theory

- Connects elements of different types of theories, including learning and bonding.
- Incorporates the life course view that behavior can change over time.

deviant behavior is the likely result. Sutherland explained that we learn deviant behavior through the same mechanisms as we learn all other behavior.

Social Learning Theory. Akers (1973) developed social learning theory as an extension of Sutherland's theory of differential association to explain how we learn behavior. Akers postulates that operant and instrumental conditioning combined are the primary mechanism for learning. Operant conditioning is the imitation aspect of Akers's theory. We model the behavior we see in others, but imitation alone cannot explain the process of recurring behavior. Akers establishes that much repeated behavior is the result of instrumental conditioning or the differential reinforcement we receive. If we receive positive feedback or our behavior is reinforced, it is likely to continue in the future. If we are punished for the behavior, future occurrences are reduced. This learning mechanism is supported by concepts of differential association and definitions. Akers believes that the people we associate with, our differential associations, expose us to varying norms, behaviors, reinforcements, and punishments. Like Sutherland, Akers expects that a person who is exposed to more law-violating norms and behaviors than law-abiding norms and behaviors will be more likely to model and imitate this behavior. Also, the behavior will be differentially reinforced, through rewards and punishments, by those around us. As this reinforcement process takes place, the individual learns and internalizes belief systems, or definitions, about criminal behavior.

Support for Social Learning Theory.   Research finds support for social learning process in connection with gang membership (Curry and Spergel, 1992; Winfree, Backstrom, and Mays, 1994; Lahey et al., 1999). Esbensen, Winfree, He, and Taylor (2001) test social learning theory predictors of gang membership and find that "the theoretical predictors from social learning theory (especially association with delinquent peers, perceptions of guilt, and neutralizations for fighting) supersede the importance of demographic characteristics" (p. 124). Research by Thornberry and colleagues (2003) finds that delinquent beliefs and prior deviant behavior partially predict gang membership. Although this research does not directly test tenets of social learning theory, these findings support social learning theory principles. Field research also supports social learning theory principles (Moore, 1991; Padilla, 1992; Vigil, 1988). One example can be found in Padilla's study of the Diamonds, a second-generation Hispanic street gang in Chicago. Members of the Diamonds recall gangs always being in the community. Padilla states that "young people have grown up witnessing and learning specific elements of gang culture" (p. 61).

Control Theory

Research has shown that gang members lack connections to family and school and embrace deviant peers and deviant value systems (Bjerregaard and Smith, 1993; Hill, Howell, Hawkins, and Battin-Pearson, 1999; Moore, 1991; Thornberry et al., 1993; Thornberry et al., 2003). These relationships can be explained by control theories, specifically Hirschi's social bonding theory (1969) and Gottfredson and Hirschi's general theory of crime (1990). Control theories are rooted in the work of Emile Durkheim and the concept of social integration. Social integration operates under the assumption that we are naturally inclined toward deviant behavior. It is because of our connections to different institutions in society that we conform. This perspective assumes that societal norms are generally agreed upon. Thus, individuals who are unable to connect to conventional society will have difficulty in integrating and will be more likely to engage in deviant behavior.

Social Bonding Theory.   Travis Hirschi (1969) builds from control theory assumptions in his development of social bonding theory. According to Hirschi, we are bonded to society through four elements: attachment to conventional others, commitment to conventional society, involvement, and belief. **Attachment** to conventional others is the element through which the internalization of societal norms takes place. This is the most important bond, according to Hirschi. If we are attached to others who are generally conforming, and if we care about what they think, we are more likely to abide by the general norms of society. If we do not care what conventional others think, then we are less likely to be constrained by norms. The latter is likely to happen when we are not attached to conventional others or when we are attached to nonconforming others. The second element of the bond that Hirschi discusses is **commitment** to conventional society. This element is based in common sense and rational choice. An individual who is committed to conventional goals will not risk losing these goals by engaging in criminal behavior. For example, people with strong conventional occupational goals will not risk losing their dreams by engaging in criminal behavior that may land them in jail. The third bond, **involvement,** is the time element of the bond. A person who is involved in conventional activities simply will not have the time to engage in criminal behavior. Those with a lot of time on their hands are more apt to engage in criminal behavior. The final element of the social bond is **belief** in societal norms. This belief system varies from one person to the next. A person who has a weakened belief system will be more likely to deviate from the general norms of society.

As applied to gang membership, Hirschi's theory can aid in our understanding of how one becomes a gang member and ultimately engages in deviant behavior. As our bonds to conventional society are capable of changing, the theory can help to explain how behavior is worsened when an individual joins a gang. It is also able to account for gang members' ability to move out of the gang and into less criminal lifestyles.

Support for Social Bonding Theory.   Research supports social bonding theory principles (Dukes, Martinez, and Stein, 1997; Mateu-Gelabert, 2002; Thornberry et al., 2003; Wang, 1995). Curry and Spergel (1992) find that youth in gangs are more likely to look to peers for self-esteem and less likely to look to the school for self-esteem. This suggests that bonds are stronger to the deviant peer group than to the conventional institution of the school, supporting social bonding. Vigil's qualitative research (1988) makes a strong case for social bonding. He explains that gang members often drop out of school, but before they do, they go through a "turning-off" process. This process, exemplified in poor grades, attendance, and behavior, demonstrates their lack of connectedness to the institution.

A General Theory of Crime.   In *A General Theory of Crime*, Gottfredson and Hirschi (1990) suggest that self-control and opportunity are the elements that propel or inhibit an individual's criminal behavior. They define crime "as acts of force or fraud undertaken in pursuit of self-interest" (p. 15). Gottfredson and Hirschi contend that in addition to criminal behavior, low self-control individuals engage in behaviors analogous to crime. These low self-control individuals also "smoke, drink, use drugs, gamble, have children out of wedlock, and engage in illicit sex" (1990, p. 90).

This self-control connection to behavior is not deterministic, according to Gottfredson and Hirschi. The connection is "probabilistic, affected by opportunities and other constraints" (1990, p. 53). If the opportunity to commit a crime is available, individuals with low self-control are more likely to engage in a criminal act than high self-control individuals. Therefore, lack of self-control does not automatically lead to crime; behavior also depends on the opportunities for criminal behavior that are present.

Gottfredson and Hirschi do not perceive self-control as a motivating force for crime. Rather, self-control is "the barrier that stands between the actor and the obvious momentary benefits crime provides" (p. 53). They identify several elements of self-control. People with low self-control seek immediate gratification, whereas people with high self-control defer gratification. Low self-control people seek "easy or simple gratifications of desires" (p. 89). They are "adventuresome, active, and physical," whereas high self-control people are "cautious, cognitive, and verbal" (p. 89). Individuals with low self-control tend to be unprepared for or not interested in long-term commitments. Gottfredson and Hirschi point out that people who lack self-control do not possess or value academic or cognitive skills. They tend to be self-centered and indifferent to the pain of others. Low self-control individuals will engage in immediate pleasures that are not criminal. They have little tolerance for irritation and are unable to "respond to conflict through verbal rather than physical means" (p. 90).

Gottfredson and Hirschi sum up their description of low self-control individuals by stating that they tend to be "impulsive, insensitive, physical (as opposed to mental), risk-taking, shortsighted, and nonverbal, and they will tend therefore to engage in criminal and analogous acts" (p. 90). They further state that self-control is a unidimensional trait that remains relatively stable throughout a person's lifetime. Once established, individual levels of self-control remain stable over the life course and are relatively unaffected by other institutions (pp. 107–8).

Support for a General Theory of Crime.   Some research has assessed the strength of self-control theory in the explanation of gang membership. Hope and Damphousse (2002) find that gang members have lower levels of self-control than nongang youth in a sample from Fayetteville, Arkansas. This is supported by Lynskey, Winfree, Esbensen and Clason's (2000) research finding that self-control influences involvement with gangs. However, Esbensen, Winfree, He, and Taylor (2001) find weak support for self-control as a predictor of gang membership when it is considered alongside learning theory indicators.

The Classical School

The principles of rational choice theory are much different than any theory discussed to this point. This theory is based in the classical school of thought established by Beccaria and Bentham, which states that people give up freedoms to ensure other rights and that the legal code represents this social contract. Beccaria believed that people were capable of making the choice to abide by the social contract with limited punishment. Bentham added the pleasure-pain principle to the classical school. He believed that we are all motivated to maximize pleasure while minimizing pain. Before engaging in any behavior, people engage a cost-benefit analysis, called hedonistic calculus. Early classical school theorists were primarily concerned with punishment and far less concerned with explaining causes of criminal behavior. The classical school was quickly altered by neoclassicalists, as they recognized individual variation in choice making (e.g., juvenile, mentally ill, and repeat offenders). Modern-day neoclassical school theorists use the basic elements of choice making and cost-benefit analysis in their theoretical formulations.

Rational Choice Theory.   Cornish and Clarke (1986) present a current extension of the neoclassical school paradigm in rational choice theory. Their theoretical specification establishes that we are rational beings with the capacity for free will. They focus more on the decision to engage in crime, rather than the motivation of the individual offender. Individuals who engage in crime do so because it is beneficial to them. This decision-making process is at times rudimentary, but it is decision making all the same. It involves a certain amount of rationality and calculation. Individuals engage in choice structuring, whereby individual needs meld with the choice to engage in particular offenses. Decisions to engage in criminal behavior are influenced by many factors, including prior learning and life experiences.

Support for Rational Choice Theory.   Regarding gangs, we see some support for the rational choice perspective. Jankowski (1991) states that individuals who do not join gangs can be "individuals who see no personal advantage in participating in a gang" (p. 59). In fact, they "see significant disadvantages" in gang membership (p. 59). This perspective is repeated by DiChiara and Chabot (2003) in their conclusion: "The more fruitful approach understands gang members as rational actors who act on the basis of economic and personal rationality" (p. 91). Gang members, in their self-accounts, discuss the "pulls" of membership in rational terms. They recognize their needs for family, money, and protection.

Interactional Theory

More recently, Thornberry's interactional theory (1987), with a life course extension, has been used as an explanation of gang membership (Thornberry et al., 2003). Interactional theory connects primary elements of traditional theories, including bonding and learning. Thornberry's theory contains a structural component, which is considered one risk factor that sets in motion individual delinquency. However, the main emphasis of the theory falls within a social psychological paradigm (see Figure 4–1). The theory operates under the assumption that behavior is not stable or set in childhood. "Behavior patterns continue to unfold and change across the person's life, in part because of the consequences of earlier patterns of behavior" (Thornberry et al., 2003, p. 83). Therefore, behavior that an individual engages in can influence conventional attachments and lead to further deviant behavior.2 The theory establishes that weakened bonds to family and school occur before delinquency. These weak bonds are more likely to occur in conditions of structural disadvantage. The combination of structure and weak bonds leads to associating with deviant peers, having deviant

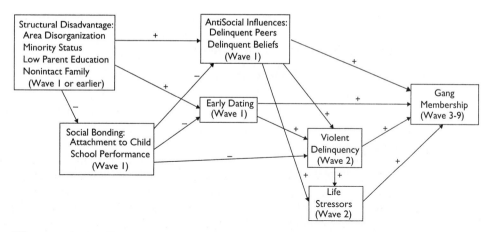

Figure 4–1   Thornberry's Diagram of Causal Processes.
(From *Gangs and Delinquency in Developmental Perspective* by Terence P. Thornberry, et al.; copyright © 2003 by Cambridge University Press. Used by permission.)

values, and early dating. These factors lead to stress and deviant behavior and then ultimately gang membership. "In brief, our model derived from interactional theory posits that structural disadvantage leads to a reduction in prosocial bonds, and both of these lead to an enhancement in antisocial influences. In turn, these earlier factors increase involvement in delinquency and violence as well as levels of stress, all of which increase the likelihood of a youth joining a gang" (p. 86).

GANG-SPECIFIC THEORIES

The theories discussed to this point mainly focus on macro- and intermediate-level explanations. However, these explanations are "not sufficient because most youths from such areas, such groups, and such families do not join gangs" (Klein, 1995, p. 75). Literature identifies individual differences between gang members and nongang youth. Klein identifies psychological factors, status needs, identity and belonging needs, social disabilities (lower social skills), and affiliative needs as differentiating between these youth (p. 200). Spergel (1995) neatly classifies these individual-level factors as "personal disorganization," including psychological deficiencies, and status and identity needs.

For the most part, gang-specific theories give particular attention to the psychological processes of adolescence (e.g., self-esteem, identity, peer acceptance). Gang membership is often thought of as an extreme in this normal pathway (Goldstein, 1991; Moore, 1991). Some researchers have explained the process of gang joining as the outcome of growing up in difficult environments. These experiences require personal adjustments and affect people's outlook on life.

TABLE 4–2

Summary of gang-specific theories

Defiant Individualistic Character
- Developed by Jankowski (1991).
- Gang members develop a unique persona as a result of growing up with limited resources.

The Hyperadolescent
- Developed by Goldstein (1991) based on Erikson's ideas on identity and adolescent development.
- Youth from marginal environments have more intense needs for peer group identification, leading to gang membership.

The Sociopathic Personality
- Developed by Yablonsky (1962).
- Poverty-based environments lead to ineffective socialization, which results in sociopathy. The sociopathic youth engages in extreme behavior to experience feeling.

Multiple Marginality
- Developed by Vigil (1988), based on Erikson's views of identity.
- Marginalized youth have difficulty in achieving a positive identity, resulting in a "psychosocial moratorium" or "ego identity crisis."
- Gang membership offers an opportunity for identity development.

The Defiant Individualistic Character

Jankowski (1991) identifies that gang members have a **defiant individualistic character** that is the result of growing up in an environment with too few resources. The lack of resources in disadvantaged areas leads to specific attributes that can be seen in gang members. These attributes are interconnected and ultimately rooted in resource deprivation. Jankowski recognizes that these attributes interact with culture, so adaptations will differ to reflect cultural values. For example, Chicano communities value family, so a Chicano's behavioral manifestation of these attributes will reflect commitment to family.

Competitiveness is most obviously seen, as families have very little, and there is constant competition over what little exists. This competition is not just at the community level but is also seen within families, where there is competition for things like food, privacy, and affection. Competition is heightened in single-parent households with many kids, in families where parents are working multiple jobs, or in living arrangements that require sibling room sharing. Competition leads to attributes such as mistrust and self-reliance. According to Jankowski, "Trust is not simply a given, but something to be calculated" (p. 24). Ultimately, competition, mistrust, and self-reliance lead to social isolation and survival instincts; an individual begins to "assume the character of predators trapping prey" (p. 25). As the individual becomes exposed to the larger world, a social Darwinist worldview will develop. Individuals in this situation compare their lives to others and see successful people getting by with values of competitiveness. This eventually leads to a defiant air, which allows them to be successful in low-resource environments. Quantitative research finds mixed support of Jankowski's theory (Jensen, 1996).

The Hyperadolescent

Goldstein (1991) also attributes gang membership to the environment. Building on Erikson's theory of identity development, Goldstein sees adolescence as a time when youth search for identity and peer acceptance. Youth spend adolescence working toward independence and enhancing self-identity. Goldstein believes this search for identity can be fulfilled in conventional and positive ways. However, youth who grow up in marginal environments have a harder time in this quest. Gang members have an "intense need for approval" and little confidence in themselves, and they are more active in their search for adult status (p. 75). As a result, "It appears that, in terms of both their prepotent needs and characteristic overt behaviors, adolescent members of delinquent gangs are what we would term **hyperadolescents**: They exhibit needs and behaviors typical of most adolescents but to a substantially intensified degree" (p. 67).

BOX 4–2: Focus on Research

Martin Sanchez Jankowski's (1991) *Islands in the Street: Gangs and American Urban Society* documents a 10-year qualitative study of gangs between 1978 and 1989 in the United States. He explores and compares different types of gangs in the long-standing gang cities of New York, Los Angeles, and Boston. Jankowski purposefully chose these cities because they best represent "different socioeconomic and political environments" (p. 6). His research generated a sample of 13 Los Angeles gangs, 20 New York gangs, and 4 Boston gangs. Jankowski also included gangs with varying race/ethnic compositions, including "Irish, African-American, Puerto Rican, Chicano, Dominican, Jamaican, and Central American" (p. 7). Interestingly, due to Jankowski's own nonwhite heritage, he more easily gained access to ethnic minority gangs. However, he was unable to gain access to Italian and Asian gangs, and his access to Irish gangs was because he was not Puerto Rican. Jankowski's study is reminiscent of Thrasher's (1927/1963) earlier work because of the variation in gangs in terms of ethnicity, size, age range, and leadership structure. Through participant observation research, Jankowski gives us a unique view of the world of gangs.

The gang member, as a hyperadolescent, is more prone to the effects of peer pressure and peer group identification.

This notion of extreme versions of normal behavior is reiterated by other researchers. Klein (1995) states that gang members have "a notable set of personal deficiencies, a notable tendency toward defiance, aggressiveness, fighting, and pride in physical prowess, greater than normal desire for status, identity, and companionship, a boring uninvolved lifestyle" (p. 76) and that "[t]heir needs and their pleasures are exaggerations of those familiar to us from a more general youth population" (p. 76). This idea is also discussed by Moore (1991) in her discussion of the behavioral continuum (see Chapter 2 for discussion).

The Sociopathic Personality

Yablonsky (1962) presents a psychologically complex portrayal of the gang member. He believes that the gang member is a "sociopathic personality" and that "[t]he violent gang . . . serves as a 'simplified' withdrawal for the sociopathic youth from the more demanding society" (p. 222). The sociopathic personality "is characteristically unable to experience the pain of the violence he may inflict on another, since he does not have the ability to identify or empathize with any others" (p. 198). This personality is characterized by one or more of the following:

(a) a defective social conscience marked by limited feelings of guilt for destructive acts against others
(b) limited feelings of compassion or empathy for others
(c) the acting out of behavior dominated by egocentrism and self-seeking goals, and
(d) the manipulation of others in a way possible for immediate self-gratification (for example, sexual exploitative modes of behavior) without any moral concern or responsibility. (p. 201)

Yablonsky details the process by which violent gangs develop (pp. 225–26). He believes that poverty-based environments do not effectively socialize youth. Someone growing up in this environment will experience "alienation from human feeling or meaning" (p. viii). The response is to engage in "**existential validation** or the validation of one's existence" (p. viii) to experience feeling. The sociopathic youth has "paranoid reactions" and engages in extreme behavior that establishes identity with similar others. The "pseudo-community" that develops provides "a channel to act out hostility and aggression to satisfy the continuing and momentary emotional needs of its members" (p. 3).

Such psychological deficits, as specified by Yablonsky, are not generally supported. The characteristics of sociopaths make it difficult for them to function in a group environment. Yablonsky's research is an example of the general lack of attention that is paid to gang member variation, even among academic researchers. It is difficult to apply his classification of "sociopath" to all gang members. Klein (1995) differentiates between hardcore gang members and other members. He states that a *"deficient-aggressive"* factor is apparent in core members. Hardcore members have lower intelligence and weaker impulse control, and they do more poorly in school than others. "Core membership, it seems, attracts the less socially capable and more antisocial youngsters" (p. 201). General themes of identity and self-esteem are present in some of the previous works, but other researchers place more obvious emphasis on these factors. McDonald (2003) states, "The imperative of self-esteem is essential for participation in the network society. It is central to the theme of 'respect,' which forms the foundation of the street cultures that have developed over the past twenty years. This imperative is the basis of new forms of gangs and of the role violence plays in the lives of marginalized young people" (p. 72).

Multiple Marginality

Vigil (1988) completes his theory of multiple marginality (see Chapter 3) with a focus on identity. Citing Erikson, he emphasizes the role of gang membership in identity development. Marginalized youth have a more difficult time fitting in and achieving a positive sense of self. They enter into a **"psychosocial moratorium"** or "ego identity crisis" (p. 151). This is not necessarily a psychological problem, but a temporary conflict that is often resolved by gang membership. "[T]he gang provides role expectations and functions to shepherd a person through this 'psychological moratorium'" (p. 168). By performing according to set expectations in the gang, the individual gains a sense of self. The gang member can more easily establish identity through deviant behavior than through conventional behavior.

CHAPTER SUMMARY

> My dad's solution was to keep me home after school. Grounded, Yeah, sure. I was 13 years old already. Already tattooed, Already sexually involved, Already into drugs. In the middle of the night I snuck out the window and worked my way to the Hills. (Rodriquez, 1993, p. 48)

It is important to study and understand the gang member. The risk factors common to gang members are useful in developing effective prevention and intervention programs. Research shows that risk factors for gang membership include the areas of community, family, school, peers, and individual characteristics. More important than any one risk factor is the cumulative effect of multiple risk factors. Theoretically, the risk of gang membership can be explained by traditional delinquency theories, including learning, social control, and rational choice. However, the fact remains that there are youth growing up in high-risk areas with many individual risk factors. Many may even be delinquent, but they do not join gangs. The question remains whether there is something different about the youth who joins a gang that cannot be explained with traditional delinquency theories.

Gang-specific theories attempt to fill this void by focusing on personality and psychological factors that may be unique to the gang member. Some common themes found in these explanations include status and identity needs. This reality of gang membership is reinforced through the words of gang members, suggesting their importance to our understanding. Overall, the theories of gang membership touch on important risk factors that are used in policy formation. Policy will be explored in Chapter 11 of this book.

KEY TERMS

attachment
belief
commitment
defiant individualistic character
existential validation

hyperadolescent
involvement
psychosocial moratorium
pull risk factors
push risk factors

QUESTIONS FOR REVIEW

1. What are the primary risk factors of gang membership?

2. How does cumulative risk allow us to understand gang membership?

3. What are the major assumptions of the traditional delinquency theories discussed in this chapter?

4. How does Jankowski's theory differ from Yablonsky's?

5. What role do identity and status play in gang membership?

DISCUSSION QUESTIONS

1. How important do you think it is to develop a gang-specific theory to explain gang membership? Do you think that traditional theories are good enough? Why or why not?

2. Vigil's theory of multiple marginality, explained in Chapter 3, examines a complex interconnection between area characteristics, family, and the individual. Do you think this is a sound explanation of gangs and gang membership? What is he missing that other theories help to explain?

NOTES

1. Thornberry et al. (2003) further expand these categories to include early delinquency and to differentiate between family sociodemographic factors and parent-child relations.

2. In research, this is referred to as a reciprocal relationship.

CHAPTER 5

GANG ORGANIZATION AND GROUP PROCESS

CHAPTER OBJECTIVES

- Understand the variation in gang activity.
- Become familiar with structural differences in gangs.
- Recognize gang organizational elements.
- Understand the process of gang organizational development.

GANG VARIATION

> Miguel and the rest of us started Thee Impersonations because we needed protec-
> tion. There were other clubs popping up all over, many challenging anybody who
> wasn't into anything. All of a sudden every dude had to claim a clique. . . . Then some
> of the clubs metamorphosed into something more unpredictable, more encompass-
> ing. Something more deadly. (Rodriquez, 1993, pp. 42, 43)

There is incredible variation between and within gangs that can be seen in the primary
behavior of gangs, the structure of gangs, and the level of gang organization. Jankowski
(1991) recognized our limited understanding of gang organization: "for the most part,
studies of gangs have not closely examined the nature, dynamics, and impact of the gang's
organizational qualities." He believed that "one of the reasons that society does not
understand gangs or the gang phenomenon very well is that there have not been enough
systematic studies undertaken as to how the gang works as an organization" (p. 5).

Most gangs are not organized (Thrasher, 1927/1963; Vigil, 1988; Hagedorn, 1988;
Klein, 1995). This may be the reason that organization is not always systematically
considered. However, research suggests that even among "unorganized" gangs, there is

variation in their group processes. This has a profound impact on the behaviors and activities of the group. It is also possible for a gang to become more organized over time. Because many researchers envision the variation in gangs differently, trying to grasp the ideas separately can create confusion. It is best viewed as a continuum of behaviors, structure, and organization that range anywhere from weakly organized **playgroups** to more clearly organized **supergangs.** Each of the elements discussed in this chapter is fundamental to understanding the group process of gangs and distinguishing groups along this continuum.

Overall, understanding the distinction in gang structure and organization is critical to developing policies and programs aimed at reducing gangs and gang violence. We run into problems if gangs are defined "in a narrow or unchanging manner," as it "neglects the process of development which different age groups within gangs undergo and ignores or undervalues variations of all sorts" (Bloch and Neiderhoffer, 1958, p. 106). This chapter will explore this variation and allow a greater understanding of the gang as a group.

BEHAVIORAL TYPOLOGIES

The most common behavior of gang members is consistently documented as "hanging out" (Decker and Van Winkle, 1996; Moore, 1978; Vigil, 1998; Padilla, 1992; Jankowski, 1991; Thrasher, 1927/1963; Short and Strodtbeck, 1965). This seemingly nonthreatening activity brings with it the ability to become more organized through the sharing of thoughts, values, and common experiences. Thrasher states that "[t]he result of this collective behavior is the development of traditions, unreflective internal structure, spirit de corps, solidarity, morale, group awareness, and attachment to local territory" (1927/1963, p. 46). As the group becomes more organized, group behaviors change. One trend in understanding gang organization has been to differentiate the group according to its prominent deviant behavior.

Cloward and Ohlin (1960) developed one of the most notable methods of characterizing gang behavior. As discussed in Chapter 3, they believe that three different subcultures can form in response to the interaction between strain and opportunity structures. The **criminal subculture** engages in moneymaking behaviors, the **conflict subculture** engages in violent behavior, and the **retreatist subculture** primarily engages in drug use. Others state that "there is no clear separation between conflict and criminal subcultures" (Short and Strodtbeck, 1965, p. 98).

A similar typology was presented by Yablonsky (1962). He distinguishes between the violent "near group," the delinquent gang, and the social gang. The violent gang mainly engages in "spontaneous prestige-seeking violence with psychic gratification" (p. 149). The sociopathic nature of its members is evident in the group's activities. It differs from the delinquent gang, whose behavior is illegal acts geared toward monetary reward. The social gang is viewed as "tough youths who band together" and whose activities are social in nature. Yablonsky also realizes that "these prototypes seldom appear in a pure form" but that they have "a central characteristic that distinguishes them" (p. 149). However, in his later writing, Yablonsky (1997) states that the activities of some gangs have "merged into a somewhat different type of gang" that he labels the "multipurpose gang" (p. 15). This later addition reflects the type of modern gang that developed in the mid-1980s.

There seems to be a pattern of more organized groups appearing in behavioral typologies since the 1980s. There is a consistency in the gang that is characterized by drug use and partying, such as "party" or "social" gangs (Fagan, 1989) and "hedonistic" gangs (Huff, 1989). Some gangs are characterized by violence, such as "predatory" gangs (Huff, 1989) and "scavenger" gangs (Taylor, 1990). The researchers of the 1980s and beyond addressed the evolving nature of gangs. The role of economic opportunity in gang life leads to less organized "delinquent" (Fagan, 1989), "territorial" (Taylor, 1989), or "street" gangs (Klein, 1995). More organized crime groups make their way into these typologies as "young organizations" (Fagan, 1989), "corporate" gangs (Taylor, 1989), and "drug" gangs (Klein, 1995). Some researchers state that less organized groups tend to be the fighters and more organized gangs tend to be criminal. This is evidenced in Hagedorn's (1988) research of Milwaukee gangs. He finds that gangs start off as fighting gangs during their "junior phase," but as the group endures, their behavior turns more criminal in nature.

Organizing gangs according to criminal behavior offers limited insight into the characteristics of the group. Overall, the gang is more than the behavior that it engages in. This is at the heart of the definitional debate previously discussed. However, there does seem to be a connection between behavior and organizational characteristics. The prominent behavior of the gang is a result of group processes. This requires a greater understanding of the mechanisms that are at work in the group.

Other typologies are based on organizational features that include age, size, structure, norms and values, role differentiation, and migration and territory (Klein, 1971, p. 64). These elements work together to form groups that differ considerably. The group process that is at work within the gang is a result of the combination of these factors.

ORGANIZATIONAL FEATURES

The Clique Structure

One difference between gangs is their **clique structure.** Some gangs have cliques or subgroups, and other gangs do not. The clique structure is more likely to appear in larger gangs. Overall, the gangs with the greatest longevity tend to have the greatest numbers (Klein, 1971; Vigil, 1988). Cliques may be age graded, or they may be due to friendship patterns that precede gang life. Even among clique-structured gangs, there seems to be loose organization, rather than a solid operational unit (Hagedorn, 1988).

One consistent distinction in the clique structure is in the age-graded composition of gangs. Researchers report that some gangs have age-graded cliques with their own names (Thrasher, 1927/1963; Moore, 1978; Hagedorn, 1988; Vigil, 1988). Some of these cliques take on a "junior" version of the gang names, such as Junior Kings and Peewee Cobras (Hagedorn, 1988, p. 91). According to Vigil (1988), these cliques or *klikas* are usually two to three years apart, although there may be more than one clique of the same age or a wider age spread.

The age-graded gang begins "as a group of friends and youth roughly the same age. As the gang ages, new age-graded groupings form from neighbors, acquaintances, and relatives" (Hagedorn, 1988, p. 88). The older members who stay in the gang have little in common with younger members, resulting in separate cliques (Moore, 1991). Klein (1971) depicts the age-graded nature of gangs as a turnip structure, with fewer members at the older and younger ends and most of the members in the middle. Some researchers state that "[e]ach age group has its own 'main group,' its leaders, and its 'wannabe's'" (Hagedorn, 1988, p. 90). Others state that the formation of subsequent cliques creates a gang unit of young and old, with older members as heads of the group (Vigil, 1988, p. 97).

The age-graded nature is less evident now than in the past. Current cliques are not clearly age graded and segregated (Moore, 1991). Decker and Van Winkle (1996) report that junior gangs were not common. Only about a third of the gangs in their study reported having a younger gang unit. In this type of gang, the activities of the younger unit were distinct from the older members. Older members were involved in moneymaking activities, and younger members reported engaging in expressive behaviors, such as fighting and property crime.

Although Decker and Van Winkle's gangs are not age graded, they have subgroups. In gangs that average over 200 members, smaller subgroups of "between two to ten friends" developed (p. 114). These subgroups were the hub of conventional and deviant activity. They suggest that group criminal behavior was subgroup sanctioned

---

BOX 5–1: Focus on Research

Hagedorn's (1988) *People and Folks* presents lessons learned from a study of gangs in Milwaukee. His research was conducted in the mid-1980s as gangs were emerging in the city. This made his research different than other research that studied gangs in chronic gang areas. The subjects of the study were 47 gang founders of 19 Milwaukee gangs. Several of these members were transplants from Chicago and were previously involved in gang activity. Each founder participated in a two-hour interview sometime between December 1985 and June 1986. Hagedorn's work was possible because of a connection with Perry Macon, the founder of the Milwaukee Vicelords. This connection allowed Hagedorn access to gang members, and it facilitated trust between him and the "top dogs." This trust was not always easy, and many interviewees were apprehensive about answering questions. At the time of the study, Hagedorn was a doctoral student at the University of Wisconsin–Milwaukee. He is currently a faculty member at the University of Illinois–Chicago.

and not gang sanctioned. The whole gang came together only when threat from a rival gang surfaced.

There are numerous ways to transition between subgroups or cliques. In some cases, "there is no clear transition; it just happens as the group ages . . . for others, this process is formalized" with rituals (Hagedorn, 1988, p. 91). Sometimes members just "jump from one clique to another" (Moore, 1991, p. 33) and participate in more than one gang (Starbuck, Howell, and Lindquist, 2001). This may be due to institutional changes of the gang and the dynamic that some gangs take over other gangs (Moore, 1991; Starbuck, Howell, and Lindquist, 2001; Vigil, 1988). This is evident in the development of the Los Angeles Crips (see Williams, 2004). This phenomenon may also stem from the prison gang culture, which may require members to switch cliques for protection. Prison gangs will be discussed in more detail in Chapter 10.

Role Differentiation

Another varying characteristic of gangs is role differentiation. Some gangs have no or little role differentiation (Decker and Van Winkle, 1996). However, as gangs become more organized and formal, there comes "[t]he presence of different roles of levels of responsibility" (Decker and VanWinkle, 1996, p. 95). The leader is the most common role defined in gangs, and it represents "the first step in role differentiation" (p. 98). "While it may sometimes be true that a gang forms about a leader, the reverse is generally true: the gang forms and the leader emerges as the result of interaction" (Thrasher, 1927/1963, p. 244).

For some gangs, there are no titles for their leaders, or their titles are borrowed from preexisting groups (Hagedorn, 1988, p. 98). In other gangs, leadership is situational and informal. "[T]he leader of the gang, even at the height of power, is not an absolute monarch, but plays his part through his response to the wishes of his followers," establishing a "crude sort of democracy which is almost universal in such groups" (Thrasher, 1927/1963, p. 247). The leaders that emerge are often diplomatic enough to fulfill the wishes of the rest of the gang (Decker and Van Winkle, 1996; Short and Strodtbeck, 1965; Thrasher, 1927/1963). They are often natural leaders who demonstrate courage and aggression (Decker and Van Winkle, 1996; Thrasher, 1927/1963) and use their ability selectively (Short and Strodtbeck, 1965).

These leadership variations are best understood as presented by Jankowski (1991). He characterizes three different authority patterns that are evident in gangs: vertical/hierarchical, horizontal/commission, and influential. The pattern evidenced in the most organized gangs is the **vertical/hierarchical** form. In this gang, leadership is divided "into three or four categories, with authority assigned to each" (p. 64). Power is dictated by place in this hierarchy, with the president holding the greatest power and others holding lesser power. This type of structure is most likely found in gangs that center around economic activity. This structure provides the efficiency and control necessary to succeed in economic ventures.

The **horizontal/commission** form is similar to the vertical/hierarchical in that there are positions of power and authority. However, in the horizontal/commission form, the positions are not ranked as in a hierarchy. The power positions usually share authority and divide responsibilities equally. The decisions arrived at in this type of group usually take longer because they are democratic in nature. This structure is more often seen in smaller gangs, in gangs that are trust based, or in those that do not seek economic gain as their primary goal. This model "represents a transitional phase in gang development" (Jankowski, 1991, p. 70) before moving to a higher level of organization or during a period of decentralization.

The final leadership structure is the **influential** model. This structure is characterized by informal leadership that is determined by charisma. Leadership is considered important, but the formality of the position is not necessary. The goals and direction of the group are influenced by the natural leaders of the group. This type of structure is seen in small gangs that have no need for formal organization, in groups that are seen as temporary, or in groups that prefer a more flexible structure.

Research shows that few gangs have any elaborate role differentiation (Decker and Van Winkle, 1996; Klein, 1995). The structure of highly organized gangs resembles a hierarchical military structure (Brotherton and Barrios, 2004; Jankowski, 1991). This type of gang has role differentiation, and it tends to be more organized, with centralized leadership and stronger communication. The roles that are assigned to other members of the organization will be discussed in Chapter 6.

Groupthink

Adolescent groups, generally, have a unique view of the world "with its own biases, predilections, attitudes, values, and jargon, from which adults, even those most closely concerned with the individual adolescent's upbringing, are sedulously excluded" (Bloch and Neiderhoffer, 1958, p. 14). This groupthink is amplified in street gangs. The gang provides a system of beliefs and symbolic views of manhood and brotherhood (Bloch and Neiderhoffer, 1958; Jankowski, 1991). The gang represents value systems and ways of thinking that provide a group mentality for its members. Gang members have shown, through gang joining, that they are ready to "surrender personal autonomy to the gang consensus" (Bloch and Neiderhoffer, 1958, p. 162).

Social Codes.   Social codes or group laws represent one of the most consistent ways that gangs represent their group mentality (Bloch and Neiderhoffer, 1958; Jankowski, 1991). Few gangs have formal, written social codes. Most gang codes are unwritten and not formally developed. They "evolved out of practice, lore, or common sense" (Decker and Van Winkle, 1996, p. 100) and are thought to have a basis in social class (Klein, 1971). Codes vary but can include rules regarding expressions of conformity and rules of prohibited behavior.

Expressions of Conformity.   The gang expresses conformity on several different levels by using rituals, such as group names, meetings, and dues. Similar to other organizational characteristics, there is great variation in these features of gang life. Just about all gangs use a name, but gang names change frequently (Klein, 1971; Starbuck, Howell, and Lindquist, 2001). Conformity is also evident in gang initiation rituals, which are "virtually universal" (Bloch and Neiderhoffer, 1958, p. 106).

Meetings and the collection of dues are less consistent among gangs. Research suggests that about 50% of gangs report holding "meetings" (Decker and Van Winkle, 1996). However, this percentage should be taken with caution because many of the meetings were simply gang members informally hanging out. Regardless of the meeting formality, group time helps to bring gang members together as a group. A less likely occurrence is the collection of dues (Hagedorn, 1988). Most gangs do not collect money from members, and most do not demand profit from individual criminal behavior (Klein, 1995).

Gang members also express group conformity in symbolic ways. Many gang members dress in certain ways to display gang affiliation (Vigil, 1988, p. 109). The movie *Colors* brought the red-blue distinction of the Bloods and Crips to the nation's attention. Hispanic gangs in Los Angeles dress in the "Cholo style," in khaki pants and a plain, long-sleeved shirt (Vigil, 1988). However, some gangs have moved toward less obvious displays of gang affiliation (Walker, 2005) in response to dress codes, stricter legal gang identification, and an attempt to avoid detection (Walker, 2005). Many gang members have nicknames, or monikers, which often suggest a highlighted feature of the member. For example, "Chesshound" likes to play chess, and "Fish" has a face that resembles a fish (Vigil, 1988, p. 114). Nicknames and gang affiliation are often displayed in tattoos and graffiti. This will be discussed in more detail in the next chapter.

Rules of Prohibited Behavior.   Other features of gang social codes include prohibited behaviors and consequences for engaging in prohibited behavior. Prohibited behaviors include "disrespecting your colors, fighting members of own gang, turning in a member of own gang, running from a fight, pretending to be a member of a rival gang" (Decker and Van Winkle, 1996, p. 101). Sometimes behavior is not prohibited in all circumstances, and rules provide a guide for acceptable behavior (Jankowski, 1991). The consequences for rule violation can include loss of gang rank or violence.

Territory and Migration

Territory is a defining characteristic of gang activity and behavior. Many gangs take on a place of their own. This "turf" identifies a specific location as symbolically important (Decker and Van Winkle, 1996). In many cases, this territory is where the gang originated and where members live. Turf, even if not owned in the fiscal sense by the gang, is defined as a place a gang will control and defend. The defense of this space is rooted in honor, respect, and loyalty (Moore, 1991; Decker and Van Winkle, 1996). It is often identified by graffiti, and in some cases it is the basis for criminal activity. This phenomenon is known as the **territorial imperative** (see Spergel, 1995, p. 87). Williams exemplifies the territorial imperative: "We proclaimed Washington High to be *our* school. This was our stomping ground. My homeboys and I ruled. Yet, we didn't financially

TABLE 5–1

Primary organizational features of gangs

One way to differentiate gangs from one another is through their organizational features. These features can be used to illustrate variation in gangs, and not all gangs have them. More organized gangs tend to exhibit more sophisticated organizational features.

The Clique Structure

- Describes various subgroups of the gang.
- Some gangs are age graded, and others' subgroups are based on friendship patterns.

Role Differentiation

- Describes varying responsibilities of members of the gang.
- Some gangs have extensive hierarchies, with identifiable leaders; others have few or no assigned roles.

Groupthink

- Describes the unique group value system of the gang.
- Most prominent are social codes. Some gangs have elaborate written codes; others are more informal.
- Usually used as identification of conformity or to establish prohibited behavior.

Territory

- Describes location of symbolic importance.
- Some gangs have identifiable territory; some turf is less rigid.

own a centimeter of property" (2004, p. 62). The location of the gang is often included in its name, such as the Westside Crips or the South End Posse.

Territory has increasingly become less rigid on account of mobility and migration. Mobility has allowed gang expansion beyond neighborhood groupings. In some cases, alliances are formed between gangs from different areas of a city (see Williams, 2004). Migration has also contributed to fluid territorial boundaries. Contrary to popular belief, gangs have not franchised themselves throughout the country. Gang migration is more expressive in nature, taking place because of "copycatting" and family relocation (Decker, Bynum, and Weisel, 1998; Laskey, 1996; Maxson and Klein, 1996). Often gang names follow gang members as their families move to different areas. Gang names are also frequently copied or mimicked, creating the illusion of expansion (Starbuck, Howell, and Lindquist, 2001).

STRUCTURAL TYPOLOGIES

Organization variations are the basis of structural gang typologies. These typologies differentiate gangs based on the combination of their organizational attributes. It has been established that those few gangs that are well organized have been around longer. They have evolved into organized entities. However, most gangs are not well-developed groups. This type of gang is short-lived, and they do not display elaborate organizational features. In fact, most gangs dissolve before displaying any advanced levels of organization. At the same time, some gangs have the ability to transform into stable organizations (Klein, 1995).

Structural classification schemes of gangs date back to Thrasher in his identification of diffuse gangs, solidified gangs, conventional gangs, criminal gangs, and secret societies. Over time, many gang researchers have classified gangs according to structure (Taylor, 1990; Jankowski, 1991; Knox, 1994; Padilla, 1992; Klein, 2002; Valdez, 2003). The basic similarities in each of these typologies focus on variations in age, size, behavior, and level of organization.

Knox's (1994) typology is one of the most extensive depictions of gang organization. He illustrates the continuum of gang development in his classification of five gang levels. As each level, Knox differentiates gangs according to group function, size, use of weapons, criminal justice system impact, meetings, leadership structure, codes of conduct, sources of income, criminal behavior, organization, and membership commitment. As the group evolves from level 0 to level 4, it displays higher degrees of sophistication and formality.

Level 0, or **pre-gangs,** are playgroups that are very small and have not been labeled as a gang. They do not yet engage in criminal behavior. Some pre-gangs evolve to Level 1, or **emergent gangs.** This informal group is recognized by their community and display developing organization in leadership and membership. Some emergent gangs evolve into Level 2, or **crystallized gangs.** This gang displays evidence of greater organizational sophistication in its leadership structure, membership, codes, and criminal involvement. Some crystallized gangs evolve into Level 3, or **formalized gangs.** These large "supergangs" are not common, but their impact is evident throughout the country. They are highly organized and represent the greatest degree of sophistication of street gangs. Knox's level 4 gangs are considered organized crime groups and are distinguished from street gangs.

Valdez (2003) offers additional insight that is important to consider, based on his research of Mexican American youth gangs. He identifies the role of adults and the emergence and fading process of gangs. In the criminal adult-dependent gang, adults offer gang members access to drugs, weapons, and networks necessary for criminal operations. This type of gang is highly organized, with a clear hierarchy and leadership structure. The adults in this relationship may be family members or prison gang members. Compared with the adult-dependent gang, the criminal non-adult-dependent gang is not as reliant on adults. Although these gangs have structure, they are more loosely knit and have a less distinct leadership structure. Gang members tend to be involved in criminal behaviors that are independent from the group. The gang is not a criminal enterprise; its function is to offer its members protection.

Other gangs identified by Valdez (2003) are barrio-territorial gangs and transitional gangs. Barrio-territorial gangs display traditional ritual activities, but they are less organized than the previously described groups. The group's primary bonding

BOX 5–2: A Closer Look

An example of a formalized gang, the Almighty Latin King and Queen Nation (ALKQN) in New York, is documented by Brotherton and Barrios (2004). ALKQN has a vertical structure with the Supreme Team, which includes five positions of President (Inca), Vice President (Cacique), Peacemaker (or Enforcer), Treasurer, and Advisor. The Supreme Team guides State and City Crown Councils, who in turn oversee local tribe crown councils, who oversee local tribe members. Each of the council levels has a similar five-position structure, although there are sometimes more than five. Each leader has a colored stone to represent rank. The Supreme Team hears "all felonious charges brought against a member," and local councils hear misdemeanor cases (p. 187). Despite this structure, it is difficult to determine clear decision-making processes.

Other organizational features are apparent. The Latin Kings demonstrate a clique or tribal structure, with subgroups in different geographic areas in New York. Membership in each tribe ranges from 50 to 300 members. There is also evidence that each tribe has subgroups based on friendship and family. Each chapter or tribe holds weekly meetings and collects $5 a week from members. As discussed in this text, ALKQN has a manifesto that specifies lessons and codes of conduct. Members of ALKQN also openly represent their gang affiliation through hand signs, beads, and exclamations of "amor de rey" or "amor de reina," meaning King Love or Queen Love (p. 84). Each of these features suggests that ALKQN has higher levels of organization than most street gangs.

element is territory, and their names often reflect their barrio location. Criminal behaviors of members are more individualized, and violence is random and interpersonal, not group related. The least organized gang, according to Valdez's schema, is the transitional gang. This type of gang is either growing or fading. This process is evident in its small numbers and minimal hierarchy and leadership.

An example of gang variation is well illustrated in research by Decker, Bynum, and Weisel (1998, p. 73). They studied differences between two gangs in Chicago and two gangs in San Diego. All gangs were identified as central gangs in the area. They found that the gangs in Chicago were similar to one another, as were the gangs in San Diego. However, there were greater differences between the two cities. This is due to the type of gang examined in each city and the longevity of gangs. Chicago gangs included the more highly organized Latin Kings and Gangster Disciples. Gangs in Chicago reported different levels of membership and identifiable leaders. Each gang reported written social codes, meetings, the collection of dues, and gang involvement in criminal behavior. In the more evolved Gangster Disciples, there was reported involvement in political activities and legitimate business ventures. San Diego gangs were emerging and did not manifest the same organizational characteristics as Chicago gangs. They did not report structured leadership, written codes of conduct, meetings, or dues.

COHESION AND GROUP DEVELOPMENT

One of the more important questions about gangs is how they evolve. How do they advance from an emergent gang to a crystallized gang? Thrasher (1927/1963) states that gangs evolve like other social groups and that evolution occurs in predictable ways. He believed that "[i]f conditions are favorable to its continued existence, the gang tends to undergo a sort of natural evolution from a diffuse and loosely organized group into the solidified unit which represents the matured gang and which may take one of several forms" (p. 47). This evolution may occur through "consolidation, reorganization, and the splintering of larger gangs" (Weisel, 2006, p. 95). Often, this change is due to adaptation to a changing environment (Weisel, 2006). Many researchers identify cohesion as a feature of adaptation that acts to unify gangs (see Jankowski, 1991; Klein, 2002). Cohesion represents the commitment of members to the gang and the group's ability to band together as a unified entity. This unification is part of the evolution in gangs.

The Role of Conflict

> To be hated and set upon by a common enemy generates a we feeling. This is the case with the boys' gang, which can survive the persecution of other gangs only if the members are loyal to one another. In the gang, therefore, is born that spirit of loyalty which lies at the foundation of most social relations. (Ross, 1919, p. 657)

Sources of cohesion can come from different places, but all sources are centered around conflict (Thrasher, 1927/1963; Hagedorn, 1988; Klein, 1971; Jankowski, 1991; Decker, 1996). Some of this conflict is **internal** to the gang and occurs through natural group dynamics (Klein, 1971; Jankowski, 1991). In some cases, internal conflict will break a group. Other times, this conflict will legitimize the organization and force it to mediate and exert control over its members (Jankowski, 1991).

Most conflict and cohesion originates from **external** sources (Klein, 1971). The effect of these sources is so strong that the elimination of external sources has been predicted to dissolve "a relatively large proportion of the gang membership" (Klein, 1971, p. 104). External sources of cohesion include societal issues, such as poverty, racism, and discrimination. Group belonging helps to compensate for societal failure (Short and Strodtbeck, 1965, p. 271). External sources of cohesion also occur through conflict with rival groups, including other gangs, teachers, police officers, and correctional officers. Ultimately, violence or the threat of violence increases cohesion (Thrasher, 1927/1963; Short and Strodtbeck, 1965; Hagedorn, 1988).

CHAPTER SUMMARY

> This forgotten generation created a quasi-culture with its own mores, styles of dress, hand symbols, vernacular, socioeconomic qualities, martyrs, rituals, blue color identification (for Crips), legends, myths and codes of silence. (Williams, 2004, p. 91)

Gang organization varies. Few gangs are highly organized, but many have minimal organizational structure. Researchers have developed typologies that allow us to classify gangs according to common characteristics. Some gang typologies focus on the type of behavior gangs engage in. This sort of typology is limited because it focuses on only one dimension of a complex group. Other typologies emphasize the varying structural qualities of gangs, such as subgroup structures, role differentiation, social codes, and territory affiliation. The evolution of gangs from loosely organized groups to more complex organizations is best illustrated by Knox's typology. This process of evolution is connected to cohesion and most effectively facilitated through conflict.

KEY TERMS

clique structure   influential leadership
conflict subculture   internal conflict
criminal subculture   playgroups
crystallized gangs   pre-gangs
emergent gangs   retreatist subculture
external conflict   supergangs
formalized gangs   territorial imperative
horizontal/commission leadership   vertical/hierarchical leadership

QUESTIONS FOR REVIEW

1. What are the main differences between playgroups and supergangs?

2. How does the behavior of gangs vary?

3. What are the different leadership styles, and how do they compare to one another?

4. What role does territory play in gang life?

5. How does conflict affect gangs?

DISCUSSION QUESTIONS

1. Groupthink plays a powerful role in gang processes. What are the different elements of groupthink? How do you think it affects gang organization?

2. Knox's typology offers a framework for understanding the evolution of gangs. Explain the process of the evolution from a pre-gang to formalized gangs. When do you think we could be most effective in preventing gang evolution?

CHAPTER 6

THE GANG MEMBER

CHAPTER OBJECTIVES

- Understand the variation in gang membership.
- Become familiar with methods of gang recruitment, initiation, and leaving.
- Know the different types of gang members.
- Recognize the effects of gang joining and the long-term consequences of gang membership.
- Become familiar with gang identity-based behavior, such as tattooing and gang signs.

GANG MEMBER VARIATION

> Gangbanging is something that I did in high school. Personally, I've never been jumped into a set. I've always been a gang affiliate. I wore the blue, but I've never been a hard-core gang member. (Ice T, 2005, p. xxi)

The previous chapter stressed the idea that there is great variation in the types of gangs that exist. The same variation exists for gang members; not all gang member experiences are the same. Many are only marginally involved in gang life, while a few are deeply immersed in their gang identity. As we discussed in Chapter 3, this variation is also reflected in the reasons for gang joining. This chapter will focus on gang member variations. It will include a discussion of methods of recruitment and initiation, different types of gang members, the effects of gang joining, noncriminal activities of gang members, how members leave gangs, and long-term effects of membership.

JOINING THE GANG

There is variation in the recruitment techniques that gang members experience. Many times the process of gang joining is a slow evolution. Potential gang members have neighborhood or school friends who are active gang members (Decker and Van Winkle, 1996). Through these associations, they become affiliated with gang life and spend time hanging out with the gang. Initiation for them just formalizes their membership. Some gangs, such as the New York City Latin Kings, have members requesting members; therefore, the gang is involved in limited recruitment (Brotherton and Barrios, 2004) but may be involved in elaborate initiation rituals.

Recruitment

Jankowski (1991) presents detailed insight into the gang recruitment process. He finds in his research that although some gangs use multiple gang recruitment strategies, many gangs rely on only one. Jankowski identifies three recruitment styles: fraternity, obligation, and coercive.

Fraternity recruitment bases its membership on reputation. The gang is solidly placed within the community, and applicants come to the group to request membership. They must demonstrate their desire and ability to fight, and this is often part of the initiation ritual. The ability to fight is important to developing a sense of trust among gang members.

Obligation-type recruitment strategies rest on persuasion to recruit members. Recruits feel that they have a duty to join the gang and that it is a community tradition to be a gang member. The recruit is often told that community members will not respect them if they do not join. Advantages of gang membership are presented to the recruit, including respect, protection, access to women, and future employment opportunities. This method may be used in conjunction with coercive methods.

As the name suggests, coercive recruitment relies on intimidation to recruit members. Intimidation can be physical or psychological and is usually aimed at potential members or their families. This method of recruitment is used to increase gang numbers quickly to protect against rival gangs or to expand criminal operations. It is also used to strengthen weakening gangs. One shortcoming of this recruitment technique is resentment by members and overall membership instability.

Initiation Rituals

Initiation rituals vary from gang to gang. However, one consistent aspect is that to gain entrance into a gang, members must display commitment and trust to the gang. This is often demonstrated in the initiation process. The ritual shows dedication to the group, serves to strengthen group bonds, and allows the individual to connect to the group (Bloch and Niederhoffer, 1958; Decker and Van Winkle, 1996; Hagedorn, 1988; Vigil, 1988). Initiation represents "group membership, social solidarity, ritualistic behavior, ceremonial processes, gender clarification, and symbolic changes" (Vigil, 1988, p. 218).

Many times the initiation process is informal, and it is sometimes waived for "members" who have already displayed the valued characteristics during a significant amount of time spent with the group (Decker and Van Winkle, 1996; Vigil, 1988). Less involved members are more likely to experience initiation rituals. Sometimes entrance into a gang is an elaborate process. Elaborate rituals or **street baptisms** are often seen in Chicano gangs (Vigil, 1988, 1996). Many initiation rituals are rooted in violence. Prospective gang members have to demonstrate that they are tough and will be able to withstand the rigors of gang life (Decker and Van Winkle, 1996). **Beating in,** also known as **jumping in** or **courting in,** is the most common passage rite. It can include the recruit getting hit as he walks through rows of gang members or enduring a timed beating by several gang members at the same time. The beating can be announced or unannounced, and the severity of the beating is often related to substance use. Cee Loc, Colton Simpson (2005), describes his beating into the Crips:

> Smiley and T.J. appear out of nowhere. Smiley punches me in the face, knocks me to the ground. Dizzy, I start swinging wildly. Big T rounds the corner. Three on one. My swing connects with a torso. Then T.J. lands five punches on my chest and I'm on the pavement struggling for equilibrium. Kicked in the stomach, the wind is knocked out of me. . . . The world swims as I received another kick and a strike. Hard spitting-punches from all angles. I'm tossed by blows like a speed-punching bag. . . . Then Smiley's arms are hard and warm around me. "You in cuz. One of us, Li'l Cee." (p. 20)

Other initiation behaviors include tattooing, property crime, and sometimes violent crime. Females may also encounter the initiation ritual of "sexing in." This will be discussed in further detail in Chapter 9.

TYPES OF GANG MEMBERS

Gang members vary in their level of involvement in gang life. This is best illustrated by the different types of gang members discussed in the literature. In its most simplistic form, gang membership can best be understood as core and fringe membership (Klein, 1971, 1995).

Many researchers discuss members within the core of gangs (Hagedorn, 1988; Klein, 1995; Taylor, 1989; Vigil, 1988). They are referred to as core or main group members, those who are most involved in gang life. They make up between a third and a half of membership. They often join the gang at early ages and remain active in gang life into early adulthood. The **hard-core** group, or "regular" members, are intensely involved in gang life. As hard-core members of the gang age, they achieve a senior gang standing, termed ancients, OGs (old gangsters), old heads, or *veteranos*. Other core members can include **peripheral members,** who strongly identify with the gang, but whose "participation in gang activities is inconsistent and tempered by interests in other areas" (Vigil, 1988, p. 98). Peripheral members join gangs later and leave earlier than hard-core, regular members. Taylor (1989) has identified core members as "corporate" and "scavenger."

Fringe membership is a category reserved for members who marginally identify with gang life. They are less committed to the gang and less involved in gang behavior. Their membership can be "temporary" or "situational." Temporary members are involved in deviant gang behaviors for short periods of time. Situational members are involved in only social aspects of gang life or in destructive behaviors when honor calls for it (Vigil, 1988). Taylor (1989) has identified similar fringe membership categories as "auxiliary" and "adjunct" membership. Gangs also have "members" who have not achieved gang member status. **Wannabes** are often gang recruits who aspire to belong to the gang. There is also the **emulator,** who tries to mimic gang behavior and "dresses or pretends to achieve goals of real gangs" (Taylor, 1989, p. 8).

THE EVERYDAY GANG MEMBER

The reason that gangs are a concern to society is the criminal behaviors that distinguish gang members from other adolescents. However, the everyday life of gang members is rather boring. Most of the time, gang members engage in regular adolescent activities (Klein, 1995; Moore, 1991; Vigil, 1988). They "sleep, get up late, hang around, brag a lot, eat again, drink, hang around some more" (Klein, 1995, p. 11), and "they talk, joke, plan social events, and exchange stories of adventure and love" (Vigil,

---

BOX 6-1: A Closer Look

Often, biographical accounts of gang members offer insight into only the world of hard-core members. Otherwise, their stories would be uninteresting. We rarely get an in-depth look at gang membership from the perspective of a peripheral member, but an exception is the life history of Ice T. Many of us know Ice T as a rapper and for his role as "Fin" on *Law & Order: Special Victims Unit.* His pre-rapper, pre-actor life was on the streets of gang-ridden South Central L.A. Some of Ice T's thoughts and experiences are illustrated in his music, his out-of-print book, *The Ice Opinion* (1994), and his foreword to *Inside the Crips* (2005). Ice T was an affiliate of the Crips; he was not hard core. It may be this level of detachment that allows him to thoughtfully and intellectually reflect on the causes of gangs and the solutions to gangs. Ice T identifies the gang as an instrument for control in an environment with little control. He also recognizes the power, the defiance, the love, and the security that come from gang membership. He states that "by the time a kid joins a gang, he's already lost all fear of what could happen to him. . . . The killing fields have destroyed his spirit" (1995, p. 151). Ice T is, by conventional society's standards, successful. He is successful despite growing up in the killing fields. There are true lessons to be learned from affiliate members. Their experiences represent the average gang life. It is with this knowledge that we can begin to understand the mechanisms at work in gang environments.

1988, p. 2). They "spend most of their time together just 'hanging around' at some special spot in the neighborhood or in smaller friendship cliques just as any group of high-school friends in any city would tend to meet regularly in the same place with the same friends" (Moore, 1991, p. 50). One method of bonding among gang members is to participate in symbolic representations of their group affiliation, such as tattoos, graffiti, and hand signs.

Gang Tattoos

Gang members use tattoos as a symbol of their group identity. Gang tattoos are linked to prison culture, and an increasing number of urban minorities wear adorning tattoos because of the meshing of prison and street gang culture (Hart and Brotherton, 2003). Tattoos are worn "with pride and gain a certain amount of status and adulation from barrio onlookers, especially siblings and younger individuals" (Vigil, 1988, pp. 114–15). The tattoo is often found on the face or the hand. It could be "a small dot or cross on their hand, between the thumb and the forefinger" (Vigil, 1988, p. 115). More committed members may have large tattoos on other parts of their body (Vigil, 1988). Many times the gang tattoo reflects the gang affiliation or nickname of the member, an affiliation sometimes hidden in numbers. For example, the Vice Lords of Chicago are often recognizable by their tattoos of the number 312, which is the Chicago area code (knowgangs.com, n.d.).

Other messages in tattoos are life philosophies, represent time in prison, or offer dedication to family and friends. A common tattoo among gang members is a small teardrop below the eye. The teardrop "usually means that the member has fought on behalf of the organization and has either shed his own blood or that of someone else" (Hart and Brotherton, 2003, p. 334).

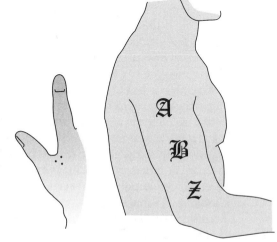

Figure 6–1   Gang tattoos may convey a message, such as "my crazy life," represented by three dots (left). Other tattoos contain an acronym for the gang name, such as "ABZ" for the Asian Boyz (right).

Tattoos have been used by criminal justice officials as one criterion to identify gang membership (see Valentine and Shoeber, 2000). However, this tactic may be problematic as tattoos become an increasing part of mainstream society. This problem of using tattoos as a singular method of identifying gang affiliation can be seen in the case of Brianna Stephenson, who was not a gang member. Brianna had a tattoo of a small cross between her thumb and pointer finger. The school district forced Brianna to remove the tattoo because of its regulations prohibiting gang symbols. Brianna was an honor student and actively involved in her education. There was no indication, other than the tattoo, that she was ever involved in gang activity (*Brianna Stephenson v. Davenport Community*, 1997). The mainstreaming of tattoos, combined with police use of tattoos as a gang identification tool, is altering tattooing in gang culture. Gang members who wish to avoid detection are not adorning themselves with tattoos or are getting preexisting tattoos removed.

Graffiti

Graffiti is similar to tattoos as a symbolic expression of identity that varies in style and quality (Vigil, 1988). It is most often placed in highly visible areas that are public property. It is most likely to be placed on property that is "characterized by the absence of anyone with direct responsibility for the area" (Weisel, 2001, p. 5). Although graffiti is vandalism and destruction of property, most gang members do not recognize the deviant nature of graffiti (Decker and Van Winkle, 1996). Graffiti is believed to give gang identity to a neighborhood (Padilla, 1992). Graffiti takes on several different forms, including gang, tagger, artistic/piecing, conventional/existential, and ideological/political (see Weisel, 2001; Alonso, 1998). Gang members are most likely to engage in the gang and tagger varieties.

As the name suggests, **gang graffiti** is the type most closely associated with gang members. The graffiti includes gang member names, gang names, or the location of the gang. It is a prominent way to identify turf and establishes territorial control. Gang graffiti is also used as a form of communication (Alonso, 1998; Decker and Van Winkle, 1996; Vigil, 1988). The messages in gang graffiti are direct and easily understood by other gang members (Vigil, 1988). For example, a crossed-out name or RIP around a gang member's name indicates intent to harm (Decker and Van Winkle, 1996, p. 132). RIP is also used to pay respect to fallen members. Many times, gang members go into rival territories to leave graffiti (Decker and Van Winkle, 1996).

Tagging tends to be more individualistic, and taggers are not always affiliated with gangs. However, some gang members engage in tagging. This form of graffiti is a way to gain notoriety or prestige (Vigil, 1988; Weisel, 2001). Many times, taggers are focused only on the goal of leaving their artistic mark for all to see. Sometimes, taggers are part of larger groups, including tagger crews or traditional street gangs. More recently, **tagbangers** have been identified (Weisel, 2001). These groups are combinations of gangs and tagging crews who are in competition with other tagbangers. It has been suggested that the competition between rival tagging crews can lead to violence (see Klein, 1995, for discussion).

Figure 6–2   Photos showing gang graffiti. The first *(top left)* is an example of graffiti that pays respect to a gang member who has died. The others show gang member nicknames and gang names.

Gang Member Movements

The identity of the gang member is also displayed in body language. Gang members are known for their physical posturing and distinctive gait (Vigil, 1988). Both are demonstrations of the cool, tough gang persona. Unique body language is also displayed in gang hand signs (Vigil, 1988).

THE IMPACT OF GANG MEMBERSHIP

There is little research on the immediate consequences of gang membership, other than increased deviant behavior. However, there is a general consensus that the gang has a negative impact on the life of the active gang member. Short (1989) states that "the gang provides no encouragement (and often discourages) the development or exercise of skills necessary to function in such conventional settings as school, work,

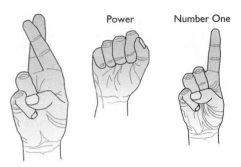

Figure 6–3   Gang hand signs can indicate gang affiliation, such as the Neta hand sign, with index and middle finger crossed *(left)*. Hand signs can also be used to convey emotion, such as power *(middle)* and being number one *(right)*.

or marriage" (p. 253). The gang member experiences a manifestation of deviant values, reductions in commitment to prosocial activities, and increases in deviance-related activities.

Values and Self-Esteem

The gang plays a role in altering the value system of the gang member. Knox (1995) states that gang membership "is a slow process that progressively erodes the value system of the potential recruit. The more time the potential recruit spends with members of the gang, the more negative behavior is reinforced" (p. 26). Gang values play the primary role in identifying goals and shaping behavior. Knox (1995) states that "the gang member becomes a person committed to success through what most consider conventional failure" (p. 18). The gang member value system, placed in the gang context, is an important link to illegal behavior (Sanders, 1994; Short and Strodtbeck, 1965; Sun, 1993). As a result of conforming to group expectations and values, gang members experience increased self-esteem through membership (Dukes, Martinez, and Stein, 1997; Sun, 1993).

Social Institutions

Gang membership interferes with involvement in conventional activities and connections to prosocial institutions, such as family, schools, clubs, and sports. Once the individual joins the gang, the influences of and involvement with conventional forces become minimal (Decker and Van Winkle, 1996; Knox, 1995; Short, 1989; Yablonsky, 1962). The gang member experiences diminishing ties to everything not gang related. "Involvement in legitimate social institutions or with nongang peers and relatives drops dramatically following gang initiation. In most cases, gang life has an obsessively deadly attraction for our subjects, one which constricts and diminishes their life to the friendship group of the gang" (Decker and Van Winkle, 1996, p. 187).

   Research finds that problematic family relationships emerge as a result of gang membership (Decker and Van Winkle, 1996; Dukes, Martinez, and Stein, 1997; Fagan,

---

BOX 6–2: Focus on Research

Decker and Van Winkle's (1996) research on gangs of the early 1990s in St. Louis, Missouri, is documented in *Life in the Gang: Family, Friends, and Violence.* Historically, St. Louis gangs have "been cyclical, emerging and fading away over time . . . correspond[ing] with the conditions . . . [of] economic change, rapid population shifts, and changes in the racial and ethnic composition of the city" (p. 36). The richness of their research findings comes from two methodologies: direct observation and qualitative interviewing. A field ethnographer directly observed gang members in their natural street environment over a three-year period. Qualitative interviews were completed by a snowball sample of 99 gang members and 34 relatives of gang members. Snowball sampling uses initial contacts to gain access to and trust from potential interviewees. The object is to use points of access to make connections to potential subjects. In Decker and Van Winkle's study, they had four points of access. They had access to a criminal sample from a previous study, and they connected researchers to gang members. The ethnographer offered the remaining three points of access. First, the field researcher had contact with gang members who knew other gang members who could be interviewed. Second, the field researcher was able to go into areas with visible gang graffiti and talk to gang members. Finally, the field ethnographer was highlighted in local media so he was recognized, and this opened the door to dialogue with families and gang members about gang activity.

1990). Despite diminished ties to the family, gang members do not completely sever their family ties (Decker and Van Winkle, 1996; Hunt, MacKenzie, and Joe-Laidler, 2000; Thomas, Holzer, and Wall, 2003).

The school experiences of active gang members are also negatively affected (Bowker and Klein, 1983; Decker and Van Winkle, 1996; Schwartz, 1989; Sheldon, Snodgrass, and Snodgrass, 1992; Wood et al., 1997). The academic success of gang members is severely limited because of their exclusion, withdrawal, or alienation from the educational experience. The active gang member invests little time and effort into school achievement (Decker and Van Winkle, 1996; Schwartz, 1989; Sheldon, Snodgrass, and Snodgrass, 1992). This separation from school eventually leads to high dropout rates for gang members (Hagedorn, 1988; Sheldon, Snodgrass, and Snodgrass, 1992).

Criminal Justice System Contact

Gang members, as a result of membership, participate in increased criminal behavior. This will be discussed extensively in the next chapter. As a result of the deviant lifestyles led by gang members, they experience increased contact with the criminal justice system. Many gang members have been arrested (Decker and Van Winkle, 1996; Klein, 1995) and have spent time in prison (Hagedorn, 1988).

Criminal and violent behavior is a core characteristic in a gang (Decker and Van Winkle, 1996). As previously discussed, it is the central feature of initiation and exit rituals. In addition to increased participation in deviant behavior, gang members experience increased incidents of victimization (Peterson, Taylor, and Esbensen, 2004) and report greater fear of harm (Dukes, Martinez, and Stein, 1997) as a result of membership. Some gang members state that they join gangs for protection. At the same time, there are serious questions regarding whether the gang is able to protect the member (Peterson, Taylor, and Esbensen, 2004). Gang members are at increased risk for violent crime victimization (Miller and Brunson, 2000; Sheldon, Snodgrass, and Snodgrass, 1992) and homicide (Curry, Maxson, and Howell, 2001; Rosenfeld, Bray, and Egley, 1999). Females generally experience less victimization than males (Miller, 1998; Miller and Decker, 2001), but they are exposed to more sex-based victimization (Miller, 1998).

The gang effect on victimization makes sense, given the fact that gang members are involved in behaviors that place them at risk for victimization, such as rival gang fights and drug dealing. However, victimization enhancement is due not only to these behaviors but also to the cumulative result of gang membership and increased participation in violent activity (Peterson, Taylor, and Esbensen, 2004).

LEAVING THE GANG

A misconception is that gang members can leave only upon death. It is true for a very few gangs, such as prison gangs, but it is not the case for most gangs. Gang membership is usually not a lifelong commitment (Esbensen and Huizinga, 1993; Thornberry et al., 2003). Most gang members are transitional, with about 50% of male gang members and about 66% of female gang members staying in the gang for one year. Only about 20% of male gang members and 5% of female gang members stay in the gang for three or more years (Thornberry et al., 2003, p. 39). Many gang members eventually conform to conventional society and do not continue criminal activity into adulthood (Moore and Vigil, 1989). This raises the question of why and how gang members leave the gang.

There are many different reasons for gang members to leave the gang. "There is no single pathway to a square adaptation" (Moore, 1991, p. 127). Some members make the conscious decision to leave, and others simply drift away from gang life. The reasons for leaving can be positive developmental processes or negative life events, such as death, the level of violence in gangs, or imprisonment (Decker and Lauritsen, 2002; Jankowski, 1991; Vigil, 1988).

More positive developmental processes that can also take gang members away include "aging out," family relocation, or the breakdown of the gang (Decker and Lauritsen, 2002; Decker and Van Winkle, 1996; Jankowski, 1991). **Aging out** refers to the natural process of gang leaving that coincides with maturing. This is more likely to occur with fringe gang members (Horowitz, 1983). The aging out process is often related to connections to prosocial institutions and conventional commitments. Positive peers are often a resource in the move away from gangs (Thomas, Holzer, and Wall,

2003). Gang members may find employment or join other organizations (Jankowski, 1991). Religious conversion and exposure to intellectual role models are not addressed much in academic research but are also turning points for gang members (Shakur, 1993; Williams, 2004).

Although connections to prosocial institutions facilitate gang leaving, it is often a difficult process. Gang dynamics and the effects of gang life make it difficult to enter the legitimate world (Decker and Lauritsen, 2002). For example, it is difficult for a former gang member to become gainfully employed because of former gang involvement. Padilla (1992) refers to this as the "Catch-22" of gang membership. Gang members gain skills while in the gang that their nongang peers do not acquire, such as wisdom, aggressiveness, survival skills, and the ability to talk to people. He states that "gang participation contributed enormously to transformation[s] into a highly competent and crafty person." At the same time, society attaches "deviant social identity" to the gang members (Padilla, 1992, p. 175). This identity limits the members' ability to gain entrance into social programming that could assist them. The result may be similar to that of Hagedorn's (1994) "homeboys" and "legits." **Legits** are able to leave gang life behind them and pursue conventional lifestyles. However, **homeboys** often move between gang activity and conventional activities and never fully renounce gang membership.

Most gang members experience no consequences for leaving the gang. In some cases, a gang member may endure exit rituals to formally leave the gang. This ritual is usually in the form of **jumping out,** that is, experiencing a physical confrontation to exit the gang (Vigil, 1988). Padilla (1992) refers to this as the "V ritual." This ritual is more important when the leaving gang member is expected to have continued contact with the active gang members.

LONG-TERM EFFECTS

The gang does not adequately prepare its members for adulthood. The gang is a group that offers to its members the chance to be tough, aggressive, and streetwise. These qualities do not translate well into adult roles (Short, 1989). The gang "serves the youth poorly, as a rule, in preparing him for a legitimate career and for a personally satisfying long-term life experience" (Spergel, 1990, p. 222). For gang members, "at the end of the journey, they are even more disadvantaged than when they first began" (Padilla, 1992, p. 182).

The gang member's experiences as an active gang member are pivotal in altering his life course (Decker and Van Winkle, 1996). Many gang members continue to experience the negative repercussions of gang membership, even after moving away from the gang, because of the cumulative effects of active gang membership, including school problems and criminal records. These effects are most often seen in employment, education, and family relationships. Despite this consensus regarding the impact of gang membership on adulthood, several researchers question whether the negative impact is equal for all members. Stable gang members are thought to experience more negative adulthood consequences that stem from long periods of cumulative disadvantage (Thornberry et al., 2003; Vigil, 1998).

Gang members have difficulty in establishing stable employment patterns (Decker and Van Winkle, 1996; Hagedorn, 1988; Padilla, 1992; Thornberry et al., 2003). They are more likely to be unemployed, to work in low-wage jobs, and to receive public assistance. The problem of unemployment is evident for the gang founders in Hagedorn's (1988) study. None of the gang founders held a job three months before and three months after their interviews. The irony of the situation is that gang members have high expectations and optimistic outlooks on their future (Hagedorn, 1988; Padilla, 1992; Short, 1989).

An obstacle to achieving lucrative employment is lack of education among gang members. Many gang members drop out of school (Decker and Van Winkle, 1996; Hagedorn, 1988; Thornberry et al., 2003). Hagedorn's (1988) study finds that all of the founding gang members had dropped out of school, and a small percentage had earned a GED. Many of the gang members had been kicked out of school on account of their gang activities.

As previously discussed, adult responsibilities are one way that gang members mature out of gang life. Gang members are more likely to experience pregnancy at earlier ages, become parents, and cohabit with partners (Thornberry et al., 2003). However, this does not necessarily mean that their adult relationships are successful. Spergel (1990) states that it is difficult for adolescent gang members to find personally satisfying long-term life experiences. Many gang members are not married in adulthood (Hagedorn, 1988).

CHAPTER SUMMARY

> At sixteen I felt like twenty four . . . I recognized early that where I lived, we grew and died in dog years. (Shakur, 1993, p. 102)

Gang membership involves many unique experiences that can have long-term effects. The experiences and effects for any two gang members are never the same. The decision to join the gang is sometimes the result of varying recruiting techniques. Gang membership is often accompanied by initiation rituals, the development of a gang identity, and associated behaviors. Some gang members are more invested in their gang identities, and others are only marginally associated with gang life. The impact that gang membership has on an individual's life is connected to the level of gang involvement. Many gang members experience reduced attachments to conventional society and increased experiences with victimization and the criminal justice system. Research suggests a bleak outlook for gang members once they reach adulthood. Even if they leave the gang, adolescent gang membership continues to influence their lives. Many are unprepared for adult roles because of their lack of skill, lack of education, and criminal records. A continued pattern of deviant behavior may result for some.

KEY TERMS

aging out

beating in, jumping in, courting in

coercive recruitment

emulator

fraternity recruitment

fringe membership

gang graffiti

hard core

homeboys

jumping out

legits

obligation-type recruitment

peripheral members

street baptisms

tagbangers

tagging

wannabes

QUESTIONS FOR REVIEW

1. What are the differences between the three gang recruitment techniques?

2. Describe the different types of gang members.

3. What are the main types of gang identity behavior?

4. What effects does joining a gang have on a gang member's life?

5. Explain the process of gang leaving.

DISCUSSION QUESTIONS

1. There is incredible variation in the experiences of gang members. What do you think are the commonalities of the hard-core and peripheral members? What are the differences?

2. The decision to join a gang is met with unanticipated immediate and long-term consequences. Do you think the prospective gang member understands this future? If so, why do you think they still join a gang? If not, do you think this insight would make a difference?

CHAPTER 7

CRIMINAL BEHAVIOR

CHAPTER OBJECTIVES

- Know the effects of gang membership on criminal behavior.
- Become familiar with the gang context that leads to criminal behavior.
- Understand the nonviolent criminal behaviors of gangs and gang members.
- Understand the violent criminal behaviors of gangs and gang members.
- Recognize the interrelationship between guns, drugs, and violence.

GANG CRIME

> Math can't stop a bullet, or put money in my pocket. What am I doing this for? I'm conditioned to simple things. You shoot me; I shoot you. You make money; I take it. You play the pig and I play the criminal. You yell "Stop!" and I run. Life in South Central is uncomplicated. It doesn't take a brain surgeon to figure out what to do during a war. (Simpson, 2005, p. 64)

Gangs are a concern to the public because of the criminal behavior that gang members engage in. "However, it is impossible to study gangs without also looking at individual gang members, and similarly it is impossible to look at individual gang members without considering the importance of the collective" (Decker and Van Winkle, 1996, p. 32). This interwoven nature of gang dynamics is most important in understanding gang crime. Individual gang members vary in the behaviors they engage in, and gangs vary in the behaviors they support (Fagan, 1990). The resulting deviant behavior is a coupling of the gang and the individual member.

This chapter will discuss the variation in gang member behavior and the group context in which this behavior takes place. Evidence will be presented that suggests the gang is a group that can reinforce and amplify the deviant behavior of its members.

The criminal behavior that results includes nonviolent behavior, such as substance use and drug dealing, and behavior that is violent and sometimes lethal. The relationship between economics, guns, and gang activity will also be explored.

THE GANG MEMBER

Research consistently finds that gang members have considerably higher levels of criminal behavior than their nongang peers (Curry, 2000; Thornberry et al., 2003). Gang members contribute "a lion's share of delinquent acts, especially for the more serious delinquent acts" (Thornberry and Burch, 1997, p. 3). As discussed in the previous chapter, most of the activities that gang members engage in are not criminal, and far fewer are violent. However, the violent activities of gang members are "disproportionately violent when compared with the activities of other youth groups or individual persons" (Klein, 1995, p. 75).

Individual behavior varies, and "[e]ven within a successful drug-selling gang there may be divergent beliefs held by members; some will prefer social activities and participate in economic activities minimally and reluctantly, while others will try to detour the gang away from recreational pursuits and into new markets and new underground economies" (Venkatesh, 2003, p. 9). Gang members who are fully immersed in the gang are more likely to be involved in more serious criminal behaviors than less committed members or nonmembers (Curry, Decker, and Egley, 2002; Esbensen, Peterson, Freng, and Taylor, 2002; Fagan, 1990).

The Individual Process

A debate exists about the developmental process of gang member deviant behavior. Some consider gang members to be "defiant individuals" (Jankowski, 1991) and the gang a group of "sociopaths" who come together (Yablonsky, 1962). Others consider the unique nature of the gang as a nurturing environment for the criminal behavior of members. Thornberry, Krohn, Lizotte, and Chard-Wierschem (1993) framed this debate in their distinction between the selection, facilitation, and enhancement effects. These effects have been extensively addressed in recent research.

The **selection model** is a "kind of person" model. It suggests that youth at high risk of delinquency are drawn to and recruited into gangs. This type of individual engages in delinquent behavior whether or not they are gang members. The gang does not "cause" delinquent behavior. The gang is merely a group of highly delinquent persons who are drawn together. In this model, individuals display high rates of deviant behavior before joining the gang that continue while they are gang members and remain stable after leaving the gang. Little support is found for the pure selection model (see Thornberry et al., 2003). Research shows that gang members have risk factors for membership (Dukes, Martinez, and Stein, 1997, and other research discussed in Chapter 3). However, "[t]he most consistent finding is that gang members do not have significantly higher rates of general delinquency, violence, drug use, and drug selling than the nonmembers unless they are actively involved in the gang" (Thornberry et al., 2003, p. 120). The deviant behavior of gang members is not stable across pregang, gang, and postgang time periods (Esbensen, Freng, et al., 2002; Thornberry, Krohn, Lizotte, and Chard-Wierschem, 1993; Thornberry et al., 2003). Their behavior is elevated only during active gang membership and decreases after leaving the gang.

The **facilitation model** is a "kind of group" model. It suggests that something about the gang fosters delinquent behavior among gang members. Without the gang, the youth is no more likely to engage in criminal behaviors than those who never join the gang. The gang members' criminal behavior is a function of a gang's group process. The mechanisms for this increase will be discussed in the next section. In this model, gang membership is considered the "cause" of deviant behavior. "Crime and delinquency are more the product than the goal of gang joiners" (Klein, 1995, p. 27). The facilitation model is strongly supported by research (Battin-Pearson, Thornberry, Hawkins, and Krohn, 1998; Dukes, Martinez, and Stein, 1997; Esbensen and Huizinga, 1993; Esbensen, Freng, et al., 2002; Hill, Howell, Hawkins, and Battin-Pearson, 1996; Thomas, Holzer, and Wall, 2003; Thornberry, Krohn, Lizotte, and Chard-Wierschem, 1993; Thornberry et al., 2003). Active gang membership consistently increases criminal behavior by gang members. "When they leave the gang, their behavior changes again; involvement in deviant behavior decreases with the exception of involvement in drug selling" (Thornberry et al., 2003, p. 120).

BOX 7–1: Focus on Research

Several longitudinal studies add to our understanding of gangs. One such study, the Rochester Youth Development Study (RYDS), provides rich information regarding the nature of gang member violence (see Thornberry et al., 2003). The data gathered about gang members were part of a larger longitudinal study of delinquent behaviors in a high-risk sample of adolescents drawn from public school students in Rochester, New York, an emerging gang city. The uniqueness of RYDS is that it is a longitudinal panel study, which means it follows the same group of subjects over many years. Students who were at high risk for deviant behavior were oversampled to ensure that they were included in the study. The original sample was 1,000 students who were in seventh and eighth grades during the 1987–1988 academic school year. For the first three years, the subjects and their primary caretakers completed a face-to-face survey interview every six months with questions about community, family, school, peers, criminal behavior, and individual experiences and values. After a two-year lag in data collection, interviews occurred once a year. The information gathered about gang membership spans the period of early adolescence through young adulthood. The study has high retention rates (80% in young adulthood) and a fairly large percentage of self-identified gang members (30.9%). The RYDS offers insight into the criminal behavior of varying types of gang members during different phases of gang life.

The **enhancement, or "mixed," model** suggests that "both selection and facilitation effects operate to account for the high levels of delinquency and violence observed for gang members" (Thornberry et al., 2003, p. 99) and that individuals at high risk for delinquency will be attracted to and recruited by gangs. Upon gang joining, members experience an increase in their already elevated levels of criminal behavior. Because research shows some support for selection and strong support for facilitation, this model is supported (Dukes, Martinez, and Stein, 1997; Esbensen, Freng, et al., 2002; Gordon et al., 2004; Thornberry, Krohn, Lizotte, and Chard-Wierschem, 1993; Thornberry et al., 2003). Gang youth engage in higher levels and more diverse delinquent behaviors than nongang youth, even before entering the gang. This behavior increases after they join the gang and then falls to pregang levels after they leave the gang.

THE GANG

The fact that criminal behavior increases during active gang membership suggests that there is something about the gang that enhances this behavior. The group context allows for learning criminal behavior (Bjerregaard and Lizotte, 1995; Fagan, 1990; Huff, 1998). As previously stated in Chapter 2, this learning environment within the gang is greater than in even highly deviant nongang peer groups. Although gangs are involved in more deviant behavior than other groups, "even during the most violent epoch, there was considerable variation in the levels of lethal violence from one clique to another of the gangs we study, and even within the gang" (Moore, 1991, p. 58).

The Group Process

The gang atmosphere supports criminal behavior. The structure of the gang provides a foundation of values and attitudes that create groupthink. In this value system, a gang member's "violent behavior is often aggrandized rather than stigmatized with a pathological label" (Yablonsky, 1962, p. 217). Short and Strodtbeck's (1965) work examines "hypotheses relating to mechanisms by which norms and values associated with structural variation become translated into behavior" (p. 269).

As discussed in Chapter 5, the more cohesive the group, the more systematic this groupthink will be. It is within this normative system that the gang member achieves status and a sense of belonging. The gang member will engage in behaviors that are supported by the group, including criminal behaviors, as a way to gain status: "The need for interaction with the group can therefore stimulate even more delinquent and violent activity" (Spergel, 1995, p. 98). This is further supported by Hughes and Short's (2005) research, which finds that status concerns outweighed other factors in the decision to engage in criminal behavior.

In addition to supporting and perpetuating a deviant value system, the gang opens the door to criminal behavior. "Gang membership plays a substantial role in increasing the level of criminal and delinquent behavior. The group context of gang behavior may provide support and opportunities for its members to engage in both more illegal behavior and more serious illegal behavior" (Curry and Decker, 2003, p. 61). These opportunities include nonviolent behavior, such as substance use and illegal economic ventures.

The connection between gang structure and illegal activities is well illustrated in Decker, Bynum, and Weisel's (1998) research. They find similarities in the criminal activities of highly organized Chicago gangs and less organized San Diego gangs. In both gangs, there was little specialization in criminal behavior. The greatest differences seemed to be in the organizational structure of criminal activities. For example, in Chicago gangs, members were likely to get drugs from leaders of the group, specific roles in the drug trade were assigned to members, and members gave a portion of their profits to the gang. On the other hand, the criminal behavior of San Diego gang members tended to be more autonomous. The criminal activities of the gang were not organized, and the group did not financially profit.

The gang also exposes members to violent behavior in a number of ways. First, the increase in access to nonviolent illegal behavior increases members' exposure to risky situations that may result in violence (Miller and Brunson, 2000; Rosenfeld, Bray, and Egley, 1999). This will be discussed in more detail later in this chapter.

Increased violent behavior also stems from the function of the gang as protection against violence in the neighborhood (Decker and Van Winkle, 1996; Williams, 2004), resulting in the "public and participatory nature of gang conflicts" (Rosenfeld, Bray, and Egley, 1999, p. 514). According to Decker (1996), the gang becomes a "safe haven" against violence in this type of environment. The gang member bonds to the collective for protection against a "symbolic enemy." However, this safe haven often leads to further gang violence, including fights over turf control, violence from rivals, and the escalation of behaviors because of status threats and retaliation (Decker and Van Winkle, 1996; Hughes and Short, 2005; Miller and Brunson, 2000; Rosenfeld, Bray, and Egley, 1999). Decker (1996) explains that gang violence is collective behavior that occurs as part of a process of escalation and retaliation, known as **contagion** (see Loftin, 1984). Loftin's "contagion" suggests that in certain areas, initial assaultive violence is met with retaliation, creating the reciprocal nature of violence. As stated by Williams (2004), "The more we fought, the more we had to fight—a continuing escalation of violence" (p. 85). Many gang members draw parallels to a war that "is no stupider than any other war" (Ice T, 2005, p. xix). They identify their gangs as "armies" (Shakur, 1993) and report "sincerely th[inking] I was a soldier in a legitimate necessary war" (Simpson, 2005, p. 308). They report feeling like "a war veteran, with a sort of post-traumatic street syndrome" (Rodriquez, 1993, p. 251).

THE GANG MEMBER AND THE GANG

Gang criminal behavior is the result of two different mechanisms: the gang member and the gang. Each gang member is an individual with different levels of connectedness to the gang. The gangs that members are connected to also vary. As discussed in Chapter 5, some gangs are highly organized and provide opportunity structure to successfully navigate lucrative criminal paths. Other gangs have less opportunity but create an environment where gang status and respect are gained through violent encounters. Some gangs are evolved playgroups, where members engage in substance use and nonspecialized deviant behavior. The behavior of a hard-core gang member in a supergang may be more serious and more frequent than that of a hard-core gang member in an emergent gang. The behavior of the hard-core member in the emergent gang may be more frequent and severe than that of the fringe member of a supergang.

NONVIOLENT CRIME

As previously stated, much of the gang member's time is spent hanging around. However, it is the criminal behavior of gangs that brings negative attention. Gangs do not specialize in a particular type of criminal behavior. They tend to engage in **cafeteria-style offending,** which means they dabble in several types of criminal activities (Klein, 1995, p. 132). Many of these activities are nonviolent. Increasingly, some activities are economically motivated. Gangs and gang members are also involved in violent behavior.

Substance Use

The social aspect of gangs brings with it alcohol and drug use. Substance use plays a primary socializing role in gang life (Hagedorn, 1988; Moore, 1991; Vigil, 1988). Alcohol and drugs "facilitate the broadening, deepening, and solidifying of group affiliations and cohesiveness" (Vigil, 1988, p. 126). This central feature of gangs has led some to identify gang types characterized by substance use (Cloward and Ohlin, 1960; Fagan, 1989; Huff, 1989).

One myth of gang life suggests that gangs negatively view substance use. However, many gang members regularly use drugs (Decker, 2000; Hagedorn, 1988), and some gang members are drug addicted (Moore, 1978, 1991). Substance use is becoming an increasing problem that is suggestive of greater alienation from conventional society (Hagedorn, 1988). The increase in substance use and abuse among gang members is also important because of its link to violent behavior (Hunt and Laidler, 2001). At the same time, this problem should be cautiously stated. Heavy drug use and abuse seem to be more characteristic of core gang members (Vigil, 1988), and research of arrestees shows that gang members used less serious drugs than nongang arrestees (Decker, 2000).

Property Crime

Gang members also engage in property crime at higher rates than nongang peers. Property-related crimes include stealing and vandalism. One of the main distinctions of property crime, compared with other gang activities, is its individual nature. "While the criminality attached to liquor consumption, drug use, and fighting is strongly embedded in gang patterns requiring group efforts and support, it appears that property related crime is more of an individual nature" (Vigil, 1988, p. 137). Commission of property crime is also a way to prove oneself for entrance into a more lucrative drug business (Padilla, 1992).

Drug Sales

One of the great debates involves the immersion of gangs, or their lack of immersion, in the drug market. Some suggest that gangs are not organized and/or do not have any significant role in the drug economy (Curtis, 2003; Klein, 1995). Others suggest that gangs, as a group, have a stake in the drug economy (Padilla, 1992; Taylor, 1989; Venkatesh, 1999). The debate may be best understood by recognizing the variation in gangs, a concept that has been reinforced so far in this book.

Some individuals who are gang members sell drugs. Research finds that drug sales increase upon gang joining (Thornberry et al., 2003). Some gang members sell drugs to generate income (Hagedorn, 1988; Vigil, 1988). This is consistent with other research (Howell and Gleason, 1999). This type of individualized drug dealing is not a group activity, and the gang may not profit in any way. In fact, gang members who are involved in drug dealing make up only a small proportion of overall drug arrests (Klein, Maxson, and Cunningham, 1991; Maxson, 1995). At the same time, drug dealing is profitable for gang members. They make more money, with fewer customers, than their nongang competitors (Huff, 1998). This individual behavior also increases gang-related homicides (Rosenfeld, Bray, and Egley, 1999). "Gang members sell drugs, and gang members kill and are killed selling drugs. However, even in situations where gangs, drugs, and homicide coincide, the motivation for those homicides was much more likely to stem from an argument over quantity/quality of the drugs, payment, or robbery of a drug dealer or customer than from two entities fighting for market control" (Tita, Riley, and Greenwood, 2003, p. 109).

In the same respect, some gangs are organized enough to profit from its members' drug sales (Decker, Bynum, and Weisel, 1998; Jankowski, 1991). The 1995 National Youth Gang Survey finds that gangs and gang members are involved in widespread drug distribution. However, it seems to be concentrated in areas with more persistent gang problems, and it is more likely to occur among young adults, not juvenile members (Howell and Gleason, 1999). Thus, it is imperative to recognize their existence. Klein (1995) distinguished street gangs from drug gangs. However, delineating the two groups leads to a misconception about street gang dynamics. This distinction may be better understood as a natural evolution of gangs. Gangs that are immersed in illegal entrepreneurial activities, such as drug dealing, tend to have a longer history and leaders who coordinate drug supplies (Decker, Bynum, and Weisel, 1998; Jankowski, 1991). This coincides with Knox's typology, discussed in Chapter 5. Gangs can become more organized and goal oriented over time. Padilla's (1992) research on the Diamonds is an example of this gang evolution from drug use to drug dealing. Padilla states that the gang's activity "demonstrates unquestionably that the Diamonds represent a very highly organized, hierarchally [sic] arranged business enterprise" (p. 116).

Jankowski recognizes the delicate balance between the behavior of gang members and gangs and the "complicated relationship" that ensues (1991, p. 136). Gang members often work as individual agents in an environment that supports criminal behavior. This business sense can be beneficial to the gang. However, too much individualism can undermine the group. The balance that results is often seen as group disorganization, but this is not always so. Some gang members are drug dealers, and some gangs are involved in coordinated drug sales. The similarity in these behaviors is economics, and those who fail to recognize this underlying feature "have generally misunderstood gang economic activity" (Jankowski, 1991, p. 136).

The economic tenet of gang drug dealing is reinforced by research. Since the 1970s, continued bleak economic prospects have led to its increased popularity for members and groups. Weak economic prospects have fostered the evolution of some less organized gangs into the corporate realm. For example, the profits from crack cocaine sales constituted 70%, or $196,000, of the yearly revenue of one such gang (Venkatesh, 1999). On the individual level, the economic benefit is supported in research that finds drug selling is the only behavior that does not decrease upon gang leaving (Thornberry et al., 2003). This is further reinforced by research that shows that selling drugs does not increase the likelihood that gang members will test positive for drugs (Decker, 2000), which suggests that gang members are not selling drugs to support their own drug habits but for other economic reasons. At the same time, most gang members do not get rich while in the gang, and eventually the gang offers no other levels of economic advancement for the older member (Venkatesh, 1999).

VIOLENT CRIME

Gang membership is not without risks. As previously discussed, gangs have a culture of violence. Violent behaviors such as initiation rituals, territorial fighting, and violence associated with criminal behaviors are prevalent within gangs. Two types of violence were classified by Block and Block (1993) as expressive and instrumental violence. In **expressive violence,** violence itself is the goal. This is the violence that is seen in gang fights over territory and in initiation rituals. In **instrumental violence,** the primary goal is not violence, but money or tangible property. Violence results as a secondary behavior, such as killing a rival drug dealer. According to Block and Block (1993), this translates into three types of gang-related violence hot spots: turf, drug, and the combination of the two. In turf hot spots, expressive violence results from exerting control over territory. This is the most common type of gang violence. In drug hot spots, instrumental violence results from drug offenses. Both instrumental and expressive violence are found in turf-drug hot spots.

TABLE 7–1

Types of violence

Instrumental

- Tangible object or property is the goal; violence is secondary.
- Includes behavior such as harming rival drug dealer.

Expressive

- Violence is the goal.
- Includes behavior such as initiation rituals and fighting over territory.

The reasons for violence are numerous, including fear and ambition (Jankowski, 1991). Most gang members do not enjoy fighting. Those who do are dispersed throughout different levels of gang membership (Jankowski, 1991). As stated in Chapter 6, many gang members ultimately leave the gang because of violence (Decker and Lauritsen, 2002; Jankowski, 1991; Vigil, 1988). Most of the time, violence is directed at other gang members. It may be violence against a member's own group or against rival gangs (Jankowski, 1991; Vigil, 1988). However, this is not always the case. Sometimes nongang members are the victims of gang violence. Gangs such as MS-13 are known for using violence to intimidate witnesses in court cases (Briscoe, 2005). Other times, gang members target family members of rival gang members. In some situations, innocent members of the community are caught in the cross fire (Moore, 1991; Vigil, 1998).

Guns

One of the notable changes in gangs over the past several decades has been the increase of gang members with guns (Howell and Decker, 1999; Huff, 1998). Gang members are significantly more likely than their nongang peers to own guns and other weapons (Bjerregaard and Lizotte, 1995; Thornberry et al., 2003). Most gang members' guns are illegally obtained and owned (Hagedorn, 1988; Lizotte et al., 2000).

Gun carrying is elevated before gang joining (Bjerregaard and Lizotte, 1995). However, the situational elements of gang life necessitate carrying a gun. For some gang members, gun carrying brings status, particularly for young members (Short and Strodtbeck, 1965). This is evidenced in Rochester, New York, where younger gang members were most likely to be involved in gun violence (Lizotte et al., 2000). As stated in Chapter 4, gang members often join gangs for protection, and thus weapons become a necessity. Gun ownership is also compounded by the illegal business dealings of some gang members, which will be discussed at the end of the chapter.

Gun carrying has changed the landscape of gang violence. The increase in gun carrying is connected to increased lethality in gang encounters (Block and Block,

1993). Another dynamic in gun carrying is that even the weakest fighters are powerful with guns. "'Men' no longer use sticks and stones but guns and knives. These are the legendary 'equalizers' which make the smallest adolescent the match for the biggest man" (Bloch and Neiderhoffer, 1958, p. 168). Once gun carrying begins, there is an escalation of gun carrying. Loftin's (1984) "contagion" is also used to describe this escalating feature of the gang-gun connection (see Lizotte et al., 2000). Lizotte and colleagues (2000) state, "If one travels in a dangerous world of youth armed illegally and defensively with firearms, it only makes sense to carry a gun" (p. 830). Williams's (2004) depiction of gang life exemplifies this changing dynamic of gang life. He states, "Though I continued the old style of gang fighting and avoided toting a gun, I found security in knowing that those closest to me were carrying" (p. 85).

Drive-by Shootings

The playing field of gang violence has also dramatically changed because of drive-by shootings. Greater availability of automobiles, coupled with increasing gun carrying, developed into a new method of gang violence in the 1970s (Howell and Decker, 1999; Moore, 1991; Sanders, 1994). In drive-bys, "gang members drive through a rival gang neighborhood, shooting into a target house or a corner gathering of teenagers" (Moore, 1991, p. 60).

Drive-bys alter the state of gang violence through the expansion of rival gangs. "A gang can hit a target miles away from its home territory, and then speed away unscathed" (Sanders, 1994, p. 84). Drive-bys also can enhance the prowess of gang members. Drive-bys give gang members more courage to strike against rival gangs. "In these situations, gang members can build an identity as having 'heart' and live to tell about it. While risky in terms of counterstrikes by the rival gang and police apprehension, a drive-by can be conducted by virtually anyone who can ride in a car and shoot a gun" (Sanders, p. 1994, 84).

Homicide

Homicides make up a small portion of gang-related crime (Maxson and Klein, 1990). At the same time, approximately 20% of homicides in large cities involve a gang member, with this percentage reaching over 50% in Los Angeles and Chicago (Egley, Howell, and Major, 2006). Although this gang crime reached its peak in the early to mid-1990s (Maxson and Klein, 1990, 1996; Rosenfeld, Bray, and Egley, 1999), it has lasting effects on our understanding of gangs that need to be discussed. There is evidence that gang membership facilitates homicide, both as victims and offenders (Maxson and Klein, 1990, 1996; Rosenfeld, Bray, and Egley, 1999). As discussed in Chapter 2, there is some question as to whether it is important to distinguish between gang-motivated crimes and gang-affiliated crimes. When a gang-motivated definition is used to classify homicide, there is a reduction of 50% in the gang-affiliated homicide rate (Maxson and Klein, 1990).

BOX 7-2: A Closer Look

Gang violence in Los Angeles took an interesting twist on account of activity in Highland Park, a predominantly Latino neighborhood in northeast Los Angeles. Four members of the Avenues, a gang that dates back four generations, have been charged and found guilty of federal hate crimes offenses based on the killing of a young African American man (Mozingo, 2006). The use of hate crimes legislation to charge "gang crime" was disputed by defense attorneys, who claim that the violent behavior was gang behavior, not racially motivated behavior (Murr, 2006). Other evidence submitted by the prosecution presented a case that the behavior was targeted toward only black individuals, and many were not gang members (Murr, 2006). This violence further escalated just days before the verdict was reached. A nongang Latino youth was fatally shot while trying to assist a nongang black youth who was fighting with a suspected Avenues member. This pattern of targeting non-gang members with violence is a typical gang behavior. Police have stated that since they targeted the Avenues gang, this type of violence has decreased (Clark, 2006).

Regardless of the definition used, the characteristics of gang homicides are similar, and they are distinguishable from nongang homicides. Gang homicide is seen in more specific areas than general crime patterns. Gang homicide rates are higher in socially disorganized, high-poverty areas. General crime is only elevated in high-poverty areas without disorganization (Curry and Spergel, 1988). The distinct situational elements of gang homicide are also found in research by Maxson and Klein (1990, 1996) and Rosenfeld, Bray, and Egley (1999). Suspects and victims of gang homicide are more likely to be young, minority males than are people involved in nongang homicides. Gang homicides are more likely than nongang homicides to take place in public and involve a firearm. The suspect in gang homicides usually has a group present during the commission of the act. Finally, the gang homicide is less likely than nongang homicides to involve drug use but more likely to involve drug sales.

The Connection

This chapter has so far established that gang members engage in more criminal behavior as a result of their gang membership. This behavior may increasingly involve drug selling as economic disparity continues. Gang members carry guns at higher rates than nongang youth for protection and status. Guns are more lethal than traditional gang weapons, such as fists and knives. The carrying of guns empowers youth to use violence in situations where they might not otherwise use it. Each of these factors makes it critical to discuss the connection, if any, between crime, guns, and gangs.

Thornberry and colleagues (2003) find a linkage between guns, gangs, and crime. They find that guns affect levels of crime for all youth in their sample. However, the compounded effect of gang membership and gun carrying increased all types of criminal activity more than the simple effect of either gang membership or gun carrying alone. This connection is less consistent for drug selling. Lizotte and colleagues (2000) find that "selling drugs significantly increased the probability of carrying a hidden gun at all but the youngest ages under consideration" (p. 829). This effect is even greater for those who sell large quantities of drugs, independent of gang activity. They find that gang members are more likely to carry a gun for protection rather than for business. This is similar to the conclusions of Howell and Decker (1999), whose review of research shows mixed support for the connection between gangs, drugs, and violence. Gang members are likely to have guns. There is overlap between drug trafficking, violent crime, and gang membership. "Drug trafficking is an indirect contributor to youth gang homicide" (Howell, 1999, p. 227). However, gangs and gang members play a minimal role in the world of drug trafficking. "Most gang violence is endemic to gang life, separate from drug trafficking" (Howell and Decker, 1999, p. 8). Therefore, the connection between gangs, guns, and crime seems to be most solidly based in the violent atmosphere of gangs, not in drug dealing.

CHAPTER SUMMARY

> Most gangs are defensive units. Now if you're selling dope that's a survival scenario as people are trying to get paper and they will defend that. There's a small portion of the ghetto who are "jackers" and that's their way to get money. When the gang decides "we're tough so we're going to move," it becomes predatory.... When someone is hit in gang warfare, it's retaliation. It's not an offensive move. Retaliation is a reaction to murder. (Ice T, 2005, p. xviii)

Gang members are involved in disproportionately more crime than nongang members. This elevated crime rate is found across categories of substance use and abuse, drug selling, property crime, and violent crime. There is variation in criminal behavior based on the type of gang member and the structure of the gang. In most cases, the criminal activity of gang members is facilitated by the gang; it increases upon gang joining. In most cases, crime levels decrease after members leave the gang, with the exception of drug selling. Therefore, there is something unique about the gang that is at the heart of this increase.

This chapter explored several ideas to account for elevated levels of criminal activity. Although much criminal activity is individualistic, the gang offers an environment that is supportive of the behavior. They provide a value system and confer status on members who engage in crime. The gang also supplies access to criminal opportunities that may not have been available to members before they joined the gang, such as drug selling. It is the violent behavior of gang members that raises public alarm. The gang culture is rooted in violence, as evidenced by initiation rituals and rival gang fighting. Although lethal violence is far less common within gangs, there are distinct features of this violence that make it identifiable. One of the more important dynamics of gang culture is the interconnection between the gang, guns, crime, and violent behavior.

KEY TERMS

cafeteria-style offending
contagion
enhancement, or "mixed" model
expressive violence

facilitation model
instrumental violence
selection model

QUESTIONS FOR REVIEW

1. What is the difference between the selection, facilitation, and enhancement models of gang member behavior?

2. How does the group process of gangs lead to criminal behavior?

3. How are drug sales and gangs connected?

4. What is the difference between expressive and instrumental violence?

5. How have guns changed the gang environment?

DISCUSSION QUESTIONS

1. Do you think it is important to distinguish between gang members and gangs when discussing criminal behavior? Why or why not?

2. How would you propose breaking the cycle of gang violence?

CHAPTER 8

RACE AND ETHNICITY

CHAPTER OBJECTIVES

- Understand gang variation based on race and ethnicity.
- Become familiar with early and modern Hispanic and black American gangs.
- Know the changes in Asian gangs since the 1970s.
- Recognize the current emphasis on American Indian gangs.
- Become aware of the role of white gangs in the United States.

UNDERSTANDING THE PROBLEM

> Never did I take into account that first and foremost the Italians had a clear sense of who they were. That is, they overstood [sic] their heritage and their relation to the world as European people. We, on the other hand, were just Crips with no sense of anything before us or of where we were headed. We were trapped behind the veil of cultural ignorance without even knowing it. (Shakur, 1993, p. 208)

Although the issue of race and ethnicity is discussed in this chapter separately, it is enmeshed with other factors and profoundly influences the gang landscape. We have already noted that many of the factors that contribute to gangs and gang membership are rooted in urban economics. Minority group members are more likely to live in communities with "unemployment, poverty, welfare dependency, single-headed households, and other socioeconomic conditions" (Valdez, 2003, p. 16). As minority populations are disproportionately affected by these factors, addressing race and ethnicity in our discussion of gangs is imperative. The NYGS finds most gangs reported are Hispanic (46%), followed by African American (34%), Caucasian (12%), Asian (6%), and 2% other (NYGC, 2000).

Ethnic gangs share similarities in their marginal status in American society. Many are considered on the fringe of mainstream culture. Many ethnic gangs also experience difficulties as a result of immigration and migration. Recall from Vigil's multiple marginality theory (Chapter 3) that ethnic gangs develop out of this marginal status. Despite these similarities, gang experiences vary for different ethnic groups. "[M]inority groups are distinct from one another reflecting difference in economic situation, social status, generations and cultural characteristics" (Valdez, 2003, p. 16).

This chapter will explore some of the commonalities and differences among five types of ethnic gangs: Hispanic, black, Asian, American Indian, and white. Although many gangs no longer maintain exclusivity based on ethnicity, much of gang culture is rooted in unique ethnic histories. Moreover, many times there are regional variations in ethnic gangs based on localized experiences. However, this book provides a broad overview, and delving into these intricacies is beyond its scope. The history and distinctive features of each ethnic gang are discussed. The discussion of Hispanic/Latino and black gangs will emphasize Los Angeles and Chicago, which have had the most gang activity for the longest duration. Specifics of more organized ethnic gangs will also be discussed because they have had a far-reaching impact on national gang activity.

HISPANIC/LATINO GANGS

The History

Hispanic/Latino ethnic gangs have members whose ancestry is rooted in Spanish-speaking regions, such as Central America, Puerto Rico, the Dominican Republic, and Mexico.[1] They have characteristically been immigrants with poor connections to school who have encountered difficulties in assimilating into American culture. As Vigil's multiple marginality theory specifies, gang members from Hispanic communities are on the fringe of their Hispanic culture and families and on the fringe of mainstream society. This creates an environment prime for gang activity, where "street socialization results when home and school socialization have failed" (Vigil, 2002, p. 45).

Gangs of the 1930s and 1940s.   As discussed in Chapter 1, Hispanic gangs were the first "modern" street gangs, originating in Southern California in the late 1930s. The precursor to the modern Hispanic gang is identified as sports clubs affiliated with churches in Mexican **barrios,** a Spanish term for neighborhoods (Moore, 1991). The groups were integrated into the community and would not be classified as gangs today. Many older members of the prosocial sports clubs were sent to fight in World War II, which left a gap in the socialization of younger males in the community (Moore, 1991). Their "abrupt departure created sharp discontinuities for the boys who remained to carry on neighborhood traditions" (Moore, 1991, p. 27). Increased segregation contributed to the phenomenon that was about to evolve because it made integration into mainstream culture more difficult (Vigil, 2002). Mexican barrios were culturally isolated and poor. One such barrio was El Hoyo, or "The Hole," named for its lack of water and sewer services (Vigil, 2002, p. 34).

With few positive role models and social isolation, young males formed groups such as El Hoyo Maravilla and the violent White Fence. These groups, soon to be gangs, developed a **pachuco, or zoot suiter,** lifestyle, which came with a distinctive physical appearance: oversized suits and hair worn in ducktails (http://www.pbs.org/wgbh/amex/zoot/index.html). Pachucos also participated in gang-related fighting, which brought negative attention from the public (Moore, 1991). The Zoot Suit Riots of 1943 were the direct result of this negative attention and race-based conflict between whites and Mexicans. The riots helped to band together Mexican pachucos and introduced the cohesion necessary for furthering group identity. In the 1940s, Chicago was also experiencing the escalation of gang activity, with the origination of clubs that would eventually give birth to more organized gangs. As with Los Angeles gangs, forerunners to the "modern" gang were attributable to discrimination and prejudice (Perkins, 1987).

Gangs of the 1970s.   The uniqueness of the gangs that developed in the 1930s was that they did not dissolve and move on as prior ethnic gangs had. The areas where they resided never experienced the invasion and succession of new ethnic groups that had occurred before (Vigil, 2002). Immigration from Hispanic countries into Southern California has been continuous. By the 1970s, a stable gang environment was established, and in some cases gangs were multigenerational (Vigil, 2002). New gangs, such as 18th Street, developed in areas where whites were displaced by Hispanic immigrants (Vigil, 2002). This current wave of gangs adopted a **cholo subculture,** which is in many ways similar to the pachuco subculture of the 1940s. The cholo subculture embraces a culture that is outside mainstream society. It is an expression of "cultural identification tied to street identity" (Vigil, 2002, p. 44). Most gangs today, regardless of ethnicity, also adopt the cholo lifestyle (Vigil, 2002). Today, Los Angeles still has the most Hispanic gangs (500), including Mexican and Salvadoran ethnicities. Their distinctive style of dress includes "white t-shirts, thin belts, baggy pants with split cuffs, a black or blue knit cap (beanie) or a bandana tied around the forehead similar to a sweat band" (Los Angeles Police Department, n.d.). The largest Hispanic gang in Los Angeles County is 18th Street, with 20,000 members. This gang encompasses a very large area, so it's also the most fragmented gang (http://www.streetgangs.com).

Hispanic Gang Experiences

Ethnic experiences shape gang life. The distinctions of ethnic gangs are often due to the unique circumstances that each group faces (Valdez, 2003). These experiences also vary by region. Historically, Hispanic gangs have been most known for their turf-oriented nature. This is due to the gang developing around a protective role (Valdez, 2003). Hispanic gang members are more likely than black gang members to report joining a gang for protection (Freng and Winfree, 2004). As a result, Hispanic gang members are more likely to engage in fighting and graffiti (Freng and Winfree, 2004;

Spergel, 1995). Hispanic gang members are also more likely to report mixed-gender gangs and the use of symbols and colors in gang identity (Freng and Winfree, 2004) and more likely than black gang members to engage in substance use (Curry and Spergel, 1992).

More recently, the role of territory for Hispanic gangs has been less pronounced. In emerging gang areas, territory is less important because the gang is more focused on monetary pursuits. Also, as the economy changes, even in areas that used to host multi-generational turf-oriented Hispanic gangs, there seems to be a shift to more economic-centered illegal activities (Valdez, 2003). This makes Hispanic gangs less distinguishable from other ethnic gangs. The prison experience has also changed the dynamics of Hispanic gangs. Members are now more likely to jump from one gang or clique to another.

Contemporary Hispanic Gangs

Latin Kings.   The Latin Kings emerged in Chicago in the 1940s as clubs. In the 1960s, the Latin Kings developed into a more problematic "gang" (Knox, 2000a). Why this occurred is unclear, but it may have to do with ineffective intervention pro-grams that fostered negative behavior (Knox, 2000a). Although membership originally included only Puerto Rican members, the group has expanded to include other Latin ethnicities. As a result of the gang's longevity, they are extremely organized (Knox, 2000a), as shown by their leadership hierarchy and the rules and regulations set forth in their constitution. They abide by a tradition of respect, loyalty, love, wisdom, and obedience, each represented by a point on a five-point star (Brotherton and Barrios, 2004). The organization is predicated on the "tradition of secrecy, lessons, rules, sanc-tions, prayers, record-keeping, and representing" (Brotherton and Barrios, 2004, p. 63). The constitution specifies celebration of "King's Holy Day" on January 6 and "King's Week" during the first week of March (Knox, 2000a). The Latin Kings are the second largest gang in Chicago, with approximately 18,000 members (Knox, 2000a).[2]

The Chicago model of the Latin Kings became an inspiration for two inmates serving time in a Connecticut correctional facility in the 1980s. Felix Millet and Nelson Millan developed the "King Manifesto," which was based on the Chicago con-stitution. In 1986, Luis Felipe, also known as "King Blood," expanded this manifesto in the formation of the New York State Latin Kings (Brotherton and Barrios, 2004). The end result was the creation of the Almighty Latin King and Queen Nation (ALKQN). Since its inception in the 1980s, the ALKQN has expanded into many areas in the Northeast. Its chapters, called tribes, include membership numbers in the thousands. The Northeast variant is notably different from the Chicago Kings in that they are more involved in political activism (Brotherton and Barrios, 2004; Knox, 2000a). The ALKQN are loosely connected to the Chicago Latin Kings, and the "Motherland" is referred to in prayers and other gang rituals (Brotherton and Barrios, 2004). Gang identifiers, including hand signs, colors of black and gold, a crown, or five-pointed star, are common across all Latin King groups.

Figure 8–1 A crown is often used in Latin King tattoos and graffiti *(left)*. The Latin King hand sign *(right)* is made with the pinkie, index finger, and thumb.

As the Latin Kings and the ALKQN continue to organize, their message focuses on community awareness. Leadership in the ALKQN emphasizes moving away from secrecy and creating more openness around gang rituals. In Chicago, a Latin King leader states they are a "street organization [trying] to move ahead, be a little bit more positive on things" (The Latin Kings Speak, 2002). In 1995, Antonio "King Tone" Fernandez, of the New York ALKQN, asked the gang to move beyond its past violence (Brotherton and Barrios, 2004). King Tone was subsequently convicted on drug charges, and the gang has had difficulty in securing a legitimate leader to take his place (Brotherton and Barrios, 2004).

MS-13.   Mara Salvatrucha, more commonly known as MS-13, is fast becoming the most notorious gang of modern times. The knowledge we have on MS-13 is primarily based on law enforcement information and newspaper reports. MS-13 began in the 1980s in Los Angeles as a gang of El Salvadoran immigrants fleeing their war-torn country (Castro, 2005). These immigrants banded together to protect themselves from established Hispanic gangs, and they soon became the bitter rival of 18th Street (Campo-Flores, 2005; Grascia, 2004). They took on their own gang identifiers, such as hand signs and blue-and-white bandanas (Castro, 2005; Grascia, 2004; McPhee, 2005; Valdez, 2000). Their name suggests familiarity with the cholo subculture. *Mara* means "posse," and *Salvatruchas* means "street-tough Salvadorans" (Campo-Flores, 2005). The "13" has different interpretations, one referencing the 13th letter of the alphabet, "M," and the connection of the gang to the Mexican Mafia (Grascia, 2004). They easily involved themselves in a variety of criminal behavior, including drug sales and car theft (Campo-Flores, 2005). The youth involved in MS-13 grew up surrounded by violence in El Salvador, and many of their activities demonstrate this culture (Grascia, 2004; Valdez, 2000). In the Boston area, MS-13 members are tied to extremely violent behaviors, such as machete attacks, home invasions, and rapes (McPhee, 2005).

One of the more startling inconsistencies of this gang is its extensive organization despite its relative youth. Since the 1980s, they have developed an elaborate organization of local gangs divided into cliques and further smaller divisions (Castro, 2005). MS-13 has had impressive proliferation into at least 27 states nationwide (Grascia, 2004), with more than 100 cliques (Castro, 2005) and 8,000 to 10,000 estimated U.S. members (Campo-Flores, 2005). Some of this expansion is due to relocation and avoiding arrest (Campo-Flores, 2005). MS-13 has also expanded into Mexico and Central

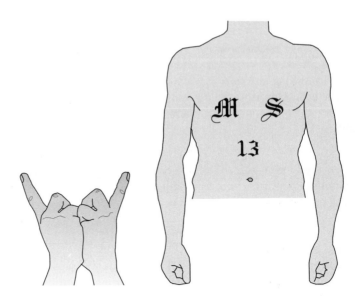

Figure 8–2 The complex Mara Salvatrucha, or MS-13, hand sign uses two hands to form an upside-down "M" *(left)*. Mara Salvatrucha members are often heavily tattooed *(right)*. These tattoos usually contain "MS" and "13" or "X3."

America. Some suggest that the expansion of the gang is partly due to deportation of MS-13 gang members (Castro, 2005; Papachristos, 2005a). In 1994 and 1995, more than 100 MS-13 members were deported in an effort to remove gang members from the United States (Valdez, 2000). The gang has quickly spread throughout Central America and then back into other areas throughout the United States (Lopez, Connell, and Kraul, 2005). It has been suggested that this international connection allows MS-13 access to sophisticated weapons (Castro, 2005), terrorist activities (McPhee, 2005), and elaborate South American car theft rings (Valdez, 2000).

BLACK AMERICAN GANGS

The History

Black American gangs emerged a little later than Hispanic gangs. Los Angeles and Chicago first experienced black gang emergence in the 1940s (Alonso, n.d.; Perkins, 1987). Many of these gangs were black immigrants arriving from the rural South to urban areas throughout the United States (Perkins, 1987; Spergel, 1995; Vigil, 2002). Like Hispanic gangs, black gangs began as small clubs (Perkins, 1987). The history of Los Angeles suggests that as the black population increased, whites felt threatened. The KKK resurfaced, and blacks became the target of white violence (Alonso, n.d.;

Vigil, 2002). As a result, black gangs formed to protect against this threat (Alonso, n.d.). The urban environment changed dramatically in the 1950s, as white flight began (Alonso, n.d.; Vigil, 2002). Interracial violence soon became intraracial violence (Alonso, n.d.). Chicago history suggests that incarceration of blacks and the breakdown of public and social institutions in the 1940s and 1950s created an environment prone to gang formation (Perkins, 1987). In both Los Angeles and Chicago, black gangs had their Hispanic gang predecessors to emulate. In Los Angeles, gangs such as the Gladiators and the Slausons developed for protection and support (Alonso, n.d; Williams, 2004). In Chicago, the Coons and the Dirty Sheiks formed (Perkins, 1987). Early on, there were differences between black gangs and their Hispanic peers. Hispanics were more turf oriented, but because of proximity to white spaces, the behavior of black gangs was more violent (Vigil, 2002). This gang environment remained stable until the 1960s.

Los Angeles Black Gangs

In Los Angeles, the Watts Riots of 1965 brought black youth together for political mobilization (Alonso, n.d.). Prior intraracial violence was harnessed and directed toward the government. This activism drew attention from criminal justice officials, and soon key activists and leaders were incarcerated and effectively "removed from the community . . . leav[ing] a power vacuum" (Alonso, n.d; see also Vigil, 2002). The riots and removal of role models in the Los Angeles black community are not unlike the history of the Hispanic community a generation before. The removal of activist role models and decreasing social programming created an environment primed for powerful gang emergence (Vigil, 2002).

Some black gangs remained active throughout the Black Power Revolution (Vigil, 2002; Williams, 2004). The still-active street gangs were violent. By the end of the 1960s, small gangs developed throughout Los Angeles for protection against more established gangs. Two such groups were the Baby Avenues, headed by Raymond Washington, and a myriad of "nongang" friends of Stanley "Tookie" Williams (Williams, 2004). Williams was focused on avoiding the "the divide-and-conquer mistakes made by other street gangs. It didn't take a mathematician to see that when a structure is divided into factions, each individual part loses its potency and thus is exposed to possible annihilation. I didn't want to make that mistake" (Williams, 2004, p. 75). This consolidation included a union with Washington's East Side gang in 1971, creating "the Cribs," with Washington and Williams as the identifiable leaders. This name would quickly turn into "the Crips." According to Williams, gang members mispronounced "Cribs" while drinking, and the new name stuck (Williams, 2004). Soon after, independent gangs, such as the Pirus and Brims, aligned themselves to form the "the Bloods" to protect against the Crips (Vigil, 2002). "While Black economic programs experienced a full downswing, the gang factor and its circle of violence were experiencing a surge. This was a growth industry!" (Williams, 2004, p. 72). By 1982, there were 18 black gangs in Los Angeles, which expanded to 155 gangs in 1992, and by 1996 there were 274 black gangs. All of these gangs allied themselves with either

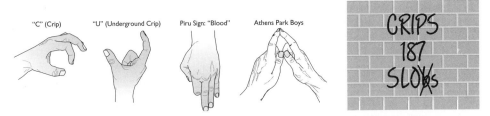

Figure 8–3 Crip hand signs use the letters "C" or "U" (for Underground Crip), while Blood hand signs use the "Piru" sign or other symbols, such as an "A" for Athens Park Boys. Graffiti often serves as a warning, as here, where a Crips "put down" warns Bloods to stay away.

the Bloods (75 gangs) or the Crips (199 gangs) (Alonso, n.d). The Crips' blue color is a tribute to a gang member killed in 1973 (Williams, 2004); the Bloods' red color is symbolism based on the gang's name. A fierce rivalry exists between the two "gangs," with Bloods refusing to use the letter "C" and Crips refusing to use the letter "B" in writing. After the Rodney King Riots in 1992, the two gangs called a short-lived truce and proposed a reconstruction plan for their community (Gangresearch.net, n.d.).

Chicago Black Gangs

By the 1960s, there was a massive gang eruption in Chicago. They "had grown to such proportions that they not only posed a threat to themselves but to the Black community as well" (Perkins, 1987, p. 32). Gangs merged to become more powerful and engage in more deviant behavior. Prominent gangs that emerged during this time were the Black P. Stone Rangers and the Gangster Disciples. The Black P. Stone Rangers were organized in 1960s under the leadership of Jeff Fort. Throughout their enduring history, they have also been known as Black P. Stone Nation and El Rukns (Knox, 2001a). The Gangster Disciples emerged in the 1970s, first under the leadership of David Barksdale and eventually led by Larry "King" Hoover (Knox, 2001b). Recruiting efforts increased gang membership in the 1960s and 1970s, and the age range of gang membership was widening (Perkins, 1987). The gangs had an appeal for marginal youth. "Being a gang member had become a status symbol" (Perkins, 1987, p. 33). Even the Black P. Stone Rangers were thought to have political connections and were "wooed by many special interest groups" (Perkins, 1987, p. 35). By the mid-1990s, the Gangster Disciples expanded its operation to more than 30,000 members in Chicago and to other members throughout the country (Knox, 2001b).

In the 1970s, there was a lull in street gang activity as key leaders were incarcerated. However, this led to a displacement of gangs from the streets to prisons, and it led to the formation of more powerful gang "nations" in the 1980s (Perkins, 1987). Some say the alliances were a way to quickly identify friends and foes (Florida Department of Corrections, n.d., pp. 4–12). It has also been suggested that prison policies

Figure 8–4 People Nation sets tend to use five-pointed stars, pyramids, and crescents in their tattoos and graffiti. Folk Nation sets tend to use six-pointed stars, pitchforks, and winged hearts in their tattoos and graffiti.

banning gang activity required an alternate identification system. The two prominent **Nations,** or alliances of gangs, that emerged were People and Folks. They are not exclusively Chicago gangs or black gangs. These alliances have been compared to baseball's National League and American League (Florida DOC, n.d., pp. 4–12). Some of the gangs in the People Nation are Black P. Stone, Vice Lord, Familia Stones, and Bloods (Florida DOC, n.d., pp. 4–12). Latin Kings used to be part of the Nation, but "Latin Kings left the People Nation. Cause there could be People and there could be Folks but we're gonna be Latin Kings" (The Latin Kings Speak, 2002). Some of the gangs that belong to the Folks are Black Gangster Disciples, Black Disciples, Gangster Disciples, Spanish Cobras, Two Six, and Crips (Florida DOC, n.d., pp. 4–12).

Black Gang Experiences

As previously discussed, black gangs formed under different conditions than Hispanic gangs. These differences are reflected in the nature of black gangs. Black communities d hit by the economy. Therefore, black gangs tend to take on activities ~ially lucrative (Valdez, 2003). In a national study, they are most likely to ; gangs for money (49%) (Freng and Winfree, 2004). The economic ; activity keeps blacks in gangs longer than other ethnic groups (Freng 2004; Spergel, 1995). Research finds that black gang members are over-..... gang members (Spergel, 1995) and are more likely to be male than other groups (Freng and Winfree, 2004). Some research finds that black gang members are involved in more delinquent behavior (Curry and Spergel, 1992); other research shows no significant difference in criminal behavior (Freng and Winfree, 2004).

ASIAN GANGS

The History

The category of Asian gangs includes many ethnicities, including Chinese, Southeast Asian, Japanese, and Korean. This is further complicated by the distinction in literature between Chinese from Hong Kong, Taiwan, and mainland China and Southeast Asian gangs from Vietnam, Cambodia, and Laos (see Wang, 2000). Southeast Asian gangs have a unique, more recent history that makes their gang experiences different from their Hispanic and black predecessors. Early Asian gangs were able to model themselves on and, in some cases, work with Asian organized crime, unlike Hispanic and black youth gangs. Like earlier ethnic gangs, Southeast Asian immigrants formed gangs in the face of hardship and adversity. In some cases, discrimination came at the hands of other Asians (Toy, 1992; Vigil, 2002). Asian immigrants experience barriers to financial success in the United States, and many live in communities that are plagued by social disorganization (Vigil, 2002; Wang, 1995, 2002).

Asian immigration was minimal throughout much of the 1900s, due to immigration restrictions. This restriction limited the number of Asian youth who resided in the United States and kept youth gangs at bay. Some Asian gangs began to appear in Chinatown areas of San Francisco in the late 1950s and early 1960s and in New York in the 1960s (Chin, 1996; Toy, 1992). Youth banded together in the face of discrimination and alienation as protection from mainstream society (Chin, 1996; Lee, 2003). They engaged in fighting and minor criminal behavior (Toy, 1992). There was extensive change in the Asian gang landscape throughout the 1960s. The 1965 Immigration Act altered the quotas for Asian immigrants, opening the door to an influx of Asians into the United States (Chin, 1996). As Asian immigration continued, distinctions were made between American-born Chinese (ABCs) and newly arriving immigrants, fresh off the boat (FOBs). Resources in Asian communities were limited, and the ABCs felt threatened by the arrival of competitors (Toy, 1992). This led to conflict between different Chinese groups and ultimately to intense gang activity. A similar pattern of activity is noted among Vietnamese immigrants in Los Angeles in the 1970s and 1980s (see Vigil, 2002). While the first wave of Vietnamese immigrants were adapting to life in the United States, the newer wave of less educated, poorer "boat people" faced more difficulties.

Asian Gangs in the 1960s, 1970s, and 1980s.   What we know about Asian gangs is derived from a limited amount of academic research, journalistic accounts, and law enforcement agencies (Mark, 1997). Much of this information comes from gangs in San Francisco and New York. The gangs in these cities developed in the 1960s and remained stable for several decades (Tsunokai and Kposowa, 2002), and they received attention on account of their close associations with organized crime. In both cities, the street gangs of the 1950s and early 1960s developed into predatory gangs who engaged in extortion and violence. By the 1970s, street gangs became affiliated with **Tongs,** adult organized crime. In New York, the Ghost Shadows, developed in 1966, worked for the On Leong Tong, and the Flying Dragons, developed in 1967, worked for the Hip Sing gambling houses (Chin, 1996).

Toy (1992) offers an in-depth historical account of the emergence of violent youth gangs in San Francisco. These groups expanded in size and began engaging in serious violent behavior, including extortion and strong-arm robberies. Early on, immigrant youth were supported through their work for Chinese Tongs. However, Yow Yee, a group of Asian youth, was formed in an effort to improve conditions for immigrants. Because they did not have support from Tong elders, they had to find money and resources themselves, and they established themselves as a street gang that relied on extortion for money. The Tongs formed an alternate youth gang, Suey Sing, to gain control of the streets. This group eventually left San Francisco and banded with a small gang in Oakland (Toy, 1992; Mark, 1997), essentially spreading Asian gangs. By the 1970s, the Tongs were able to split Yow Yee into several different factions, and the Tongs effectively utilized the gangs in criminal ventures. Intense rivalries and gang warfare plagued much of San Francisco Chinatown in the 1970s, culminating in the Golden Dragon Massacre in 1977. The massacre is named for the restaurant where open fire left 5 dead and 11 injured, none of them gang members (Toy, 1992). A lull in gang activity ensued, but the Wah Ching hung on and emerged as a powerful force in the 1980s. By the 1980s, the Wah Ching membership merged ABCs and FOBs, creating friction that would lead to disorganization, splintering, and a loss of control. Since the 1990s, the Suey Sing has been the youth gang that is believed to control the economic markets of gambling and protection in San Francisco. It is suggested that they also have close ties to Tong organized crime.

Asian Gang Experiences

The common experiences of Asian immigrants set the stage for gang activity. Unique to Asian gang joining is the role of family. Family values stress educational and economic success. Asian parents work very hard to succeed in the United States, often long hours away from home (McPhee, 2003a; Vigil, 2002; Zhang, 2002). Their children experience difficulties in school (Vigil, 2002; Zhang, 2002). Youth left with pressure to succeed, little adult guidance, frustration, and a desire for making money find gang joining a viable option (Zhang, 2002).

Much of Asian gang history suggests a connection between street gangs and Asian organized crime and Tongs. Often law enforcement suggests that Asian gangs maintain distinctive features that warrant their inclusion as organized crime, such as profit orientation and older leadership structure (Chin, 1996). Most research finds that some Asian youth gangs are associated with organized adult groups, but these associations are loose, and they are not fully integrated into this world (Joe, 1994a; Chin, 1996). Most violence committed by Asian gang members is done independently of Tongs (Chin, 1996).

The connection between Asian street gangs and adult criminal organizations does influence the behavior and values of the gang. Traditionally, Asian gangs have not included female members (Chin, 1996), and the gang is not turf oriented (Vigil, 2002). Most Asian gang members are older, in their late teens and early twenties (Tsunokai and Kposowa, 2002; Vigil, 2002). Asian gang members rarely use drugs and engage in minimal drugs sales, but they are more likely to engage in violence than members of other ethnic gangs (Chin, 1996; Tsunokai and Kposowa, 2002; Vigil, 2002). Younger members of the gang are often given the most violent tasks (Chin, 1990). In some cases, this violence is connected to childhood exposure to violence, such as in Vietnam (Vigil, 2002).

Asian street gangs are "more sophisticated and pragmatic" in their activities (Vigil, 2002, p. 115). They are primarily motivated by money, and much of their criminal behavior reflects this goal. This ethnic street gang is distinct from others because they victimize their own communities (Chin, 1996). Asian gangs exist in communities that have greater wealth than other ethnic groups. As a result, they are more likely to

---

BOX 8–1: Focus on Research

Chin's study of Chinese gangs is presented in *Chinatown Gangs* (1996). His study was conducted in the early 1990s in New York City's Chinatown. To explore the unique nature of these ethnic gangs, Chin used multiple methodologies and gained information from businesses, gang members, law enforcement, and community leaders. All of the information Chin gathered came from face-to-face interviews. His business survey was designed to gain information about victimization. More than 600 business owners completed the survey in 1990 and 1991. A follow-up study of 50 victimized businesses was conducted one year later. Chin's study also included interviews with 70 gang members to assess the organization and criminal behavior of gang members. The study is further enhanced by interviews with 23 law enforcement officers to understand control of Asian crime and interviews with 15 community leaders to become familiar with the history and activities of Asian crime. The multiple methods approach is beneficial to Chin's study because it allows a greater understanding of a unique ethnic experience.

engage in profit-oriented crimes, such as extortion, fraud, and computer crime (Chin, 1996; Chin, Fagan, and Kelly, 1992; Wang, 2000). Asian street gangs are also known for engaging in home invasion robberies (Vigil, 2002; Wang, 2000). Because of their distrust for the banking system, Asian business owners keep large amounts of cash in their homes (Chin, 1996; Vigil, 2002). Asians also lack trust in the criminal justice system and often do not report criminal victimization. Southern California police estimate that 90% of all home invasion robberies in Asian communities go unreported (Vigil, 2002, p. 112). This combined distrust makes Asian business owners and families vulnerable targets for crime.

Contemporary Asian Gangs

Today, the number of active Asian gang members is quite small. In 1990, Chin (1990) stated that there were no more than 2,000 members nationwide. McCurrie (1999) found that 25% of police agencies reported active Asian gangs in their communities, which represented 6% of gang membership (NYGC, 2000). Only 21% of Asian gang members belonged to ethnic Asian gangs; the remainder belonged to mixed gangs (McCurrie, 1999). Asian gangs exist in many large cities throughout the United States, including San Francisco, Chicago, Los Angeles, Boston, and New York. They have also expanded to areas outside main cities, including Oakland, Queens, and suburban areas surrounding Boston. Some groups throughout the United States are splinter groups of the larger Ghost Shadows and Flying Dragons (Chin, 1990). Others are homegrown groups, such as the Asian Bloods and Asian Crips in Florida and Massachusetts (Florida DOC, n.d.; Massachusetts DOC, n.d.). There is much variation because of regional differences and affiliation (or lack of affiliation) with Tongs.

In the late 1980s and early 1990s, RICO (racketeering in corrupt organization) statutes were used to dismember prominent Asian street gangs (Chin, 1996). Some suggest that this virtually eliminated the Asian street gang problem; others state that the reduction in activities is more complicated and influenced by other changes in Asian communities (Lee, 2003). Asian immigrants were able to assimilate into mainstream culture, which reduced gang activity. For example, Lawrence Wu was a member of an Asian street gang who was arrested for serious crime. He is a corporate lawyer and former editor of the *Columbia University Law Review* (Wilson, 2000). The organized crime landscape in Asian communities also changed the dynamics of street gangs. Transportation to other gambling communities reduced the necessity for protection of organized crime gambling houses in U.S. Chinatowns, as did the shift in the drug trade (Lee, 2003). However, its continued presence in Asian communities allows some street gang members to move on to other opportunities. For example, Ceng, a former member of the Ghost Shadows, assists in the operation of a nightclub in Queens that is believed to be connected to organized crime (McPhee, 2003a).

However, not all Asian street gangs are enmeshed with organized crime. These groups tend to be smaller and more cohesive than Tong-affiliated groups because the lack of competition allows them to operate effectively in newly established Asian communities

(Chin, 1996). These newly forming groups tend to take on more traditional gang identifiers such as tattoos and colors, mimicking Hispanic and black gangs (Vigil, 2002).

These newly established gangs tend to be less organized than those connected to organized crime. McPhee (2003b) describes the Asian Eagles or Asian Empire (AE), the first new gang since the 1980s in New York City's Chinatown and Queens. This gang is made up of about 50 teenagers, both ABCs and recent immigrants. They operate like other ethnic gangs in that they are primarily involved in assaults, but some suggest that larger organized crime is waiting in the wings to work with them.

AMERICAN INDIAN GANGS

The History

American Indian gangs have been some of the most neglected in research and "have been largely absent from survey findings" (Major, Egley, Mendenhall, and Armstrong, 2004, p.1). Their systematic exclusion from national databases is due to nonmandatory reporting on Indian reservations. However, several initiatives have increased our knowledge. In 1999, the National Youth Gang Center targeted Indian reservations for information, and a research team out of California State University at Sacramento is completing a study of youth gangs on the Navajo Indian reservation (Armstrong et al., n.d.). This, along with several other pieces of research, gives us some insight into the world of American Indian gangs.

Like other ethnic gangs, American Indian gangs experienced a period of "non-gang" youth group activity before the era of modern gangs. The precursors to Indian gangs were partying groups that engaged in substance use, primarily alcohol, and other petty behaviors (Armstrong et al., n.d.; Henderson, Kunitz, and Levy, 1999). It was not until the 1990s that Indian communities experienced an emerging gang problem (Major and Egley, 2002). In a relatively short period, youth gang activity on reservations dramatically increased. The Bureau of Indian Affairs reported 181 known gangs in 1994, and by 2000 there were 520 gangs with more than 6,000 members (Beiser, 2000). Youth gangs are now found in more than 23% of reservations (Major and Egley, 2002). The Navajo reservation, the largest in the country, has been reported to have between 50 and 75 gangs (Armstrong et al., n.d.; Beiser, 2000; Henderson, Kunitz, and Levy, 1999), and the Tohono O'odham reservation in Arizona, the second largest, has 25 gangs with approximately 2,000 members (Khoury, 1998).

Proliferation of gang activity is tied to the influence of mainstream urban gangs (Henderson, Kunitz, and Levy, 1999). This influence occurs in several ways. Some American Indian youth are influenced by the media, similar to proliferation across the country (Beiser, 2000). Unique to Indian gangs is **cross-fertilization** from schooling, imprisonment, and migration patterns. Some American Indian youth are sent away to school or prison outside their reservations, which enables them to experience gangs in urban environments and bring their knowledge back to the reservation (Henderson,

Kunitz, and Levy, 1999; Khoury, 1998; Beiser, 2000). Similarly, some families move from the reservation to outside areas, allowing contact with urban gangs (Armstrong et al., n.d.). Thus, many of the gangs on reservations mimic Hispanic and black gangs, and some have urban gang names (Khoury, 1998). In some cases, there is continued contact between reservation gangs and urban gangs (Armstrong et al., n.d.). The expansion of youth gangs is attributed to the limited ability of tribal police to handle a growing crime problem. Reservation police have a limited number of officers, who must monitor a very large amount of land (Beiser, 2000; Martinez, 2005; Joseph and Taylor, 2003). One solution to this problem has been for tribes to create gang task forces (Beiser, 2000).

American Indian Gang Experiences

The structure of American Indian gangs is not much different from the structure of gangs in other communities of a similar size (Major et al., 2004). Native communities with large populations have greater problems than those with smaller populations. Comparisons across Native and non-Native communities find that Native gangs have similar gender composition and engage in similar activities (Major et al., 2004). As Indian gangs are emerging, few report a leadership structure capable of controlling membership (Armstrong et al., n.d.). Many American Indian gangs are of mixed gender (Armstrong et al., n.d.; Major and Egley, 2002). Research using data from the National Longitudinal Survey of Adolescent Health finds that American Indians were most likely among all ethnic groups to report membership in a gang that was named (12%) (McNulty and Bellair, 2003).

American Indian gangs engage in relatively minor turf-oriented crime, such as graffiti and public disorder offenses (Major and Egley, 2002). They are more likely than nongang youth to engage in substance use (Whitbeck, Hoyt, Xiaojin, and Stubbin, 2002). American Indian communities have experienced violence attributable to gangs since the 1990s (Armstrong et al., n.d.; Joseph and Taylor, 2003; Major et al., 2004). Window Rock, the capital of the Navajo nation, was reported to have a homicide rate that was higher than either Los Angeles or Chicago (Beiser, 2000). Although most gang members report that violence is not a regular gang activity, many report carrying firearms (Armstrong et al., n.d.). Gang membership explains more criminal behavior for American Indians than for other ethnic gang members (McNulty and Bellair, 2003).

Like other ethnic gangs, American Indian gangs exist in communities of poverty and other disorganization, including widespread addiction (Major et al., 2004; Martinez, 2005). Youth on reservations experience marginality from conventional society (Armstrong et al., n.d.; Beiser, 2000; Major et al., 2004), and some experience a lack of connection to Indian culture as well (Armstrong et al., n.d.; Henderson, Kunitz, and Levy, 1999). At the same time, their experiences are different in that their oppression has existed far longer than that of other ethnic groups and they do not face the same experiences with mobility (Major et al., 2004). Reservations have the added effect of a young population: "The median age of American Indians is 24, as opposed to 22 for other Americans. On many reservations, half the population is under the age of 18" (Beiser, 2000, p.15). The community also lacks the leadership for advocacy that other ethnic groups have (Martinez, 2005).

Although few Indian youth join gangs, those who do tend to live in troubled households with single parents, alcoholism, and more life transitions than nongang Indians (Armstrong et al., n.d.; Whitbeck, Hoyt, Xiaojin, and Stubbin, 2002). Reasons for gang joining are similar for American Indian youth and other ethnic gang members. They report joining gangs for status, prestige, protection, and family (Armstrong et al., n.d.; Beiser, 2000; Henderson, Kunitz, and Levy, 1999).

WHITE GANGS

The History

There is much debate in the discussion of white gangs as street gangs. Part of this debate is rooted in the tendency to include racist skinheads in this category. As will be discussed, many experts believe that skinheads are a different phenomenon that should not be considered street gangs. The fact remains that the NYGS, which excludes hate groups in their definition of *gang*, finds that 12% of youth gang members are white (NYGC, 2000). It is also a fact that the very first gangs in the United States were Caucasian. As discussed in Chapter 1, immigrant groups from European countries were the first to form gangs in the late 1800s. They formed gangs as a way to cope with discrimination and the difficulties of adjusting to a new culture. Their reasons for gang formation and gang joining were themes that would echo for more than a century.

Today, it is more difficult to find exclusively white street gangs. Some white gang members are part of mixed-race groups. Those exclusive white gangs that are documented often fall into the category of "stoner" gang, a group that bonds over drug and alcohol use (Jackson and McBride, 1992; Korem, 1994; Sanders, 1994). This type of gang is similar to other groups that have been discussed in that members come from families that have broken down and the group occasionally engages in violence. At the same time, they are different because they often do not claim territory or engage in behaviors that express their identity (Korem, 1994), although some may connect through a music-based identity and wear clothes expressing their subculture (Jackson and McBride, 1992).

The Case of Neo-Nazi Skinheads

Some researchers and practitioners believe that neo-Nazi skinheads should be characterized as a street gang. According to Knox (1994), a gang is a group that reaps some benefit from its members' behavior. Therefore, skinheads should be considered a gang. Other researchers find patterned similarities between street gangs and skinheads. Blazak's research focuses on the role that blocked opportunity plays in a skinhead's decision to join the group (Wooden and Blazak, 2001). He stresses that these youth experience threats to their status as white males living in a lower income environment. They are unable to find work and experience role confusion as our society continues to strive toward equity. These threats are similar to those felt by the "traditional" street gang member. Grennan and Britz (2006) present other similarities between street gangs and skinheads. Both groups are found in economically depressed areas, and both experience expansion during economically difficult times. Both groups also tend to identify institutional discrimination as the cause for their economic difficulty. Both traditional street gangs and skinhead groups offer their members a sense of belonging and family, with recruitment into the group occurring through family lines. Like street gang members, skinheads come from single-parent households, experience environments of physical abuse, and have low educational attainment (Grennan and Britz, 2006).

Other prominent researchers identify key differences between street gangs and skinheads that raise questions about skinheads' inclusion in the street gang category. Hamm (1993) explores the ideological differences between the two groups. The fundamental cornerstone of skinhead groups is racism. This ideology is not found in street gangs, and it creates a dynamic that clearly differentiates the two groups. For skinheads, this ideology gives their group strength and cohesion (Grennan and Britz, 2006). The skinhead group also utilizes mass media and computers to spread their message and draw membership from the larger society (Hamm, 1993; Grennan and Britz, 2006). Therefore, skinheads do not share neighborhood or community ties (Hamm, 1993). The ideology of racism also leads to instrumental violence against the

---

BOX 8–2: A Closer Look

White Aryan Resistance (WAR), led by Tom Metzger, is one of the more prominent examples of the racist skinhead movement. Metzger, a former Klansman, effectively used the British-based skinhead music culture to cultivate a hate-filled group of disenfranchised youth. This led to the later development of the Aryan Youth Movement (AYM) headed by John Metzger, Tom's son. Youth in AYM and similar neo-Nazi movements adorn themselves with shaved heads, Doc Martens, and leather jackets and sport swastika tattoos.

WAR maintains an elaborate communication system, including a quarterly paper with monthly newsletters, a Web site, radio shows, and a telephone hotline. The paper, *The Insurgent,* is touted as being "the most racist newspaper in the world." The Web site is filled with racist jokes, cartoons, games, and merchandise for sale. More startling is the presentation of the group's philosophy, which advocates "lone wolf" and leaderless resistance. This form of organization recognizes each person as his own leader and calls for individual or small-cell behavior in achieving the group's goals. Metzger also advocates using the phrase "I have nothing to say" when being questioned by police. This type of organization is one of the differences between traditional street gangs and racist skinheads.

Source: The Insurgent (2006).

perceived problem, and this violence is an inherent part of the subculture (Hamm, 1993). This leads to the conclusion that neo-Nazi skinheads are something different and deserving of their own classification (Hamm, 1993; Sanders, 1994).

CHAPTER SUMMARY

My cultural awareness was zero. I needed a complete Black history course and a thorough deprogramming. I had been duped into believing that all Black people were inhuman and inferior, that we had made no contribution to the forward thrust of civilization. . . . [C]ountless delusional Blacks . . . believed the myth of Black inferiority. Their contempt for their own Blackness was so dynamic, they had subconsciously stepped outside themselves to assimilate with any cultural group other than their own. (Williams, 2004, p. 35)

The purpose of this chapter was to develop an understanding of the impact of ethnicity on gangs and gang members. Ethnic experiences add more layers to our understanding of gang variation. By examining race and ethnicity, we explored similarities and differences in gang experiences. Each ethnic gang has a unique history that shapes the world in which gangs form. At the same time, there are apparent consistencies in gang development. All ethnic gangs develop in environments where youth experience marginalization from mainstream society. For some gangs, this marginalization is the result of recent immigration, and for others marginalization has become part of their cultural identity. All ethnic gangs experienced pregang youth groups that eventually emerged as street gangs. For ethnic gangs with longer histories, there was a lull in gang activity, followed by a resurgence in activity. The longevity of Hispanic and black gangs in Los Angeles and Chicago should raise our awareness that gangs can and do evolve into more organized groups. These commonalities and features of gang development are important in understanding the problem of street gangs.

KEY TERMS

barrios
cholo subculture
cross-fertilization

Nations
pachuco, or zoot suiter
Tongs

QUESTIONS FOR REVIEW

1. What are the common experiences among the race/ethnic gangs?

2. What are the pachuco and cholo subcultures? How are they related to gangs?

3. How are the experiences of Los Angeles and Chicago black gangs similar to and different from one another?

4. How are Asian youth gangs different from their ethnic counterparts?

5. What is cross-fertilization, and how does it contribute to American Indian gangs?

DISCUSSION QUESTIONS

1. Our insight into gangs focuses primarily on economics and community structure. How is this knowledge enhanced by considering issues of race and ethnicity?

2. Which of the ethnic gangs would be easiest to control? The most difficult? Why?

NOTES

1. Mexican gangs are also referred to as Chicano.

2. The Gangster Disciples are the largest Chicago gang (Knox, 2000a).

CHAPTER 9

THE FEMALE GANG MEMBER

CHAPTER OBJECTIVES

- Be familiar with our historical knowledge of female gang members.

- Understand our current knowledge of female gang members.

- Recognize how the female gang experience has similarities and differences compared with that of males.

- Become aware of the different types of female gangs.

- Understand how the structure of the gang influences the female gang experience.

UNDERSTANDING THE PROBLEM

> We ladies, we not dudes for real. . . . We don't got to be rowdy, all we do is fight. A dude, he is quick to go get a gun or something, a girl she quick to pull out a knife. Still, [girls] just want to fight one-on-one. (J. Miller, 2001, p. 140)

Our understanding of female gang members has been refined in the past 20 years. As discussed in Chapter 1, virtually all research shows a higher percentage of male gang members than female gang members. Statistics from the 1998 NYGS report that only 8% of gang members were female (National Youth Gang Center, 2000, p. 18). However, research consistently suggests fairly high percentages of female gang membership, from 20% to 38% (see Bjerregaard and Smith, 1993; Esbensen, Deschenes, and Winfree, 1999; Esbensen and Huizinga, 1993; Esbensen and Winfree, 1998; Moore and Hagedorn, 2001; Thornberry et al., 2003). This discrepancy is not surprising, given the historical framework for understanding female gang membership.

Historically, the role that females played in gangs was systematically downplayed. Today's knowledge has opened our eyes to the consistent place females have had in the gang world.

This chapter will provide insight into the role of the female gang member. Many experiences are similar to what has been discussed in this book already. They are gang members. However, sometimes the female experiences the gang differently because of the overlapping effects of gender, race, ethnicity, and class. Female experiences are also influenced by the type of gang they join. The result is a "complex experience" (Portillos, 1999) that is manifested in similarities and differences with male gang members, including risk factors for joining, their criminal behavior, and the long-term consequences of membership. It is these differences that will be the focus of this chapter.

THE HISTORICAL FOUNDATION

Early studies of gangs minimized the role of female gang members. Some researchers reported gangs as a "male sanctuary" where "one rarely sees gang members with a girl" (Bloch and Niederhoffer, 1958, p. 100). Others acknowledged female gang members but reported them as "present but invisible" (Chesney-Lind and Hagedorn, 1999, p. 6). Thrasher's (1927/1963) early work represents this role in his depiction of female gang members as "tomboys," sexualized, or a combination of both. According to Short and Strodtbeck (1965), their researcher described gang girls as "a loud, crude group of girls who not only curse and are sexually active, but who take no pride in the way they dress" (p. 242). The tomboy role assumed that females would demonstrate their physical ability and hang out and fight alongside males (Thrasher, 1927/1963; Quicker, 1999). Thrasher believed this was more evident at younger ages. However, as gang members aged, the sexualized aspect of female members was inevitable. The obvious sex role of female gang members comes in their offering sexual favors to male members (Brown, 1977; Fishman, 1995; Quicker, 1999; Short and Strodtbeck, 1965). Bernard (1949) describes the "revolting" sex practices of the "gangsterettes." Less obvious exploitation of "sex" is also evidenced in early gang literature. Femininity was reported to advance the cause of the gang. Females carried weapons because they were able to avoid detection by police; they were less likely than males to be stopped and frisked. Female gang members were also able to bait rival gangs through flirtation with rival male gang members (Brown, 1977; Quicker, 1999).

Researchers report that all-female gangs were rare (Bernard, 1949; Brown, 1977; Thrasher, 1927/1963). Females were by and large viewed as a supplemental feature to a predominantly male phenomenon (Quicker, 1999). Early gang research consistently portrays them "as 'pale imitations' of the male genuine article" (Chesney-Lind and Hagedorn, 1999, p. 8). This is evidenced in Rice's (1963) reporting on the auxiliary role of the Persian Queens and Bernard's (1949) discussion of the "fierce loyalty" that females give to their supporting male gang.

Stereotyping Females

This historical view of female gang members is rooted in the stereotypical female views of the time. Their full immersion in gang activities was believed to be hindered by the close supervision females were under (Thrasher, 1927/1963). Females were believed to lack the "gang instinct" and did not join conflict groups that evolve into gangs (Thrasher, 1927/1963). These gender stereotypes even led to female-based rehabilitation policies, such as modeling lessons (Short and Strodtbeck, 1965) and charm school to teach manners (Campbell, 1999; Chesney-Lind and Hagedorn, 1999).

These early accounts have been criticized because female gang members were largely ignored and "defined by the male experience" (Chesney-Lind and Hagedorn, 1999, p. 245). Our knowledge was based on information "by male gang members to male researchers and interpreted by male academics" (Campbell, 1990, p. 166). Male gang members have something to gain by talking about females in a sexual capacity; it enhances their masculine identity (Campbell, 1990). Moore (1991) directs our attention to **cognitive purification** (p. 137), referring to the popular image of gangs as a male-dominated phenomenon. This offered a skewed vision of female gang membership.

OUR CURRENT KNOWLEDGE

Research into the female gang experience has increased considerably since the 1970s and led to a more thorough understanding of female gang members (Curry, 1999). In alternate analysis, there is evidence to suggest that early interpretations of female gang members were inaccurate. Chesney-Lind and Hagedorn (1999) find that earlier work overlooks obvious information that sheds a different light on female gang participation. There is historical evidence to suggest that females are more than sexual objects for male gang members. Females were consistently reported as engaging in gang fighting and other violent acts (see Brown, 1977; Fishman, 1995; Miller, 2002). Female gang members were reported as subservient to males, but there was also evidence that they were fairly independent and formed strong same-sex bonds (see Chesney-Lind and Hagedorn, 1999). Females had some degree of independence from male gangs.

This research brought with it a plethora of interest in understanding female gang members. As such, the current status of females in gangs endures considerable debate. Some suggest that we were misinformed and that females were always actively engaged in gangs. Others suggest that females still play a minimal role in gangs but that this role may be changing, as reflected in increases in recent years. The clear fact is that there is variability in the experiences of female gang members, within and across gangs.

The Extent of Female Involvement

Many researchers agree that there has been relative stability in female gang membership over time (Chesney-Lind, Sheldon, and Joe, 1996; Curry, 1998; Miller, 2002). This

> **BOX 9–1: Focus on Research**
>
> In *One of the Guys: Girls, Gangs, and Gender* (2001), Jody Miller presents the results of qualitative research that explored the lives of female gang members. She conducted her study in Columbus, Ohio, and St. Louis, Missouri. Miller gathered her sample primarily from detention facilities, shelter programs, and community agencies. Interviews began in Columbus in early 1995 and were completed the year following. The St. Louis interviews began in the spring of 1997 and were completed by fall. Between the two cities, Miller interviewed a total of 94 girls, 48 of whom were gang members. All participants completed a survey, and gang members engaged in follow-up semistructured in-depth interviews. Supplemental data were also gathered about neighborhood characteristics. An interesting ethical dilemma arose in the research. Study participants were given financial compensation. In one case, a female joined a gang so that she could participate in the study and get the money. This is obviously not the intended purpose of studying gang members. However, it is one of the many difficulties in research. Despite the potential pitfalls of any research, Miller's work specifically provides valuable insight into the lives of female gang members and enriches our knowledge.

research also suggests that female gang members have always been active participants in the gang world (see Miller, 2002). Miller (2002) states that "the proportion of gang members who are girls, and the nature of girls' gang involvement, does not appear to have shifted substantially over the years" (p. 176).

Other researchers suggest that females are still only marginally involved in gangs (see Curry, Ball, and Fox, 1994). However, females may be becoming more enmeshed in the gang lifestyle because of economic pressure (Anderson, Brooks, Langsam, and Dyson, 2002; Taylor, 1993). This is supported by officially reported female gang membership (see Moore and Hagedorn, 2001). This increase may be due to the increased willingness of law enforcement to identify and arrest female offenders (Chesney-Lind, Sheldon, and Joe, 1996). As will be discussed, female gang member involvement in serious crime remains minimal and stable, which allows them to categorically avoid detection by official measures (Chesney-Lind, Sheldon, and Joe, 1996; Curry, 1998; Esbensen, Deschenes, and Winfree, 1999). This effect is also enhanced by the age dynamic of female gang members (Curry, 1998; Miller, 2002).

The Age Dynamic

The age dynamic of female gang membership is not the same as that of males. Female gang members start hanging out with gangs at ages as young as 12 or 13 (Miller, 2002;

Portillos, 1999), younger than their male counterparts (Chesney-Lind and Hagedorn, 1999; Miller, 2002). They are also more apt to leave gangs at younger ages than males (Chesney-Lind and Hagedorn, 1999; Thornberry et al., 2003). Gang leaving is facilitated by pregnancy, marriage, incarceration, and desire to be prosocial (Harris, 1994). This results in age dynamics that limit females to shorter periods of membership in early adolescence (Campbell, 1984; J. Miller, 2001; Moore and Hagedorn, 1996; Thornberry et al., 2003).

Gender Composition of Gangs

Miller (1975) identified three types of female gangs: auxiliary, coed, and independent. The **auxiliary gang** operates as a support system for a main male gang. The female group of this gang has its own leadership structure but tends to defer to the primary male gang. They usually take on a feminine version of the male gang name (Quicker, 1999); for example, the Latin Queens are associated with the Latin Kings. Early research identifies this type of gang as the most common type of female gang (Miller, 1975). This is supported by current research findings that 32% of female gangs were affiliates of male gangs (Nurge, 2003). As a word of caution, the notion of the auxiliary role of female gang members reinforces views of females as subservient to males within the gang. It also reinforces the idea that females play a minor role in gang life. This is not the case. Auxiliary gangs have their own norms, and this type of gang member is actively involved in gang activities.

The **coed gang** includes both male and female gang members. In this gang, there is no gender separation within the organization. Males and females coexist in a gang that has one leadership structure. Some research finds an evolution of females from their auxiliary role (Fishman, 1995), and many female members maintain they have equal status in their gangs (Lurigio, Schwartz, and Chang, 1998). Nurge (2003) finds that only 16% of female gangs were coed and another 28% were loosely connected to male gangs. She emphasizes the variation in the ratio of males to females.

The **independent gang** is exclusively female and not connected to a male gang. As previously stated, early research found this type of gang to be rare, even nonexistent (Bernard, 1949; Brown, 1977; Thrasher, 1927/1963). Some research still finds this pattern today, as only 2% of gangs were female dominated (NYGC, 2000). Some suggest that auxiliary gangs are evolving into independent groups (Lauderback, Hansen, and Waldorf, 1992; Taylor, 1993). This is supported by the moderate percentage (24%) of independent female gangs reported in Boston (Nurge, 2003). It is still the case that independent gangs make up the smallest percentage of female gang members (Miller, 2002). Interesting research by Hagedorn and Devitt (1999) finds that some of the variation in the reporting of independent female gangs may be due to females' traditional views. They found differential reporting for females within the same gang based on individual female views. Females who were more traditional saw their gangs as auxiliary; less traditional females saw the gang as independent.

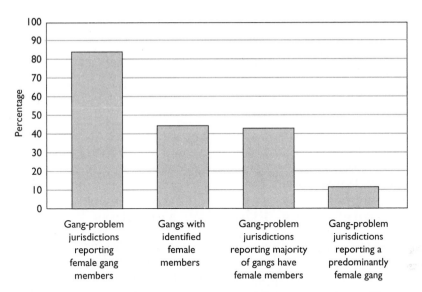

Figure 9–1   Characteristics of Female Gang Membership in Various Jurisdictions.
National Youth Gang Survey (2006).

Beyond Sexual Exploitation

The role that female gang members play in relation to male gang members is varying and changing. Historically, female gang members were viewed as either tomboys or sex objects (Campbell, 1990). This dichotomy suggests a gender-based understanding that may be "insufficient" (Miller and Brunson, 2000). Research finds that females do not engage in promiscuous sex more than males, and they do not specialize in sex-based behaviors while in the gang (Bjerregaard and Smith, 1993; Campbell, 1990). Although the gender-based portrayal may be exaggerated, it is also the case that females are not always treated as equals within the gang context (J. Miller, 2001; Portillos, 1999). The female gang member is "expected to construct a femininity that serve the purposes of the gang" (Portillos, 1999, p. 244). This often leads to double standards for female gang members. They are expected to maintain monogamous relationships (Portillos, 1999). Yet, "there are reports from females that they have been sexually exploited by males within the gang" (Moore and Hagedorn, 2001, p. 4). "The gang is not, ultimately, a place where they can escape gendered expectations" (Portillos, 1999, p. 233).

The variation in the role of female gang members is shaped by the views of male gang members and the types of gangs to which females belong. The reputation of young males is strengthened through the exploitation of females, whether real or imagined. Males may hold stereotypical views of females that translate into their interpretation of gang experiences (Miller and Brunson, 2000; J. Miller, 2001; Moore, 1991). Moore (1991) finds that 41% of older male members and 56% of younger male members believe that males treat females as possessions (p. 53). Those who do not buy into the dominance argument are more likely to see the gang as a family.

The view of females is also related to the variation in the types of gangs that females belong to (Moore, 1991). Research finds that male-only gangs have the most stereotypical view of females. On the other hand, coed gangs have more balanced gender views, with the exception of sex stereotypes (Miller and Brunson, 2000). The greater the ratio of females in a mixed-gender gang, the more support there is for female members. At the same time, few females held positions of power in coed gangs (National Gang Crime Research Center, 1997).

Gender, Race, Ethnicity, and Class

The final concept necessary for understanding female gang members is the interrelatedness of gender, race, ethnicity, and class (Miller, 2002). Despite equity, traditional views of females still permeate the gang world (Portillos, 1999). These views are compounded by race, ethnicity, and class. "Because girls in the gang collectively experience their everyday world from a specific position in society, they construct femininity in a uniquely race and class appropriate way" (Messerschmidt, 1999, p. 131).

Many female gang members join gangs because of their experiences with racism, classism, and poverty (Fishman, 1995). These experiences differ for different gang females. In a study of Latin Queens, Brotherton and Salazar-Atias (2003) find that many held traditional views of motherhood and commitment to male partners. Few Latin

---

BOX 9–2: A Closer Look

We know that female gang members have unique life histories that are important to understand. Their experiences are layered with gender, race, ethnicity, and class issues. Therefore, some gang prevention programs recognize this overlap through the creation of female-targeted programs. This is the case for the Movimiento Ascendencia (Upward Movement) program implemented in Pueblo, Colorado (OJJDP Model Programs Guide, n.d.b.). This program is designed to prevent gang involvement and substance use in Hispanic at-risk and gang-involved females. The program centers around "cultural awareness, mediation or conflict resolution, and self-esteem or social support." Girls age 8 through 19 voluntarily participate in activities including mentoring, recreation, tutoring and homework support, and cultural enhancement programs. There are additional components of case management, family involvement, and a "safe haven." Evaluation research finds that the program is effective. Program participants have greater decreases in delinquency and higher grades in school than nonparticipants. No programmatic effects on self-esteem were found.

Queens reported middle-class aspirations. Views of male dominance and independence may be based in racial and ethnic experiences (Moore and Hagedorn, 2001). The traditional views held by Latina gang members are not as evident in black American female gang members (Chesney-Lind and Hagedorn, 1999; Moore and Hagedorn, 1996, 2001). Fishman (1999) explains that these differences exist because black females "are socialized to be independent and assertive and to take risks" (p. 83). They have endured "force emancipation" that allows them to be more involved in gang life (Fishman, 1999).

JOINING THE GANG

Risk Factors

Risk factors for female gang membership are generally consistent with those of male gang members (Bjerregaard and Smith, 1993; Miller, 2002; Thornberry et al., 2003). They are likely to experience multiple risk factors that distinguish them from nongang females (Miller, 2002; Thornberry et al., 2003). Like male members, female gang members are likely to come from low-income areas with gang presence (Miller, 2002; Thornberry et al., 2003). Peer delinquency and early sexual activity also elevate risk for gang joining, similar to males (Bjerregaard and Smith, 1993). The peer effect for females manifests itself differently. For females, the peer effect on gang membership includes the influence of boyfriends and male relatives (Campbell, 1990; Miller, 2002). Female gang members have also been found to have lower levels of self-esteem and higher levels of social isolation than male gang members and nongang females (Esbensen, Deschenes, and Winfree, 1999). Female gang members are also more likely to have problems with school (Harris, 1994; Thornberry et al., 2003).

Family dynamics as a risk factor for female gang joining is inconsistent, but this is similar to male research (Campbell, 1990; Miller, 2002). Some research shows that females are more likely to come from troubled families with weak attachments (Harris, 1994; Moore and Hagedorn, 1996). Other research reports that females are more likely than males to report strict parenting (Moore, 1991). National research of incarcerated gang members finds that female gang members are more likely than males to come from father-only households (National Gang Crime Research Center, 1997). Still other research reports that family attachment is not a risk factor for female gang joining (Bowker and Klein, 1983; Bjerregaard and Smith, 1993). The most consistent research shows domestic violence as a major risk factor for female gang involvement. Female gang members, more than males and nongang females, come from households where they have experienced or seen physical and sexual violence (Joe and Chesney-Lind, 1995; Harris, 1994; Miller, 2001, 2002; Moore, 1991; Moore and Hagedorn, 2001).

Reasons for Joining

There are females with multiple risk factors who never join gangs. Thus, our understanding of female gang joining is incomplete without a discussion of reasons for joining beyond risk factors. Like males, many females join gangs for identity, family, and acceptance (Brown, 1977; Campbell, 1984; Harris, 1994). Others join for protection from their violent backgrounds (Chesney-Lind, Sheldon, and Joe, 1996; Joe and Chesney-Lind, 1995).

At the same time, there is something unique to females that we understand through research. The gang phenomenon "reflects the attempts of young women to cope with a bleak and harsh present as well as a dismal future" (Joe and Chesney-Lind, 1995, p. 428). Gangs are an avenue for girls to unite to confront a common destiny (Harris, 1994). "The gang represents for its members an idealized collective solution to the bleak future that awaits" (Campbell, 1990, p. 173). Campbell (1990) specifies this "bleak future" in her summarization of research on Hispanic female gang members from backgrounds of poverty. She states that for these girls, the future is "meaningless domestic labor" as homemakers and caretakers of children who face "subordination to the man of the house" (pp. 172–73). This is compounded by "social isolation" and the "powerlessness" of poverty. The gang offers a respite from the drudgery of their future.

Gang Initiation

As with other aspects of female gang membership, there are similarities and differences with males. Like males, they are recruited to gangs through peers. Sometimes this recruitment is coercive and obligatory in nature (National Gang Crime Research Center, 1997; Turley, 2003). Others report that females are not pressured to join (Brown, 1977; Quicker, 1999).

The method of initiation varies by gang, and how the female enters determines the level of respect she will have while a gang member (Portillos, 1999). Jumping in is the same ritual as for males. Females must endure a fight with active members to prove toughness. This is the most frequent method of initiation (Quicker, 1999). It allows females the male gang members' respect because they have demonstrated that they are equals (Quicker, 1999). Less violent versions of jumping in are "fair fights," in which the prospect fights one female.

Gangs that rely on obligatory recruitment strategies may be more inclined to have members who are "born in" the gang. This type of initiation is neighborhood based. Females grow up and hang out with gang members during childhood (Portillos, 1999). They are essentially "walked in" through a process of group agreement (Quicker, 1999).

Female gang members are given the least amount of respect if they are initiated through being **trained in** or **sexed into** the gang (Portillos, 1999). In this ritual, membership is earned by having sex with multiple male gang members. The lack of respect is apparent in the label "hood rat" given to females who join the gang in this fashion (Portillos, 1999; see also J. Miller, 2001). There is some debate as to how common this ritual is. Decker and Van Winkle (1996) report that males report sexing in as a ritual but most female gang members discount this idea.

Female Identity

There are differences in how females and males identify with the gangs. This is due to the female identity that they bring into the gang with them. "They are female, adolescents and young adults, of colour, poor, living under stressful family conditions and trying to negotiate a sense of identity, including what it means to be feminine" (Laidler and Hunt, 2001, p. 675). Females are more likely than males to have strong attachments to the gang and to see the gang as family (Brotherton and Salazar-Atias, 2003; Campbell, 1984; Esbensen, Deschenes, and Winfree, 1999). This effect is more than just a gender effect; it is enhanced within the gang (Esbensen, Deschenes, and Winfree, 1999). Within the gang, females find a balance between traditional female roles and individualism (Laidler and Hunt, 2001). They act like a female with males but also protect themselves if necessary. This is probably due to the backgrounds of violence that gang girls come from (Brotherton and Salazar-Atias, 2003; Laidler and Hunt, 2001). The strong same-sex bonds that are formed by female gang members aid in their "self-definition" by providing a reference group for comparison and identity (Campbell, 1984, 1987, 1990; Giordano, 1978; Laidler and Hunt, 2001). Female gang members are also more involved than males in prosocial gang activities (Joe and Chesney-Lind, 1995). Interestingly, female gang members still maintain relationships with their own families while in the gang (Decker and Van Winkle, 1996; Hunt, MacKenzie, and Joe-Laidler, 2000). Their membership may cause conflict with their families, but family members are still identified as important in the gang girl's life (Decker and Van Winkle, 1996; Hunt, MacKenzie, and Joe-Laidler, 2000).

CRIMINAL INVOLVEMENT

Level of Offending

Female gang members engage in more delinquent behavior and more frequently than nongang girls (Bjerregaard and Smith, 1993; Campbell, 1990; Deschenes and Esbensen, 1999; Thornberry et al., 2003). They engage in a variety of offenses but less frequently than their male gang peers (Amato and Cornell, 2003; Esbensen and Winfree, 1998; Thornberry et al., 2003). However, female gang members engage in a greater proportion of female crime than male gang members do male crime (Thornberry et al., 2003). Female gang members are also more delinquent than nongang males (Esbensen and Winfree, 1998; Moore and Hagedorn, 2001). These findings hold true regardless of race (Esbensen and Winfree, 1998).

The Group Influence

For females, delinquent involvement is influenced by the type of gang to which they belong. Research by Peterson, Miller, and Esbensen (2001) finds an interesting relationship between the gender composition of the gang and delinquency rates. Members of independent female gangs had the lowest levels of delinquency of gang members. Females in coed or mixed-gender gangs with gender balance had the next lowest levels of delinquency. Females in majority-male gangs had the highest levels of delinquency, even higher than all-male gang delinquency. This is consistent with research by Giordano (1978) that finds that mixed-gender gangs fostered delinquency. However, Giordano also finds that black females in all-female gangs had fairly high delinquency rates. These studies suggest that delinquency is more than just being a gang member; issues such as gender and race come into play in group dynamics. It may be that females "learn" to be deviant in groups with more males. It could also be that both males and females are playing out gender-specific roles within the gang.

Females also tend to bring a feminine identity into their deviant behavior (Fishman, 1995). They are less enthusiastic and less committed to deviant behaviors than males (Turley, 2003). Although "[g]ang membership appears to be significantly related to neutralization of violence and to lack of guilt, for both males and females" (p. 88), female gang members experience more guilt, and they are less likely than male members to neutralize their actions (Deschenes and Esbensen, 1999). The behavior that results is a balance that allows them to be gang members while maintaining their female identity (Swart, 1991; Laidler and Hunt, 2001). But many times they are "demonized" for their behavior, particularly for violence (Chesney-Lind, 1993).

Violent Crime

Research finds that female gang members have always been involved in violence (Chesney-Lind and Hagedorn, 1999). Female gang members engage in more violent behavior and more frequently than nongang females (see Thornberry et al., 2003). At the same time, female violent behavior is less serious and less frequent than that of male gang members (Deschenes and Esbensen, 1999; Thornberry et al., 2003).

Fighting is one type of violence with gender equity. Both males and females show similar rates of past fighting (Deschenes and Esbensen, 1999). Other research finds that females are not as quick to engage in these violent interactions (Joe and Chesney-Lind, 1995). Within the gang, a female who is willing and able to fight is valued (Harris, 1994). Some research finds that female gang members like to fight more than males do (Hagedorn and Devitt, 1999). They are less likely to use weapons or have lethal encounters (Hagedorn and Devitt, 1999).

Several researchers suggest that the willingness of female gang members to engage in violence is due to their backgrounds of family violence (Campbell, 1999; Joe and Chesney-Lind, 1995). The gang provides the skills necessary for the female gang member to protect herself (Joe and Chesney-Lind, 1995). This function of aggression differentiates gang girls from nongang girls. Campbell (1999) contends that most female aggression is expressive, "to release the unbearable anger that they could no longer suppress" (p. 249). Male violence is generally instrumental, "to cause the other person to back down" (pp. 248–49). However, within the gang, the function of violence changes for females to instrumental. It serves as a way to protect them, and it allows them to control others in a world where protection and control do not exist. Being a "fighting female" also offers gang members a way to fight the socially constructed view of gender (Hagedorn and Devitt, 1999).

Economic Crime

Economic changes, including welfare reform, also affect the behavior of female gang members (Moore and Hagedorn, 2001; Taylor, 1993). In an environment with little public assistance, they are presented with opportunities for engaging in economic crimes. This opportunity structure is enhanced as more male gang members are incarcerated (Moore and Hagedorn, 2001; Taylor, 1993). Consistent with other behaviors, the levels of economic crime for females remain lower than those of their male counterparts (Miller, 2002; Moore and Hagedorn, 1996), but they are very much involved in criminal economic activities (Lurigio, Schwartz, and Chang, 1998). The "new" female gang is more independent and entrenched in illegal economic ventures, notably drug sales (Anderson, Brooks, Langsam, and Dyson, 2002; Lauderback, Hansen, and Waldorf, 1992).

THE EFFECTS OF GANG MEMBERSHIP

The decision to join a gang is not without risks and repercussions. However, there is debate as to the magnitude of these effects. Female gang members' backgrounds are more troubled to begin with, so "they are not leaving Brady Bunch for the Hell's Angels" (Moore and Hagedorn, 1996, p. 215).

The **liberation perspective** suggests that the gang offers a place where female members can gain safety and independence (Chesney-Lind, 1993). The advantages of gang membership outweigh the negative effects. As previously discussed, the gang is an escape from the reality of female members' present and future lives. Female members come from backgrounds of victimization, and the gang offers family and protection. Research on the Latin Queens finds that the gang offered assistance with children and employment (Brotherton and Salazar-Atias, 2003).

In contrast, the **social injury perspective** believes that female gang membership has a long-term negative impact (Curry, 1998). The social costs of gang joining have a devastating effect on the female gang member. This perspective is supported in much research. Miller (2002) finds that gang membership intensifies lives that are already troubled. Female gang membership does increase risk of victimization (Knox, 2004a; Miller, 2002; Portillos, 1999). It also interferes with family relations (Decker and Van Winkle, 1996; Hunt, MacKenzie, and Joe-Laidler, 2000). In addition, females face negative labeling more frequently than male members do (Moore and Hagedorn, 1996; Swart, 1991). Most gang members are not involved in the gang into adulthood (Hagedorn, 1988; Thornberry et al., 2003). However, they experience long-term

TABLE 9–1

The effects of female gang membership

Liberation Perspective (Chesney-Lind, 1993)

- The gang offers a place where female members can gain safety and independence. Therefore, the advantages of gang membership outweigh the negative effects.

Social Injury Perspective (Curry, 1998)

- Female gang membership has long-term negative effects because of the social costs.

Enabling Perspective

- The gang may allow the female to escape her home, but joining the gang comes with costs.

consequences after leaving the gang. Many former gang members have children (Campbell, 1990; Hagedorn, 1988; Moore, 1991; Thornberry et al., 2003). Most, if not all, are unmarried, and they raise their children alone (Hagedorn, 1988; Moore and Hagedorn, 1996). Work involvement is minimal (Moore, 1991; Thornberry et al., 2003), and many rely on public assistance (Hagedorn, 1988).

There are others who suggest that social injury and liberation are not mutually exclusive and that a little bit of both may be apparent (Curry, 1999; Nurge, 2003; Portillos, 1999). The gang may allow the female to escape her home, but joining the gang comes with costs (Portillos, 1999). This view has not been formally termed in the literature. For the purposes of this text, we will term this the **enabling perspective** (see Curry, 1999, p. 152). This is supported by research on female gangs in Boston (see Nurge, 2003). Gang members look on their gang experiences with mixed reactions. The gang was viewed as a place for social support when it was needed. At the same time, members recognize the risk of membership and report that they would not want their family members to join. This reaction may be gender based, as females tend to view their experiences more negatively than males (Moore and Hagedorn, 1996).

CHAPTER SUMMARY

> If girls have an opportunity to attend good schools; if we can build on the cultural strengths present in their neighborhoods; if we can protect children from sexual and physical violence; if we can provide youth who cannot stay at home with safe places to live; if we can help resource strapped families nurture their children; if we can offer economic security for all parents and hope for the future for their children— only then will our nation's gang problem shrink to more manageable proportions. (Chesney-Lind and Hagedorn, 1999, p. 5)

We have come a long way in our understanding of female gang members. Females are active gang members, and they do engage in both violent and economic criminal activities. Although they engage in less serious forms of crime than do male members, they have higher levels than nongang females and, in some cases, nongang males. Females enter into gangs at earlier ages than males. Their entrance into gangs seems to be intrinsically tied to their neighborhoods and their experiences with family violence. This suggests that prevention for female gang members needs to begin earlier than for males (Miller, 2002). It also suggests that these prevention efforts need to address the reality of female experiences with physical and sexual abuse.

The experiences of the female gang member are laden with socially constructed views of gender. These views are evidenced in their perceptions of self and perceptions by males, the community, and other females. This is entangled with views of race, ethnicity, and class. The types of gangs to which females belong also affect the gang experience. The result is much variation within and between gangs and members.

Females leave gangs earlier than males, many times because of children. Despite their short time in gangs, the impact of membership stays with them into adulthood. They are faced with the stigma of membership. They enter into parenthood early, without partners, and without gainful employment. The results are troubling because, as mothers, former gang members have greater influence over their children than fathers do (Moore, 1991). The long-term impact may ultimately affect the next generation.

KEY TERMS

auxiliary gang	independent gang
coed gang	liberation perspective
cognitive purification	social injury perspective
enabling perspective	train or sex in

QUESTIONS FOR REVIEW

1. What is our historical understanding of female gang membership?

2. How do the different types of gangs that include females differ from each another?

3. What are the primary differences between male and female risk factors for gang membership?

4. Compare and contrast the social injury, liberation, and enabling perspectives of gang membership consequences.

5. What are the long-term effects of female gang membership?

DISCUSSION QUESTIONS

1. Based on your understanding of female gangs, do you think the criminal justice system should treat them differently? Why or why not?

2. The experience of the female gang member is a culmination of the type of gang to which she belongs, the gender composition of the gang, and gender stereotyping. If you were a female gang member or if you were a member of a gang that included females, which type of gang would you be most comfortable in and why?

CHAPTER 10

PRISON GANGS

CHAPTER OBJECTIVES

- Know the extent of the prison gang phenomenon.
- Become familiar with the overlap between prison gangs and street gangs.
- Be aware of the differences between prison gang members and nonmembers.
- Recognize the strengths and weaknesses of prison gang control strategies.

UNDERSTANDING PRISON GANGS

Today's street gangs are becoming tomorrow's prison gangs. (Carlson, 2001, p. 12)

For many years, prison gangs were regarded as a separate problem from street gangs. Prison gangs developed in prison and stayed in prison. Street gangs developed on the street and stayed on the street. More recently, this phenomenon has changed. Although many prison and street gangs are still distinct, some gangs overlap in the two environments. Prison gangs are no longer isolated in the prison environment, and street gangs are no longer just a street issue. Perkins (1987) stated that prison offers gang members a sabbatical from street life. However, with the relationships between prison and street gangs, there is no time out (Jacobs, 2001). The gang member's ability to separate from street life becomes difficult and undermines the goals of rehabilitation and treatment (Jacobs, 2001). Approximately 60% of "gang-problem jurisdictions reported the return of gang members from confinement" (Egley, Howell, and Major, 2006, p. 35). These returning gang members are identified as contributing to increases in violence and drug sales (Egley, Howell, and Major, 2006). Therefore, we must understand prison gangs to fully understand street gangs. This chapter will examine the unique characteristics and challenges of prison gangs. The connection between prison and street gangs will be explored, and prison gang control strategies will be discussed.

Definition

Prison gangs, sometimes known as **security threat groups** (STGs), are "two or more inmates, acting together, who pose a threat to the security or safety of staff/inmates and/or are disruptive to programs and/or to the orderly management of the facility/system" (American Correctional Association, 1993). This definition allows a broader identification of threat groups than the traditional street gang definition. The STG definition includes groups that form around political and religious ideology, such as white supremacist and extremist groups.

Extent of Prison Gangs

We actually know very little about prison gangs throughout the country. They remain "gang researchers' final frontier and prison managers' biggest nightmare" (Fleisher and Decker, 2001a, p. 2). There are several reasons for this lack of knowledge, as specified by Fong and Buentello (1991). One reason is that prison administrators do not allow researchers access to facilities because of security issues, which has allowed prison officials to minimize or deny the presence of gangs in their facilities. There are also problems with acquiring accurate information, even if access is granted, because of a lack of documentation and the incredible secrecy of prison gang members. This secrecy is imperative to prison gang members in order to avoid detection by prison officials (Fong, 1990). The information that we do have comes from a handful of national surveys (Camp and Camp, 1985; Knox, 2000b; Knox, 2004b), from some statewide assessments (Fong and Buentello, 1991; Fong and Vogel, 1995), and from prison gang defectors (Fong, 1990).

The Gypsy Jokers are the first known prison gang. They were formed in a prison in the state of Washington in the early 1950s. This gang was a weak predecessor to the better known Mexican Mafia that emerged in California before the end of the 1950s (Orlando-Morningstar, 1997). Many of today's prison gangs emerged in California correctional institutions (National Institute of Corrections, 1991). Although prison gangs began on the West Coast, by the 1960s they became apparent in other large cities, such as Chicago (Ralph et al., 1996). Throughout the 1960s and 1970s, a more widespread presence of prison gangs became apparent (Orlando-Morningstar, 1997). However, the "problem" of prison gangs remained minimal. A study by Camp and Camp (1985) found 114 gangs with just over 12,000 members in 29 prison systems. This was less than 3% of the prison population. By 1993, a study by the American Correctional Association (ACA) found that this percentage of gang members increased to 6% of the prison population. A continued increase is suggested by Knox's (2000b) study, as he finds about 25% of prison inmates reported to be gang members in 1999. The increased prison gang membership was seen throughout the country in the 1980s, including Texas, Massachusetts, and North Carolina (Fong, 1990; Jackson and Sharpe, 1997; Kassel, 2003).

BOX 10-1: Focus on Research

The best-known research on prison gangs was conducted by Camp and Camp (1985). Their study, *Prison Gangs: Their Extent, Nature and Impact on Prison,* provided a comprehensive and rare insight into prison gangs at the state and federal levels in the United States. Their research has three primary goals: "Produce a national overview of the nature and extent of prison gangs," "ascertain the impact of gangs in prisons, prisoners, and administrators," and "ascertain what strategies are being used to cope with and manage prison gang situations" (pp. 3–4). The target sample included "all 50 state prisons, the District of Columbia, and the Federal Bureau of Prisons" (p. 5). Each jurisdiction received a comprehensive questionnaire that included prompts for further information on major gangs. Forty-nine of the 52 jurisdictions completed and returned the survey. Nine jurisdictions participated in an on-site follow-up interview. These jurisdictions were selected because of their extensive problems with gangs or because their gang situation was unique.

Proliferation of Prison Gangs

The proliferation of prison gangs can be attributed to several factors. One reason may be the increase in gangs on the streets. The increased presence of street gangs and accompanying gang crime inevitably leads to higher incarceration rates of gang members. Therefore, facilities may experience the "importation" of street gangs into prisons (Peterson, 2000b). **Importation** refers to individual gang members bringing their gang-banging lifestyle into prison and "doing gang time" (Ralph et al., 1996). This leads to an emergence of gangs in facilities where they were not seen before. In fact, "incarceration as a method of breaking up gangs is perhaps the worst single policy at the disposal of the public. Yet it remains the chosen policy" (Hagedorn, 1988, p. 162). For example, North Carolina has faced the importation of Blood gangs into their facilities (Jackson and Sharpe, 1997). The presence of gangs has also been reported in juvenile facilities (Knox, 2004b; Peterson, 2000b; Stone and Wycoff, 1996). Many prison gang researchers recognize that street gangs now maintain a prominent presence in prisons (Carlson, 2001; Ralph et al., 1996). In some cases, street gangs are better able to organize in prison settings; for example, Jeff Fort is believed to run the Black P Stone Rangers from prison (Knox, 2001a). In fact, the strength of the prison-street relationship gives us insight into the level of organization of a gang. In Decker, Bynum, and Weisel's (1998) research, they found that the Latin Kings and Gangster Disciples were influenced by prison gangs. Incarcerated members of their gangs directed the street gang in terms of violent activities and economic pursuits. This is especially likely if a high-level member is incarcerated. In less organized street gangs, there was no formal connection between prison and street gang members.

The proliferation may also be due to the developing connection of traditional prison gangs and street gangs. Although "[w]e have only a rudimentary knowledge of prison gangs as social groups operating inside prisons and of the interplay between street gangs and prison gangs" (Fleisher and Decker, 2001a, p. 2), we do know that there is a connection. Knox (2004b) finds that approximately 88% of agencies report that their prison gangs are also present on the street. As early as the 1960s, the Mexican Mafia began to take their dominance to the streets (National Institute of Corrections, 1991). Prison gangs used alliances with street gangs to expand their power and control criminal behavior on the streets (Ralph et al., 1996). These connections are further strengthened as prison gang members leave facilities and go "home." As prison gang members migrate, are rearrested, or are transferred to other facilities, prison gangs spread throughout the country (NIC, 1991; Ralph et al., 1996). In some areas, street and prison gangs have well-developed relationships (Fleisher and Decker, 2001a). The fluid method of communication between street and prison gangs (Jacobs, 2001) results in "a well-established communication system between incarcerated prisoners, institutions, and illicit activity in the community" (Carlson, 2001, p. 12).

PRISON GANG DYNAMICS

Reasons for Prison Gangs

Many people falsely believe that incarceration is enough of a deterrent to change criminal tendencies. This is often not the case. Given the nature of the prison environment, there is a "good chance" that an individual, even a nongang member, will join a gang when entering prison (Curry and Decker, 2003; Jacobs, 2001). Prison gangs have traditionally emerged as a result of "deprivation" (Peterson, 2000b). **Deprivation** implies that gangs develop in prison to alleviate the pains of imprisonment.

The deprivation hypothesis is supported by the fact that gangs often are surrogate families that "offer a way to beat the man" (Ralph et al., 1996, p. 126). Prison gangs are an adaptation to the "austere circumstances" and "thrive" on the conflict with authority (Scott, 2001). Inmates are an identifiable part of the institution and make greater demands than they would outside (Regulus, 1991). The fight for control undermines the authority of the institution (Jacobs, 2001). "Left unattended, small acts of gang-involved disorder and small signs of prison ganging create a social and cultural environment that either encourages or fails to negatively sanction more serious gang-related offenses against property and person" (Scott, 2001, p. 30). Often, older gang members cooperate with authorities so that they can engage in illegal activities. In some cases, the authority of prison gangs "supplants that of the institution" (NIC, 1991, p. 3).

Prison gangs also offer protection (Ralph et al., 1996), which suggests that incarcerated people encounter safety deprivation. The proliferation of prison gangs in Texas resulted from the removal of the building tender system. In this system, inmate guards monitored inmate activities, establishing a system of control. However, as a result of the

Ruiz v. Estelle decision (1980), this system was removed, leaving a void in the power structure. Inmate violence increased as a result, and prison gangs were established for self-protection (Fong and Buentello, 1991; Fong and Vogel, 1995). Essentially, "judicial intervention has escalated violence in prisons" (Fong and Buentello, 1991, p. 66).

Deprivation is also seen in the types of behaviors that prison gangs engage in. Prison is a criminogenic environment characterized by overcrowding (Fleisher and Decker, 2001a; Regulus, 1991; Scott, 2001) and understaffing (Fleisher and Decker, 2001a). Prison gangs are motivated by power and money (Fleisher and Decker, 2001a). Therefore, prison gangs gain control of illegal resources within the institution (Ralph et al., 1996; Fong and Buentello, 1991). They engage in financial-based crimes, including drug trafficking, extortion, prostitution, and gambling (Fong, 1990; NIC, 1991; Ralph et al., 1996). This activity also includes corrupting staff to secure the continued availability of illegal goods and services (NIC, 1991).

Prison Gang Members

Studies that examine the similarities and differences between gang members and nonmembers in prison find that prison gang members are poorly educated (Kreinert and Fleisher, 2001), but their education level is similar to that of nonmembers (Fong and Vogel, 1995; Ralph et al., 1996; Sheldon, 1991). Prison gang members are less likely to be employed than nonmembers (Kreinert and Fleisher, 2001; Sheldon, 1991). Prison gang members are more likely to have a prior criminal record (Ralph et al., 1996; Sheldon, 1991) that is evident in adolescence (Ralph et al., 1996; Sheldon, 1991). This record includes a history of violent offenses (Kreinert and Fleisher, 2001; Ralph et al., 1996). This history may explain why gang members are more likely to be serving longer prison sentences (Ralph et al., 1996) or life sentences (Fong and Vogel, 1995). Their deviant conduct continues while they are incarcerated, as gang members are involved in more rule infractions and more violent misconduct in prison than nonmembers (ACA, 1993; Fong and Buentello, 1991; Jackson and Sharpe, 1997; Ralph et al., 1996; Sheldon, 1991). This involvement is enhanced by gang embeddedness, and core members are more likely to be violent then peripheral members (Gaes et al., 2002).

Structure and Rules

Prison gangs are more organized than traditional street gangs (Carlson, 2001). Some penal institutions report gangs that are connected to political institutions (Knox, 2004b). At the same time, there is variation in the level of organization that each gang displays (Regulus, 1991; NIC, 1991; Fong and Vogel, 1995). Well-organized prison gangs have a stable hierarchy of leaders, lieutenants, and soldiers (Fleisher and Decker, 2001a; Fong, 1990; Fong and Vogel, 1995; NIC, 1991). The leader is more powerful in a prison setting because he has the ability to constantly supervise the activities of members (Jacobs, 2001), and he is able to recruit and lead through power and coercion (NIC, 1991; Fortune, 2004). More organized prison gangs often recruit along ethnic lines, and potential members often have a "homeboy" connection to current members (Fong, 1990; Fong and Vogel, 1995).

Often, prison gangs have codes of behavior, clearly written rules, and procedures for rule violation (Fong, 1990; Ralph et al., 1996). Traditional, well-organized prison gangs operate under a *"blood in, blood out"* oath (Carlson, 2001; Fong, 1990; Fong and Buentello, 1991; NIC, 1991), which refers to the requirement of violence for gang joining and lifetime commitment to the gang. This demonstration of loyalty is imperative for gang membership (Fleisher and Decker, 2001a). Some prison gangs are more democratic than others. Gangs such as the Texas Syndicate require unanimous votes in gang decision making (Fong, 1990). In other gangs, leaders have the ultimate decision-making power (Fong, 1990; Fortune, 2004). The primary means of communication among gang members are mail, telephone, cell phones, and visits (Decker, Bynum, and Weisel, 1998; Fong, 1990). As previously stated, prison gangs demand absolute secrecy (Fleisher and Decker, 2001a), and communication is often coded to avoid detection (Fong, 1990).

Traditional Prison Gangs

The most notable traditional prison gangs are the Mexican Mafia, the Black Guerilla Family, Texas Syndicate, La Nuestra Familia, and Aryan Brotherhood. Each of these gangs developed in the 1950s and the 1960s in the California prison system. Their impact is experienced in many regional and federal correctional facilities throughout the country. More recently, Neta has been identified as a prison security threat in Florida, Connecticut, and Massachusetts.

The most enduring powerful prison gang is the Mexican Mafia (NIC, 1991). This gang was formed in 1958 in Deuel Vocational Center in California (Orlando-Morningstar, 1997). As the name suggests, membership in this group is rooted in Hispanic ethnic heritage, primarily Mexican, and prospective members must be sponsored. The primary goal of the group is economic activity, including drug trafficking and gambling. They are able to effectively control illegal activity in prison because of their "mafia style" chain of command (Orlando-Morningstar, 1997). The Mexican Mafia is well connected to the street (NIC, 1991). The group is not involved in a political agenda. However, sources suggest that the Mexican Mafia has tried to infiltrate legitimate business ventures to front for illegal activities (NIC, 1991).

The Black Guerilla Family is a bit different than the Mexican Mafia. This prison gang was formed in 1966 by a Black Panther member, George Jackson, in San Quentin (NIC, 1991; Orlando-Morningstar, 1997). Membership is open to black prisoners with sponsors. The group is highly organized, with an elaborate leadership structure, a well-executed constitution, and a code of ethics (NIC, 1991). The Black Guerilla Family seeks to maintain dignity during incarceration, and their primary goals are political in nature. The Black Guerilla Family educates black inmates about racism, based on revolutionary ideas of Marxist-Leninist-Maoist philosophy (NIC, 1991). They emphasize the message of government overthrow. Because of their distrust for the establishment, they tend to engage in the most violent acts against staff (NIC, 1991). This political orientation has them less involved in illegal criminal ventures within prison.

TABLE 10–1

Characteristics of traditional prison gangs

Black Guerilla Family

- Originated in 1966 at San Quentin State Prison.
- Members are black and take a strict death oath.
- Politically aligned, due to Black Panther roots.

Mexican Mafia

- Originated in late 1950s in Deuel Vocational Center, California.
- Members are Mexican American/Hispanic, and they take a death oath.
- Use killing for discipline or respect.

La Nuestra Familia

- Originated in mid-1960s in Soledad Prison, California.
- Members are Mexican American/Hispanic, and they take a strict death oath.
- Connected to street gangs.

Texas Syndicate

- Originated in early 1970s in Folsom Prison, California.
- Members are Mexican American/Hispanic.
- Established in response to threats from other prison gangs.

Aryan Brotherhood

- Originated in 1967 in San Quentin State Prison.
- Members are white, and they take a death oath.
- Many follow supremacist and neo-Nazi philosophies.

Neta

- Originated in 1970 in Rio Pedras Prison, Puerto Rico.
- Members are Puerto Rican and Hispanic, and they do not freely admit membership.
- Connected to street gangs.

Information taken from Florida Department of Corrections (n.d.: pp. 14–15).

POLICIES AND PROGRAMS

Identification of Problem

As recently as 1992, many correctional institutions did not have specific policies for prison gangs or STGs, and units for gathering intelligence were not widely accepted (ACA, 1993). This does not mean that prison gangs were not present; rather, it suggests that often the first approach to prison gangs is denial (Carlson, 2001). This creates a problematic situation because gangs are easier to manage and control earlier in their development, when they are small and less organized (NIC, 1991).

The key to addressing the problem is to identify prison gang development in its early stages. Several identifying activities indicate the development of prison gangs. Some of the most consistent activities are requests for protective custody and transfer (Fong and Buentello, 1991; NIC, 1991), increased numbers of gang tattoos (Fong and Buentello, 1991; NIC, 1991; Stone and Wycoff, 1996), and more frequent violations for contraband (Fong and Buentello, 1991; Stone and Wycoff, 1996). Less obvious indicators of gang activity include secret race-based groupings (Fong and Buentello, 1991; Stone and Wycoff, 1996) and frequent gatherings of inmates with connections from the street or ethnicity (NIC, 1991). This activity can be confirmed by prison informants (Fong and Buentello, 1991). As a prison gang gains control of illegal activities, incidents of disruptive behavior increase, including verbal threats and physical assaults on staff and inmates (Fong and Buentello, 1991; NIC, 1991; Stone and Wycoff, 1996) and extortion (Fong and Buentello, 1991).

Once a prison acknowledges a problem, they move to the second stage of assessing the problem. The difference between occasional disruptions in prison settings and more organized gang activity is the frequency of the activities (Fong and Buentello, 1991). Knox (2004b) suggests that gang density can be used to identify a gang problem. *Gang density* refers to "the percentage of inmates who are now or who have ever been members of a street or prison gang" (p. 4). Research shows that when gang density approaches 17%, prison gangs become a problem (Knox 2004b).

Suppression Strategies

Carlson (2001) identifies that once a prison acknowledges and assesses their gang problem, they move to other approaches to control prison gangs, such as neutralizing leadership and preventing gang activity. These approaches, as implemented in corrections, can be classified as **suppression techniques.** Suppression strategies are the most widely used method of dealing with prison gangs, but many recognize that this strategy alone is ineffective (Knox, 2000b). The most commonly used suppression methods include inmate transfer, segregation, monitoring inmate communication, and monitoring by gang task forces (Knox, 2004b).

Validation Process.   To implement suppression strategies, correctional facilities must be able to identify, or "validate," gang members. In the **validation process,** prison gang members are identified (Knox, 2004b). This process varies across institutions, and many facilities recognize that their gang classification procedures could be better (McEwan, 1995).

Some institutions have strict identification procedures, as in Florida and California. In Florida, only 4,000 of their 73,000 inmates are validated gang members (Carlson, 2001). The inmate collects points in a validation procedure that differentiates suspected members from known members (Florida DOC, n.d.). Some agencies exercise more caution in identifying gang members. Some take no action against a member for status, only behavior (Carlson, 2001; Kassel, 2003). In New York, members are sanctioned for individual behavior because they do not want to empower the status of gang membership (Carlson, 2001).

Other institutions more broadly identify prison gang membership. In Massachusetts, inmates are considered gang affiliated through different criteria. They may be only suspected of gang affiliation by socializing with known gang members. Often the gang member is told only that they have been identified by a confidential informant. About 90% of identified gang members are Latino, and staff members indicate that only one of six are gang leaders (Kassel, 2003). Currently, an inmate can dispute STG status. In a dispute, the chief of the intelligence unit or a designee meets with the inmate, reviews the identification information, and decides whether the identification is validated (Massachusetts Department of Correction, n.d.).

Validated gang members may be **jacketed,** meaning that a notice of gang affiliation is placed in the inmate's file (Knox, 2000b). Identification and information sharing becomes an important tool for correctional administrators (Carlson, 2001; Regulus, 1991). Once a gang member is validated, he faces more scrutiny by prison officials. The validated STG member may have communication more closely monitored (Regulus, 1991). He may also have restrictions on activities. The Connecticut Department of Correction does not allow STG members to participate in group activities in the hopes of preventing gang activity (Carlson, 2001). In other systems, STG members may be placed in segregation, or they may be transferred or housed in gang units. This will be discussed in more detail in the following section.

Segregation and Isolation.   Many jurisdictions rely on segregation and isolation to deal with prison gang members (Carlson, 2001; Kassel, 2003). **Segregation** and **isolation** refer to separation of inmates from the general inmate population. Sometimes, all gang members are housed in a particular facility. For example, in California, STG members are housed at Pelican Bay, Corcoran, and Tehachapi (Carlson, 2001), and in Massachusetts they are housed in MCI–Cedar Junction (Kassel, 2003). In the Federal Bureau of Prisons, members of problematic STGs are placed in high-security facilities (Carlson, 2001).

Prison administrators use segregation and isolation as a bartering tool. Many facilities require the gang member to renounce gang membership in order to be placed back in the general inmate population. For example, in Texas, STG members are placed in a long-term special housing unit unless they renounce membership. The Department of Corrections offers protection to gang members who renounce. Members of "blood oath" prison gangs have not renounced (Carlson, 2001). However, "[a]dult gang members may be unwilling to relinquish a gang identity even if they are not active gang members" (Fleisher and Decker, 2001b). This has led to policies that allow STG members to be moved back into the general population without renouncing membership if they have been inactive for a period of time (Carlson, 2001).

Institutions also use segregation and isolation to neutralize gang membership. The idea is that by removing leaders from the general population, the prison gang will be weakened. However, neutralization may not be effective. By the time the problem

BOX 10-2: A Closer Look

In December 1989, California opened Pelican Bay State Prison, a facility designed to house violent offenders. As presented in its mission statement, such offenders include "validated gang members/associated and other inmates who pose a threat to the safety and security of mainline facilities" (California Department of Corrections and Rehabilitation, n.d.). This innovative facility, known as a "supermax," allows minimal contact between inmates, through remote-controlled cells and solitary confinement for all but one to two hours a day (Montgomery, n.d.).

One would think that this type of facility would curb gang activity. However, this is not the case at Pelican Bay. Prisoners have developed elaborate communication systems to send messages, known as "kites" or "wilas" (Geniella, 2001). These messages use exotic foreign languages and microwriting, which is the practice of cramming large amounts of print into a tiny space (Montgomery, n.d.). This has allowed prison gangs such as Nuestra Familia, Aryan Brotherhood, and the Mexican Mafia to flourish in prison.

In the case of Nuestra Familia, they have been able to take operations to the streets and utilize street gang members for their prison gang profit (Montgomery, n.d.). In fact, prison gang leaders have been able to order hits of street rivals (Geniella, 2001). This connection between prison and street gangs is troublesome. Some street gang members idolize their prison counterparts for their intellect and ability to flourish in the most difficult circumstances. These gang members see incarceration as a time to learn more about criminal enterprise from seasoned prison gang members. They learn "vocabulary, how to speak properly, how to dress properly, blend in with society so that way you can do your criminal activity on the under" (Montegomery, n.d.).

has been acknowledged and identified, the gang is often organized. They may be prepared for the removal of leaders and have new leaders waiting in the wings (Carlson, 2001). This is an example of failing to understand the difference between gang members and the gang as a group. If the group is strong enough, removing a member will make very little difference. Other problems with this method of suppression are that it can lead to inmates becoming "profoundly embittered" (Kassel, 2003, p. 231) or it can lead to status enhancement of gang members (Carlson, 2001).

A Midwest correctional department created a "gang-free" facility. Research explored the perceptions of inmates in this facility with interesting results (Rivera, Cowles, and Dorman, 2003). Those inmates who resided in the facility before and after the conversion and those who were transferred to the facility after the conversion viewed the environment negatively. Some of the criticisms were inconsistency in rule application, increased staff power, and a restrictive environment with less autonomy. According to the respondents, prison gangs monitored the behavior of inmates and staff. The respondents felt that gangs offered a more positive environment with consistency and order. Without this control mechanism, the behavior of neither group is controlled. The group of inmates who volunteered to go to the facility had more positive views of the gang-free environment.

Legal Challenges.   Suppression techniques designed to reduce gang activity have met with legal challenges. Three of four civil actions classified by Eckhart (2001) involved the techniques used to control prison gangs. The actions question the constitutionality of gang member classification, institutional grooming policies, and the prohibition of written and audio material. Eckhart finds that most legal suits are decided in favor of prison officials. However, this is not always the case.

One challenge for prison administrators came with the passage of the Religious Land Use and Institutionalized Persons Act of 2000 **(RLUIPA).** One portion of the act seeks to protect prisoners' religious freedom (Gaubatz, 2005). Prior to RLUIPA, prison officials could deny inmates the opportunity to participate in religious services for disciplinary reasons or for safety reasons (Knox, 2004b). RLUIPA successfully expands prisoners' freedom to practice religion (Gaubatz, 2005). It establishes that prison officials cannot deny religious freedom without ensuring that a prisoner's rights are not violated (Gaubatz, 2005; Knox, 2004b). It is suggested that RLUIPA gives prisoners a new way to conduct gang business by using religious services as a communication tool. Many facilities report monitoring religious services for gang activity, either through video or through guards (Knox, 2004b). RLUIPA has been extensively challenged, based on its constitutionally. With the exception of one case that is being appealed, the courts have ruled that RLUIPA is constitutional (RLUIPA.com, n.d.).

A Massachusetts policy of segregation also came under criticism and was the subject of legal intervention in the case of *Haverty v. Commissioner of Correction* (2002). The case was the result of restrictive segregation procedures instituted in 1995 that allowed the segregation of suspected gang members, even if they were not violating any prison regulations. The court decision established that segregation of inmates could not occur for non-disciplinary-related reasons. Since *Haverty v. Commissioner of Correction*, the Massachusetts DOC has established a policy that houses suspected and validated gang members in the general population at MCI–Concord. Any inmate who engages in an STG offense is referred to a disciplinary committee and must complete an STG program at MCI–Cedar Junction before being returned to the general population (Massachusetts Department of Correction, n.d.).

Alternate Strategies

Suppression strategies have been criticized, and few published studies measure effectiveness of suppression methods (Scott, 2001). As previously stated, even prison officials recognize that suppression alone is not effective (Knox, 2000b). In fact, Fleisher and Decker (2001b) caution that a "pedantic approach requiring former inmates and gang members to meet 'our conditions or else' is unreasonable and in the long run will be counterproductive" (p. 76). There are several reasons for this. Suppression policies are typically based on an inaccurate perception of prison gangs, which leads to a misidentification of gang members and to racial and cultural stereotyping. The suppression approach could also inadvertently lead to increased gang cohesion and enhanced gang status (Kassel, 2003).

Suggested alternative strategies for dealing with prison gangs include changing our perceptions of prison gangs and understanding the meaning of gang membership (Kassel, 2003; Kreinert and Fleisher, 2001; Regulus, 1991; Scott, 2001). However, prison gang members have been found to be less involved in treatment programs than nonmembers (Sheldon, 1991). Therefore, participation in any of the discussed programs needs to be strengthened. It is suggested that current policies may target gang members for status and not behaviors (Kassel, 2003). This develops a mind-set of perceived injustice and views that the staff is disrespectful (Kassel, 2003). If policies distinguish between gang and nongang inmates, they must be perceived as fair by the inmate population (Regulus, 1991). These policies can be developed with the goal of reducing disorganization in the prison environment by limiting gang affiliation indicators, such as graffiti, colors, and tattoos (Scott, 2001). Staff training can also enhance relations between inmates and prison officials (McEwan, 1995; Regulus, 1991).

Knowledge-Based Programs. Prosocial experiences that focus on social intervention have been offered as a more effective method of dealing with the prison gang problem (Kassel, 2003; Scott, 2001). One method of reducing prison gang activity is through knowledge-based programs that offer gang members proactive solutions to prison gang joining. For example, the Connecticut Department of Correction gives new inmates a pamphlet that proactively addresses what will happen to a gang-involved inmate. In Massachusetts, the Hampden County Correctional Facility offers more rigorous programming that utilizes movies, discussion sessions, and homework. In this graduated program, the inmate eventually writes a statement renouncing gang affiliation (Fleisher and Decker, 2001b). Other underutilized avenues of intervention are programs to facilitate gang resistance, including tattoo removal (Knox, 2004b).

Reintegration-Based Programs. Another issue to be addressed is that prison gang members eventually return to the community (see Egley, Howell, and Major, 2006). Many STG members are confined in segregated populations. They are often not eligible for minimum-security facilities or parole, and they are released back into the community (Kassel, 2003). Upon return to the community, the prison gang member may face challenges that the nonmember does not or face challenges with greater intensity (Fleisher and Decker, 2001b). Researchers suggest that social intervention programming that focuses on education and occupational training can "inspire fundamental personal transformation while enhancing prison security" (Kassel, 2003, p. 241; see also Regulus, 1991). Some prison gang members actually utilize their experiences in politically based prison gangs when they are released from prison (Martinez, 2003). This transition back into the community becomes an important link in reducing gang activity (Carlson, 2001). According to Fleisher and Decker (2001b), "the problem of prison gangs originates in the community and . . . community problems linked to gangs do not end when gang offenders are convicted and sentenced to prison" (p. 67).

CHAPTER SUMMARY

> In prison, one is thrown in with all the other criminals, gang members, outlaws, misfits, outcasts, and underworld people. . . . Since every jail I have ever been in seems designed to be recidivistic, as opposed to rehabilitative, the criminal culture is very strong. It saturates every level of every jail, from juvenile hall to death row. And so each individual going and coming back learns a new scheme to be used in the ever-growing arsenal of criminality. The 'hood also gains yet another expert in another field. (Shakur, 1993, p. 164)

It is important to discuss prison gangs in the context of street gangs. In the past several decades, the connection between the two groupings has been increasing. In some cases, prison gangs have taken their activities to the street. In other cases, the street gang continues its activities within prison walls. Thus, an environment that is meant for punishment, community safety, restitution, or rehabilitation is not effective at achieving any of its ultimate goals. Without addressing the prison gang problem, there will be limited effectiveness in addressing the street gang problem.

Prison gangs have become a massive problem for corrections in the United States. Although accurate information regarding the number and dynamics of prison gangs is difficult to obtain, we do know gangs are increasing. As a result, correctional facilities have begun to acknowledge prison gangs and institute policies designed to limit prison gang activity. It is expected that suppression strategies should work. The incarcerated population is a captive one. The adage "Where there's a will there's a way" seems to accurately depict this issue. Suppression is designed to take away the avenues, or the "ways," in which prison gangs do business. However, without addressing the reasons, or the "will," behind prison gangs, few advances are made. Alternate programming that addresses the motivations for prison gang activity has been slowly finding its way into correctional facilities. However, without access to the prison environment to assess the problem and propose solutions, we will continue to perpetuate the problem.

KEY TERMS

deprivation hypothesis
importation hypothesis
isolation
jacketed
RLUIPA

security threat groups (STGs)
segregation
suppression techniques
validation process

QUESTIONS FOR REVIEW

1. How are prison gangs different than street gangs?

2. What does the importation hypothesis suggest causes prison gangs?

3. What does the deprivation hypothesis suggest causes prison gangs?

4. How are prison gang members different than nonmembers?

5. Explain suppression techniques prisons use to control gangs.

DISCUSSION QUESTIONS

1. Suppression techniques may be effective at ensuring safety in prison settings. However, there is some suggestion that this technique fosters the prison-street connection. Do you think that prison administrators have a responsibility to ensure that prison gangs are not connected to the street?

2. What proposed solution could you offer to break the prison gang–street gang cycle?

CHAPTER 11

PREVENTION AND INTERVENTION

CHAPTER OBJECTIVES

- Recognize basic issues of prevention and intervention.
- Identify the steps of addressing a gang problem.
- Understand the elements of the Spergel model.
- Become familiar with effective gang prevention and intervention programs.

UNDERSTANDING PREVENTION AND INTERVENTION

> Children gone wild in a concrete jungle of poverty and rage. Armed and dangerous, prowling the concrete jungle in search of ourselves. We were children who had grown up too quickly in a city that cared too little about its young. (Shakur, 1993, p. 111)

We have a gang problem in the United States. The severity of the problem is sometimes overstated, but it is still a problem. This problem continues despite more than 50 years of attempts to address the issue. It begs the question of whether anything is effective in addressing gangs. There is evidence that gang prevention and intervention programs may be effective. Miller (1990) cites evidence of increases and decreases in gang behavior throughout history and notes that some communities with factors conducive to gangs do not have them. He suggests that gang programming could be effective because of the foundation of learning gang behavior and the prosocial function of the gang. These features, combined with some degree of visibility in gang activities, imply that there are things that we can do to effectively address gangs and gang members.

The chapter will introduce you to basic issues of gang prevention and intervention. The variation in gangs and gang members discussed throughout the book come to fruition in our approach to gang policy. Some policies address gang members, and others address gangs. This is further complicated by the varying approaches we take in prevention and intervention. These approaches have changed over time, and we have just about come full circle. However, the most current initiatives in gang prevention seem to be informed by lessons we are slowly learning. In the past 10 years, we have engaged in more thorough discussions of these issues. This chapter will orient you to prevention and intervention approaches, and promising initiatives to reduce gang membership and violent activity will be discussed.

Approaches to Prevention

The public health model may provide a most beneficial framework for understanding gang prevention (Esbensen, 2001). Papachristos (2005b) suggests that viewing gang behavior as a public health issue allows a better understanding of how it grows and spreads. The health care system focuses on the prevention of disease because it is most cost effective (Huff, 2002). Our current system only weakly embraces this idea. We spend more money on correctional institutions than on prevention efforts (Huff, 2004). "By analogy, if we pursued similar policy preference in health care, we would concentrate our public expenditures solely on those at the end of the medical care continuum—those who are dying. We would not focus on preventive health measures, even though they are much less expensive in the long run. Instead, we'd concentrate on end-of-life care, such as hospices and units for terminal cancer patients" (Huff, 2002, p. 288).

The health care model differentiates three levels of prevention: primary, secondary, and tertiary. **Primary prevention** is aimed at youth before they are involved in a gang (Greene, 2003). It applies a prevention program to a population of youth and usually selectively targets general populations at risk for gang membership. The key is that participants are not selected because of their individual precursors; rather, whole populations are identified as at risk. For example, a gang prevention program could be implemented in a low-income urban environment. **Secondary prevention** efforts target high-risk individuals who have risk factors for gang joining and who may have already been exposed to gang life (Greene, 2003). This type of prevention seeks to make youth more resilient to gang membership, and it often requires more intensive efforts. This is the suggested strategy for female gang membership prevention, beginning before the age of 12 (Miller, 2002).

In a perfect world, our primary and secondary prevention efforts would be enough to address the gang problem. However, there are youth who will join gangs and will engage in delinquency. **Tertiary intervention** efforts allow a second window of opportunity to change the course of behavior (Greene, 2003; Huff, 2002). This intervention effort focuses more on rehabilitation and aims to redirect delinquency. According to Huff (2002), this window may be more effective after a gang member engages in violence or at critical decision-making stages.

TABLE 11-1

Prevention strategies

Primary Prevention

- Goal is to prevent youth from joining gangs.
- General population is targeted.

Secondary Prevention

- Goal is to prevent high-risk youth from joining gangs.
- High-risk individuals who have been exposed to gang life are targeted.

Tertiary Intervention

- Goal is to prevent gang-involved youth from continuing membership.
- Gang members in need of redirection are targeted.

ASSESSING THE COMMUNITY

Some communities have gangs, and some do not. Most often, the initial reaction of communities with gangs is to deny that they exist (Hagedorn, 1988; Huff, 1990). This denial of a potentially serious issue creates an environment where gangs can thrive because there is no authority figure to control their behavior (Huff, 1990). Therefore, it is important to recognize gangs and move beyond denial (Trump, 1996). This is a delicate balance because too much attention to gangs during early stages can foster cohesiveness in the group (Klein, 1995). At some point, usually after a major public event, there is an acknowledgment of a gang problem (Huff, 1990). This major event is often the death of a nongang victim (Huff, 1990; Perkins, 1987). This community reaction is often one of panic and overreaction (Hagedorn, 1988; Huff, 1990; McCorkle and Meithe, 2002). Again, a delicate balance is called for. With too harsh a response, there is a risk that all gang members, even marginal members, are treated severely. Thus, it fosters the cohesion of the gang (Huff, 1990).

After denial and panic, a community begins to develop informed policy aimed at addressing gang problems. A critical step in addressing a gang problem is to understand the unique nature of local gangs. For communities with gangs, there is variation in the types of gangs that exist. Some have chronic, organized gangs, and some have emerging, loosely structured entities. Some members are well connected to the group, and others are only marginal. These different types of gangs require different types of responses. An extreme response to a loosely structured gang can inadvertently lead to greater levels of gang organization. Unfortunately, "[t]here are so many ways to feed gang cohesiveness and so few to reduce it" (Klein, 1995, p. 158). An effective response is based on an understanding of the local problem (Fearn, Decker, and Curry, 2001) and requires an assessment of the problem and not policies that are based on assumptions (Gottfredson and Gottfredson, 2001; Greene, 2003; McGloin, 2005).

Implementing Policy

Once a needs assessment has been conducted, a response to the local problem can be developed. There is no "one size fits all" program for gang prevention and intervention. The local policy should address immediate and background causes of gangs, which requires considering both individual- and community-level factors (Fearn, Decker, and Curry, 2001). The response must clearly specify what type of prevention or intervention is being implemented and who the target audience is (Greene, 2004). This response is ultimately rooted in theoretical ideas of the causes of gang formation and gang joining (Greene, 2004).

Historically, programs that have been implemented have not been adequately evaluated (Miller, 1990), and so it is difficult to assess what works and what does not. It is also difficult to determine the ideal conditions for effective programs, such as type of city, type of gang, or type of gang member. This gap in knowledge has led to a call for evaluation research in gang prevention and intervention (Decker, 2003; Hagedorn, 1988; Miller, 1990; Spergel et al., 1994). Evaluation research will not only measure outcomes of programs but also evaluate how programs are implemented. It will guide us in understanding key elements in program administration and ultimate effectiveness.

The Spergel Model

The Office of Juvenile Justice and Delinquency Prevention (OJJDP) initiated research to develop a "national" policy for gang prevention and intervention. The initial reaction of researchers was that this type of policy could not be developed because every community had different needs. A program that worked well in one community may not work well in another, and an effective program in one community may need to be modified over time because the gang landscape changes. These factors make it incredibly difficult to set a national policy. However, Irving Spergel researched what communities throughout the United States were doing to address gangs. The results of his research suggested that there were five main areas of gang policy:

1. community mobilization—programs to strengthen community institutions;
2. social intervention—programs to strengthen individual resolve against gangs;
3. opportunities provisions—programs to strengthen educational and employment opportunities;
4. suppression—programs to strengthen legal system responses to gangs and gang members;
5. organizational change/development—programs to alter the administration of agencies that deal directly with gangs (Spergel and Curry, 1993).

These five strategies became the foundation for the OJJDP comprehensive model, also known as the **Spergel model.** The framework the model provides is used as a guide for

---

TABLE 11-2

Elements of the Spergel model

Community Mobilization

- Based on social disorganization theories.
- Programs strengthen ineffective communities.

Social Intervention

- Based on biological, psychological, and micro-sociological theories.
- Programs address deficits in individuals and families.

Opportunities Provisions

- Based on strain and underclass theories.
- Programs increase opportunities and resources for education and employment.

Suppression

- Based on deterrence and rational choice theories.
- Programs increase certainty and severity of sanctions.

Organizational Change

- Based on administrative theory.
- Programs increase criminal justice system efficiency.

---

communities to develop local strategies based on their needs. A national survey, conducted by Spergel and Curry (1993), found that suppression was the most frequent strategy used, and it was used by both chronic and emerging gang communities. Although it was the most frequent strategy used, it was reported to be the least effective strategy. Chronic gang cities identified opportunities provisions as the most effective strategy, and emerging gang cities identified community mobilization. However, these strategies were least often utilized.

Community Mobilization

Community mobilization is rooted in the theoretical underpinnings of social disorganization theory (see Chapter 3; Spergel, 1995). It suggests that gang problems are the result of ineffective communities; therefore, the key to gang reduction is to strengthen communities by fostering cooperation among key social institutions (Fearn, Decker, and Curry, 2001) to allow better coordination of agencies and the services they offer. Institutional strengthening will, it is hoped, lead to a supportive environment that involves citizens and eventually enhances relationships between people (Short, 1996).

Community mobilization was one of the first strategies used in addressing youth violence and gang activity. Early efforts of community mobilization can be traced to the

Chicago Area Project (CAP), which was created in 1934 (Howell, 2000). This program used professionals to initially bring the community together, but program development came from community members, including ex-gang members. The success of this program was never formally evaluated (Spergel, 1995). Community mobilization in its pure form focuses on the development of a prosocial community. Currently, it is most often used in combination with other strategies. For example, the Philadelphia Youth Violence Reduction Partnership (YVRP) is designed to reduce homicide. The program utilizes several strategies, including mobilization, opportunities, social intervention, and suppression. The community mobilization portion of the program includes partnerships and collaboration between legal institutions, the school district, human services, the housing authority, drug and alcohol programs, a university, and public and private partners. Other recent efforts use community mobilization to strengthen suppression efforts, shifting the focus from community organization to enhancing legal system–community relations (Maxson, 2004; Maxson, Hennigan, and Sloane, 2003).

Social Intervention

Social intervention is rooted in theories that address individual-level risks for gang joining, such as family and psychological factors (see Chapter 4; Spergel, 1995). Individual deficits are believed to be a root cause of gang membership, and this approach attempts to address these individual deficits. It strives to "develop the connections, engagements, and involvements necessary to ensure its new members will conform to society's belief and value system" (Vigil, 2002, p. 159).

Social intervention was first utilized in the 1950s as community mobilization was weakening or being redirected. At its inception, social intervention relied on a detached worker program. This strategy was the one used by the Mid-City Project that operated in Boston from 1954 to 1957. Detached workers, also known as street workers, would go to the streets to foster relationships with gang-involved youth. Sometimes street workers were former gang members. Detached workers became the link between the street and mainstream society. Often gang youth were excluded from prosocial programs, and the street worker established a connection and offered services to youth (Klein, 1971). The early detached worker programs were ineffective. Some programs showed no impact on gangs (Spergel and Curry, 1993); others actually increased gang cohesiveness (Klein, 1971; Knox, 2000a). As a result, social intervention efforts shifted to prevention-based programming.

Current Programs.   Current methods of social intervention include crisis intervention, individual and family counseling, referral to social and health services, conflict resolution training, antibullying programs, and tattoo removal (Fearn, Decker, and Curry, 2001; Miller, 2002; Spergel and Curry, 1993). At the primary prevention level, social intervention programs teach youth prosocial values. This is the goal of Gang Resistance Education and Training (G.R.E.A.T). This school-based program, taught by police officers, introduces students to the consequences of gang joining. The program goals are to reduce gang membership and to foster prosocial relationships between youth and law enforcement. Evaluations of G.R.E.A.T. find moderate results (Esbensen, Freng, et al., 2002; Esbensen et al., 2004). Students who are exposed to G.R.E.A.T. do hold more prosocial values, and several years after program completion they have lower levels of victimization and more prosocial peers. However, there is no reduction in gang activity or self-reported delinquency.

For those who are at higher risk, social intervention attempts to redirect negative behavior. For example, the Boys and Girls Club of America's Gang Prevention through Targeted Outreach (GPTTO) program provides multiple prosocial activities, as well as a support system to at-risk and gang-involved youth (Van Ness, Fallon, and Lawrence, 2006). The progress of program participants is tracked to determine criminal justice system contact, school performance, and individual and family participation in program components. A study of program effectiveness revealed that active participants of the program were less involved in deviant behavior, performed better in school, and were involved in more prosocial activities.

Social intervention can also be used at the macro level to target gangs (Miller, 2002). Escalating gang conflicts can be identified, and organizations can work with gangs to resolve the conflict. This is the strategy used by the House of Umoja, a grassroots program developed in the 1970s in Philadelphia. The House of Umoja was created by the Fattahs and used their home and their own resources. Their home became a "family-centered community institution that effectively mediated gang conflicts" (Howell, 2000, p. 6). They initiated a "No Gang War '74" program, which virtually eliminated gang wars in Philadelphia (House of Umoja, n.d.). Currently, the House of Umoja has a residential program for youth referred through the Department of Youth Services. This program offers individual services of intervention and opportunity. The House of Umoja also sponsors a "Peace in the Hood" program that asks high-risk youth to commit to lives of nonviolence (House of Umoja, n.d.).

Opportunities Provisions

Opportunities provisions is a strategy based on strain and underclass theories (see Chapter 3; Spergel, 1995). This approach suggests that a main motivation for gang involvement is lack of opportunities in underclass communities. In certain environments, access to employment and educational resources is limited. Therefore, programs in this strategy focus on fostering education, job training, and career-oriented employment opportunities in economically depressed areas. Geis (2002) states, "It is an irrefutable fact that youngsters who own cars do not often steal other cars. People who enjoy a decent standard of living, a good education in a well-supplied school with first-rate teachers, and similar things that give them a stake in conformity, by and large will behave in a similar manner as do others who enjoy such opportunities" (p. 270). The origins of opportunities provisions trace back to the 1960s, when strain theory was embraced. The Mobilization for Youth Program, implemented in New York City between 1961 and 1967, is an early example of opportunities provision (Spergel and

Curry, 1993). One aspect of the program, the Youth Services Corp, employed youth who were not able to find employment. As with other programs of this time, there was no systematic evaluation to determine its effectiveness.

Of all strategies, this is the most expensive and the most challenging to implement (Spergel and Curry, 1993). As previously stated, it is also considered the most effective approach in chronic gang environments. Note that employment opportunities should be career based and emphasize long-term success. Optimally, youth should be able to achieve success in the local community. "We always tell people that you go to school cause you got to get out of this neighborhood. Why you got to leave the neighborhood? To succeed. You should be able to succeed in your own home, right?" (Latin Kings Speak, 2002). This strategy is rarely used on its own and is more often included as one component of larger programs. For example, the Building Resources for the Intervention and Deterrence of Gang Engagement (BRIDGE) in Riverside, California, incorporates employment, job training with a paid stipend, and educational assistance. Many times, opportunity-based programs are grassroots. For example, Father Gregory Boyle, also known as G-Dog, began employing youth at his church. When he realized they needed careers, his efforts escalated into "Jobs for a Future/Homeboy Industries," which is an "employment referral center and economic development program" (Homeboy Industries, n.d.). His program has also sparked the development of "Homeboy Bakery, Homeboy Silkscreen, Homeboy/Homegirl Merchandise, Homeboy Graffiti Removal, Homeboy Maintenance, and Homeboy Landscaping" (Homeboy Industries, n.d.). Similar efforts are discussed by Ice T (2005). He states that when he engages in capitalistic businesses, he employs his friends and members of the community.

Suppression

Suppression strategies are rooted in deterrence and rational choice theories (see Chapter 4; Spergel, 1995). They embrace the idea that gang membership and gang crime are the result of individual choice and seek to increase the certainty and severity of consequences for gang behavior. Suppression became the primary approach to gangs in the 1980s, when other approaches seemed to be failing and there was an overall shift toward politically conservative policy (Klein, 1995). As previously stated, suppression is the most commonly used prevention/intervention strategy, which makes sense because the criminal justice system is the most obvious resource to combat crime. However, suppression alone is not a successful gang reduction policy. It is a necessary strategy (Huff, 2002), but "[w]hen suppression occurs in a vacuum, when it is not accompanied by other, more supportive, actions, the chances of making lasting changes in gang crime are diminished" (Fearn, Decker, and Curry, 2001, p. 341).

Current suppression initiatives include metal detectors in schools, increased surveillance, saturation patrol, curfew and truancy enforcement, and increased arrest and imprisonment of gang members (Bynum and Varano, 2003; Fearn, Decker, and Curry, 2001; Huff, 2002; Spergel and Curry, 1993). In fact, curfew and other time-of-day restrictions were reportedly used by more than 60% of jurisdictions in 2001, and just under 50% reportedly used firearm suppression initiatives (Egley, Howell, and Major, 2006). Contact with the criminal justice system is also increased through the use of gang member databases and gang incidence tracking systems that identify high gang crime areas, or **hotspots** (Huff, 2002). However, gang hotspots may be different than their primary hang out area, or **set space** (Tita, Cohen, and Engberg, 2005). Increased attention to both areas can help restore defensible space (Lasley, 1998). Often the identification of hotspots and set space involves information from community members. Working with the community serves the function of empowering the community, leading to improvements in community organization and effectiveness (Maxson, Hennigan, and Sloane, 2005; Short, 1996).

Police Agencies.   Law enforcement is often the primary agency in a suppression strategy. However, pure law enforcement suppression has a weak record of success. Extreme policing that increases surveillance and targets high-risk areas without community support reinforces the "us versus them" attitude (Klein, 1995; Maxson, Hennigan, and Sloane, 2005). There are some situations where extreme policing has led to officers essentially creating a gang of their own. In Los Angeles, Community Resources against Street Hoodlums (CRASH), an elite antigang unit, was formed to control gang crime. It came under fire in 1998 and was disbanded in 2000 because of criminal charges against CRASH officers and systematic enforcement of the law through unlawful means. The charges against CRASH officers included murder, drug charges, bank robbery, shooting unarmed suspects, stealing, assault, planting evidence, and perjury. The Rampart Scandal, as it came to be known, involved a secret fraternity of more than 30 antigang unit members and supervisors. Their behavior resulted in more than 100 convictions being overturned on the basis of tainted evidence and credibility issues (see Kirk and Boyer, 2001; see also Streetgangs.com, n.d.).[1]

Currently, we have become more aware of the potential pitfalls of suppression techniques. According to Greene (2003), police have begun to recognize that effective intervention efforts require other external agencies' participation. However, other research has shown that police department participation and commitment to intervention efforts is often lessened when police are not the lead agency (Decker, 2003). Current suppression efforts include coordinated efforts with police, probation, and the court system. Often, gang leaders, hard-core members, and recidivists are selectively targeted (Kent and Smith, 2001). The Baton Rouge Partnership for Prevention of Juvenile Gun Violence, although not specific to gangs, is an example of coordinated suppression. In one element of this program, three-member police-probation teams oversee and implement conditions of probation. The program is considered effective. Despite the fact that probationers were under increased supervision, their violations decreased from 44% in 1997 to 26% in 1999 (Van Ness, Fallon, and Lawrence, 2006, p. 23).

Civil Gang Injunctions.   The judiciary, specifically prosecution, can also effectively suppress gang behavior. One avenue that has been utilized in the control of gang behavior is civil gang injunctions. **Injunctions** are a legal avenue to prohibit members of a designated street gang "from engaging in conduct which facilitates criminal activity" (L.A. City Attorney Gang Prosecution Section, 2001, p. 320). Injunctions were devised as a way to proactively control gang activity by controlling legal behavior that is connected to gang crime, such as carrying pagers, wearing colors, flashing hand signs, and congregating in problem areas (Maxson, Hennigan, and Sloane, 2005). Problematic aspects of injunctions include the prohibition of any two gang members from associating with one other (Maxson, Hennigan, and Sloane, 2005).

Research suggests that there is less gang presence in the short term when injunctions are used (Maxson, Hennigan, and Sloane, 2005). Often, injunctions are only temporary solutions to more deeply rooted community problems (Bjerregaard, 2003), and their implementation can lead to **displacement**—the movement of crime from one area to another. There is some evidence that injunctions can enhance neighborhood effectiveness and quality of life (Grogger, 2005; Maxson, Hennigan, and Sloane, 2005). These improvements are more apt to occur in areas that rely on information from community members to develop the case for an injunction (Maxson, 2004; Maxson, Hennigan, and Sloane, 2003). This requires more effort on the part of the criminal justice system.

There are other questions concerning the most appropriate circumstances for their use. Maxson, Hennigan, and Sloane (2005) find that in areas with less gang activity, injunctions were related to an increase in gang presence, greater disorder, and greater victimization. This may be an example of the "us versus them" dynamic, which increases gang cohesion in the face of external conflict. Therefore, injunctions might be most effective against groups that already have cohesion (McGloin, 2005), against traditional gangs that have definitive territory (Maxson, Hennigan, and Sloane, 2005), or in areas with severe gang problems (Maxson et al., 2003).

Organizational Change

Organizational change and development focuses on administrative changes that maximize the effectiveness of any of the previously mentioned approaches. This change can be the creation of a gang task force, which is a specialized gang unit or an integrated team of system workers. For example, TARGET (Tri-Agency Resource Gang Enforcement Team) is a team of police officers, "a probation officer, a deputy district attorney, and a district attorney investigator" who monitor high-risk offenders (Howell, 2000, p. 33). Organizational change can also include the implementation of **vertical prosecution,** which is one prosecutor seeing a gang case all the way through from beginning to end (Bynum and Varano, 2003). In many cases, organizational change is new legislation designed to more effectively prosecute gang members (Fearn, Decker, and Curry, 2001). Any organizational change should be based on a local assessment of the gang problem, and it should not simply be done because others are doing it (Bynum and Varano, 2003; Webb and Katz, 2003).

Legislation.   More than 70% of all states have created legislation related to gangs (Institute for Intergovernmental Research, 2000), such as enhanced sentences for gang members, civil remedies for gang victims, and criminalization of gang recruitment (Fearn, Decker, and Curry, 2001; IIR, 2000). Other gang-related legislation requires listing property in gang areas as "psychologically affected property" (IIR, 2000). One of the most notable pieces of gang-related legislation is California's Street Terrorism and Prevention Act (1988), which criminalizes a "person who actively participates in any criminal street gang with knowledge that its members engage in or have engaged in a pattern of criminal gang activity, and who willfully promotes, furthers, or assists any felonious criminal conduct by members of that gang" (California Penal Code §§ 186.20-27).

In regard to gang legislation, sometimes "the cure is worse than the disease" (Huff, 2002, p. 293). There has been much debate about constructing legislation that targets gang-involved youth (see Bjerregaard, 2003; see also Geis, 2002). Some suggest that legislation arises out of frustration with gang problems (Bjerregaard, 2003) and ultimately punishes status, not behavior (Geis, 2002). For example, in a debate about the Chicago antigang statute, a council member supporting that statute expressed frustration that gang members avoided arrest by engaging in crime when the police were not present. This is an illogical argument because most rational people try to avoid detection (Geis, 2002, p. 265).

Many statutes have been constitutionally challenged and found to be in accordance with due process rights (Bjerregaard, 2003). However, in *Chicago v. Morales* (1999), the U.S. Supreme Court ruled that Chicago's antigang ordinance violated due process rights because the legislation was unconstitutionally vague. In its original form, the statute allowed an officer to arrest a person loitering who was reasonably believed to be a criminal street gang member (Geis, 2002). The Supreme Court stated that the statutes had to more clearly define *gang* and *gang member* and more specifically identify the prohibited behavior of loitering.

Gang legislation may also emphasize suppression at the cost of more effective programs (Papachristos, 2005b). For example, the Federal Gang Deterrence and Community Protection Act of 2005, also known as the Gang Busters Bill, calls for an increase in gang intelligence gathering. However, the language of the bill relies on definitions of gangs that are extreme, and the suggested policies have not been properly evaluated (Papachristos, 2005b). There is also a call to extend RICO statutes, legislation designed for organized crime, to street gangs (Geis, 2002). Additionally, antigang legislation ultimately targets youth from disadvantaged groups, "who start out far behind in the social race and are not afforded reasonable opportunities to catch up (Geis, 2002, p. 269).

Important suggestions for improving a legislative approach to gang suppression include Bjerregaard's (2003) recommendation that the definitions of *gang membership* and *gang* need to be refined. The focus of legislation should be hard-core members and gang crime that involves the whole group, not the individualized behavior of a few. It has also been suggested that the legal system should rely on already existing legislation (Bjerregaard, 2003; Geis, 2002).

BOX 11-1: A Closer Look

Organizational change to curb gang activity can be found in the Gang Deterrence and Community Protection Act of 2005, also known as the Gangbusters Bill (H.R. 1279). This bill has been passed by the House and is currently being considered by the Senate Committee on the Judiciary.[1] The goal of this federal bill is "to reduce violent gang crime and protect law-abiding citizens and communities from violent criminals, and for other purposes."

To meet this goal, the Gangbusters Bill suggests altering the federal criminal statute to include street gang crime, and it institutes enhanced sentencing for such crime. The bill defines a criminal street gang as " a formal or informal group or association of 3 or more individuals, who commit 2 or more gang crimes (one of which is a crime of violence other than an offense punishable under subparagraph (A), (B), or (C) of section 401(b)(1) of the Controlled Substances Act), in 2 or more separate criminal episodes, in relation to the group or association, if any of the activities of the criminal street gang affects interstate or foreign commerce." Also included in the Gangbusters Bill is enhanced sentencing for illegal aliens who participate in gang crime.

A second method for addressing street gangs in the Gangbusters Bill is increased federal funding to enhance law enforcement and prosecution efforts in high-intensity gang areas. The stated goal of these increased resources is to "deter and prevent at-risk youth from joining illegal street gangs." These resources are to be used for training and equipment and to create gang databases and law enforcement teams that include local, state, and federal agencies.

[1]More recent action (June 2006) has been taken by this subcommittee on their similarly worded bill entitled "Gang Prevention and Effective Deterrence Act of 1995" (s.155).

COMPREHENSIVE STRATEGIES

We seem to have come full circle. Each of the five strategies has dominated a particular point in our history. We have moved on to new strategies without considering the strength of previous ones. Many researchers have stated the ineffectiveness of our strategies (Klein, 1995; Miller, 1990; Spergel et al., 1994) and the necessity for program evaluation (Decker, 2003; Hagedorn, 1988; Spergel et al., 1994). Researchers have recognized for years that "[w]ithout multiple sources of information and a coordinated response that involves suppression, community mobilization, and social opportunities provision, little progress will be made in responding to such gangs" (Fearn, Decker, and Curry, 2001, p. 342). Huff (2002) stated, "Although our children are our nation's most important resource for the future, we often pay more attention, in the public policy arena, to our physical infrastructure than to our human infrastructure" (p. 290).

At last we are taking steps to learn from our ineffective past. In 1991, Hagedorn stated that "[i]n the absence of institutional reform and guarantees that resources will get to those that need it, more resources alone will not necessarily contribute to solving gang problems" (p. 535). Important federal- and state-level initiatives, such as the Title V Community Prevention Grants Program sponsored by the Office of Juvenile Justice and Delinquency Prevention (n.d.) and the Senator Charles E. Shannon Jr. Community Safety Initiative in Massachusetts (Van Ness, Fallon, and Lawrence, 2006), are attempting to put resources into communities and programs that may actually make a difference. President George W. Bush stated that we need programs that "focus on giving young people, especially young men in our cities, better options than apathy, or gangs, or jail" (Department of Justice, 2006). Attorney General Gonzales unveiled a plan that emphasizes prevention and opportunities through the expansion of successful programs and "new comprehensive anti-gang programs" (Department of Justice, 2006).

These are steps in the right direction (see Klein, 1995). Additionally, these initiatives are emphasizing the necessity for research evaluation. The revised approach is a **comprehensive strategy** that emphasizes coordinating all of the strategies in accordance with the needs of the community. This comprehensive approach recognizes the value of primary prevention and secondary intervention (Fearn, Decker, and Curry, 2001; Huff, 2002). It strives toward interagency collaboration and recognizes that good programs require community participation in decision making (Weston, 1993). In the comprehensive model, the needs of the local community are the starting point. As program development and research evaluation continue, there will be increasingly more effective programs.

Gang Violence Reduction Project

An example of a model program is the Gang Violence Reduction Project in the 10th District in Chicago, known as "Little Village" (see Spergel et al., 2002). Little Village,

---

BOX 11–2: Focus on Research

The OJJDP Model Programs Guide offers online access to more than 175 prevention and intervention programs that have proven effective at reducing juvenile delinquency and gang involvement (OJJDP Model Programs Guide, n.d.a.). This guide was developed as part of the Title V Community Prevention Grants Program. The guide allows the user to explore programs in major categories of prevention, immediate sanctions, intermediate sanctions, residential programs, and reentry. Each major category has detailed subtopics that allow users to find programs that best suit their needs. The program guide was designed so that communities could explore potential effective programs that best match the needs of the local environment. The site (http://www.dsgonline.com/mpg2.5/mpg_index.htm) also allows users to refine their program search by gender, age, race, problem behaviors, and target settings. This amazing online source is one of many resources offered by OJJDP in the development of effective, comprehensive programs.

which houses predominantly lower income Hispanic residents, had some of the highest gang violence rates in Chicago. This violence was primarily due to two gangs: the Latin Kings and Two Six. The goal of the program was to redirect the behavior of 200 targeted high-risk youth in order to reduce gang violence and reduce the number of hard-core delinquents.

The project utilized the Spergel model and relied on a team of workers to implement programming in a highly coordinated and integrated manner. The team consisted of two police officers, two part-time neighborhood relations officers, three probation officers, a professor from the University of Chicago, and five community youth workers. The youth workers included some former gang members and some who had grown up in Little Village. They were crucial to the program's success because they understood gang dynamics and gained the trust of gang members. The youth workers only notified police of hotspots or escalating gang violence; they were not snitches. The program included referral to counseling services, access to education and job opportunities, and increased surveillance by the legal system. True to a comprehensive strategy, the program was continually adapted based on feedback from ongoing research.

Results of the five-year project find that the program "was highly effective in the reduction of serious gang violence and drug crime among individual targeted youth" (p. 97). However, "[t]he Project was less effective in changing the basic institutional pattern of ganging and gang crime in the Little Village community as a whole" (p. 97). The evaluation suggests that the local tactical police were effective in the implementation of the program. However, the centralized Chicago Police Department did not commit to the project, there was no lead agency, and this may have affected the community's overall ability to mobilize.

The Boston Miracle

Operation Ceasefire is a program that was implemented in Boston in the mid-1990s. The program approached deterrence with community policing and problem-solving techniques (see Braga, Kennedy, and Tita, 2002; see also Kennedy, 1998). The program, originally designed to combat gun violence, sent clear messages to those engaging in crime that the behavior was not going to be tolerated. It instituted a "pulling levers" approach, which was designed to ensure certainty, severity, and swiftness of response. Gang members were individually identified to receive the "pulling levers" message. Gang members were given the message that gang violence would draw attention from law enforcement, and they were also made aware of the consequences of such behavior. Rather than a typical reactive approach to policing, "pulling levers" was more proactive. The gang members were identified and told that law enforcement would be harsh if their behavior continued. This proactive approach also sent the message that the community cared about the gang member. At the "pulling levers" meetings, intervention- and opportunity-based services were made available, and community and church groups were there to support the message (Braga, Kennedy, and Tita, 2002; McDevitt, Braga, Nurge, and Buerger, 2003). The program was touted as "the Boston Miracle" because of the significant reductions in violence that resulted from the program (McDevitt, Braga, Nurge, and Buerger, 2003).

The program has been implemented throughout the country. True to a comprehensive strategy, however, communities have altered the program based on their local needs. Stockton, California, used qualitative research to gain a greater understanding of youth violence in the community (Braga, Kennedy, and Tita, 2002). Other communities modified some of the Ceasefire strategies. For example, Minneapolis includes a hospital component that warns injured gang members in the hospital about the consequences of retaliation (Braga, Kennedy, and Tita, 2002). The mayor of the city also holds press conferences to announce gang arrests that result after clear warnings. In Boyle Heights, California, the program targets one neighborhood; in Baltimore, the targeted area is a violent drug market (Braga, Kennedy, and Tita, 2002). One community expanded the levers that were pulled to include revocation of probations, housing, relinquishing ownership of property, and asset forfeiture (Tita, Riley, and Greenwood, 2003). Other times, implementation of the Boston Ceasefire components was more difficult because of a reluctance to implement a program that originated elsewhere (Tita, Riley, and Greenwood, 2003).

CHAPTER SUMMARY

> Youth gang members fall between the cracks of social services, social opportunity programs, and police sweeps. Not only do criminal acts of individuals and groups add to the problems of youth gangs, but inappropriate responses by agencies and community groups fuel them. (Spergel et al., 1994, p. 6)

We seem to be perpetually desperate for a quick fix to a gang problem that has taken several decades to create. Many of our programs have not been adequately tested, so we do not know if they are effective, and if they are effective, there is not enough information to determine the ideal circumstances for implementation. We do know that different programs target different risk levels, including primary, secondary, and tertiary.

The creation of the Spergel/comprehensive model has provided a framework that will allow us to develop more effective gang prevention and intervention policy. The model calls for coordinated strategies of community mobilization, social intervention, opportunities provision, suppression, and organizational change. More important, the model allows communities to develop policy based on their local gang problem. There is also a developing emphasis on evaluation to determine which programs are effective and under what conditions they are most beneficial. Ideally, this will lead us to more successful gang prevention programming.

KEY TERMS

community mobilization
comprehensive strategy
displacement
hotspots
injunction
opportunities provisions
organizational change
primary prevention

secondary prevention
set space
social intervention
Spergel model
suppression
tertiary intervention
vertical prosecution

QUESTIONS FOR REVIEW

1. What is the difference between primary, secondary, and tertiary interventions?

2. What is community mobilization, and how is it implemented?

3. How do injunctions reduce gang activity?

4. What is the difference between hotspots and set space?

5. How is a comprehensive strategy better at addressing the gang problem?

DISCUSSION QUESTIONS

1. Suppression brings to the forefront the balance between crime control and due process rights. Do you think that suppression strategies are unreasonable or necessary? Is there a balance that can be achieved?

2. Our approach to gang prevention and intervention has cycled, primarily because of the desire for quick fixes and the lack of programs that have been proven effective. If you were the mayor of a gang city, what would you say to your constituents to get them to buy into a comprehensive approach?

NOTE

1. In 2000, a similar but less pervasive situation occurred in Chicago. A member of the antigang unit, along with gang members, was charged with operating a cocaine ring between Chicago and Miami (see Media Awareness Project, 2003).

CHAPTER 12

THE FUTURE OF GANGS

CHAPTER OBJECTIVES

- Understand common themes in our knowledge of street gangs and gang members.
- Comprehend the connections between the elements of street gangs and gang members.
- Recognize the involvement of gangs in social, political, and economic activity.
- Anticipate the future of street gang activity.

OUR UNDERSTANDING

> And, just when we think we have closed in on some empirical "facts," new revelations pull the conceptual tablecloth right off the table . . . because gang research is not the make-believe world of magicians, all the dishes break. (Papachristos, 2005b, p. 643)

Our knowledge of the world of street gangs and the role of gang members is constantly evolving. At the same time, this dynamic phenomenon is also ever changing, making it difficult to ever truly understand gangs and members. The goal of this book was to provide you with a foundation of knowledge into street gangs and gang members as we currently understand them. In particular, we distinguished the gang as a group from the gang member as an individual. A summary of this information is presented in this chapter because it is through knowledge that the potential future of street gangs can be explored.

History

The history of street gangs informs us that this has been a relatively constant social issue. Throughout the past century, there were four gang eras with their own unique gang problems, but an understanding of the common themes of these eras can be valuable in comprehending the current situation. Although the ethnicity of gang members has changed over time, the social experiences of these members are similar. Gangs develop out of poverty, discrimination, economic changes, and related social ills. The current gang era shares these similarities. Today's gangs are predominantly in underclass, minority communities. But there has also been an expansion of gangs from chronic gang environments to emerging gang cities. This has been accompanied by changing gang demographics.

Definition

As knowledge increases, so does the debate surrounding definitions of *gang, gang member,* and *gang crime.* This debate reflects our increased knowledge and the variation and changing dynamics of gang activity. Some definitions of *gang* focus on group process; others emphasize criminal behavior. The term *gang* has also been refined to include youth gang and street gang. Membership is less a subject of controversy. Much of our knowledge relies on self-identification of gang membership, which provides insight into different levels of commitment to gang activity. It has also enabled differentiation between gang-motivated crime and gang-related crime.

The Group Perspective

Our understanding of gangs emphasizes the wide variation in the group. This is evident in the theories that explain gang formation, including strain, social disorganization, and underclass theories. Despite the variations in our explanations of gang formation, there are common themes of disadvantage offered. Variation is also evident in our understanding of the organization and process of the group. Most gangs have limited organizational elements, but some gangs are highly organized. Our understanding of group dynamics is enriched by recognizing the structural elements that distinguish gangs from one another, including leadership, roles, social codes, and territory. Knowledge of group process is also enhanced by recognizing the critical role that cohesion plays in group evolution. This knowledge of group process ultimately leads to a greater understanding of criminal behavior, including exposure to illegal economic activity and the cycle of gang violence.

The Individual Perspective

We have also expanded our understanding of the gang member. We are increasingly gaining insight into members' reasons for joining a gang, including family, protection, and money. This insight can be framed in a theoretical context that explores individual explanations for gang membership. More important, we understand that multiple factors place a person at increased risk for joining a gang. This knowledge of variation expands our understanding of individual experiences within the group context. Gang members are recruited differently and face different types of initiation rituals. There is variation in their involvement in gangs; some are highly committed, and some are not. Often, the decision to join a gang puts a gang member on a negative path that continues long after the individual has left the gang. Many times, this is due to the increased deviant behavior that a gang member engages in while actively involved in a gang. Although this behavior decreases after a member leaves a gang, gang members' experiences leave them unprepared for adulthood.

Diversity

Exploring issues of diversity has further enriched our understanding of street gangs and their members. Historic and modern ethnic experiences shape the unique gang landscape of Hispanic, black, Asian, and American Indian gangs. Each ethnic minority endures marginalization from mainstream culture. However, the social and political atmosphere that fosters gang formation leads to differences in ethnic gangs.

This contrast is also apparent in our understanding of female gang members and the gangs they belong to. Historically, a male-centered perspective skewed our knowledge of female gang membership. Although female gang members share many characteristics and experiences with male gang members, there are key differences. We have gained insight into the different types of gangs that females are involved in, and we are beginning to understand how the structure of gangs influences the female gang member's experience. Specifically, the unique female social experience is at the core of many of these differences, from sexual abuse as a risk factor for membership, to their differential experiences with violence as active gang members, to the long-term impact of early motherhood. This knowledge will allow us to develop prevention and intervention programs that better address the needs of gang-involved females.

The Prison-Street Connection

Our understanding of street gangs would be incomplete without a discussion of prison gangs. More than at any other time in gang history, this knowledge is crucial. The number of prison gangs and prison gang members continually increases, partly because of the continued gang affiliation of gang members who get sent to prison. Thus, the street gang member never gets a time out from gang life and a chance at reflection, reformation, or rehabilitation. There are also increasingly stronger ties between prison gangs and street gangs; in some cases, they are one and the same. This has led to the development of stronger, more cohesive gangs. In fact, in prison, the gang and its members become more efficient because, for the first time, they learn to function as part of an institution. The standard institutional policy for dealing with prison gangs and gang members has been zero tolerance and suppression. There are questions as to the effectiveness of such policies to the exclusion of others. Without effectively addressing the prison gang problem, we cannot effectively address the street gang problem.

Policy

Our understanding of street gangs is the foundation for developing effective prevention and intervention policies. Recognizing the variation in gangs and gang members is a key to successful programming. We have tended to develop policy that addresses one element of gangs, rather than a systematic, holistic approach. Our efforts have also been weakened by a lack of evaluation research to determine program effectiveness. The formulation of the Spergel/comprehensive model is a step in the right direction because it emphasizes the need for each community to identify its own gang problem. The policies developed should originate from this local understanding. The strength of the Spergel model is its adaptable framework of community mobilization, social intervention, opportunities provision, suppression, and organizational change and development. This multifaceted approach can be implemented in any environment. Our knowledge will continue to be strengthened as we continue to evaluate prevention and intervention programs. This research will allow us to understand the best methods of implementation, the most effective programs, and the linkage between effective programs and target populations.

THE FUTURE

Now more than ever before, we should be concerned with what gangs can become. Our national emphasis is on international terrorism, and we are once again in an economic downswing characterized by cuts in social programming and the continued movement of jobs overseas. These factors only enhance the bleak conditions that created gangs to begin with. It will be these same conditions that create the movement of some gangs into organizations that are structured and capable of mass action or mass destruction. Our current policy of sending more and more minority youth to prison for long sentences will inevitably create further solidarity and cohesion in street gangs.

Empowerment

As gangs continue to organize, they have two paths that can be followed. They can continue to stay involved in criminal behavior and more effectively organize criminal enterprises. This path could lead to organizations that look more like organized crime and less like stereotypical street gangs. The alternate, sometimes simultaneous, path offers prosocial empowerment. Note that "gangs are not ordinarily committed to or participants in social and political causes" (Spergel, 1995, p. 121). At the same time, some well-organized gangs are.

Community Support.   It is already the case that some communities with a strong gang presence have a love-hate relationship with them. "Both conflictual and contradictory relationships can form between gang and community. In such situations, the youth gang itself becomes a locally recognized community institution, decried yet supported, excluded yet relied on, loathed yet embraced" (Venkatesh, 1996, p. 243). Many conventional community residents do not appreciate criminal activities and the associated social ills, but they accept the institution of gangs and the resources they provide. The gang combines "community organizational, social support, political, and criminal business functions" (Spergel, 1995, p. 123). In some communities, street gang members offer financial support and services for needs that are otherwise unmet (DiChiara and Chabot, 2003; Venkatesh, 1996). Gangs are sometimes involved in community cleanups and fostering cultural awareness (DiChiara and Chabot, 2003). Some gang members foster community development as they invest their money in legitimate businesses (Decker, Bynum, and Weisel, 1998). Gang members who leave gang life and become successful understand what the gang is offering to its youth but recognize that the community is responsible for rising above the situation (Ice T, 2005).

Political Involvement.   One way that street gangs are empowered is through their involvement in the political world. Political involvement has been a documented gang activity since the 1800s (see Asbury, 1928). This political activity continued into the 1900s. Thrasher (1927/1963) noted that "the political boss finds gangs, whether composed of boys or men above voting age, very useful in promoting the interests of his machine" (p. 313). In the 1960s, Chicago gangs were used by politicians to calm unruly residents and "[t]hey were used by police as an auxiliary force to maintain order" (Spergel, 1995, p. 121).

BOX 12–1: A Closer Look

Los Solidos is an example of a gang that has ties to the community. This primarily Puerto Rican gang originated in Hartford, Connecticut, in the early 1990s through a merger of existing gangs. Since this time, the gang has migrated to Massachusetts, Pennsylvania, New York, New Hampshire, and Maine. Members of Los Solidos believe that their gang formed "to provide street youth with protection from victimization by others gangs, and to help deal with the negative personal and social effects of poverty" (DiChiara and Chabot, 2003, p. 87). As such, Los Solidos specifies its vision as commitment to "short-term economic survival through drug sales, family support, community development, and eventual movement into the legitimate community" (DiChiara and Chabot, 2003, p. 82). This vision, with the exception of one goal, relies heavily on commitment to conventional society. This is exemplified in some of Los Solidos's activities. In the mid-1990s, Los Solidos organized a community cleanup day, and members attended planning meetings for a youth center. Patrons in the community worked with the gang to foster the group's positive nature. The gang is also able to act as an informal control agent in the community (DiChiara and Chabot, 2003).

Yablonsky (1962) suggests that gangs only engage in senseless violence against one another and that their behavior is not directed toward those who are responsible for the plight of the underclass. However, in some instances this behavior is changing. Williams (2004) states, "[t]hough we were often seen as social dynamite, I believe we were a perfect entity to be indoctrinated in cultural awareness and trained as disciplined soldiers for the Black struggle" (p. 80). This philosophy is at the heart and core of more recent gang activity. Currently, some gangs are used as a vehicle for social change and political awareness. Both active gangs and members and reformed gang members sometimes pursue this avenue. Some gangs are at early stages of political awareness, and they simultaneously engage in criminal behavior. Others are further along in their development and move away from active illegal activities (DiChiara and Chabot, 2003).

Street gangs are connected to politics in several ways. They are involved in both temporary and stable **exchange relationships** with political institutions (Jankowski, 1991). The gang-political integration can be subtle. For example, the existence of gangs provides politicians with a platform, and their presence helps to secure grant money for the community (Spergel, 1995). In simple ways, gangs organize voter registration drives, as evidenced by the Neta in Connecticut (Curtis, 2003) and the **21st Century Vote** campaign organized by the Black Gangster Disciples (Decker, Bynum, and Weisel, 1998). More direct relationships between gangs and politics are often found in cities that have a political machine (Jankowksi, 1991), such as the El Rukns' support for political candidates in Chicago (Spergel, 1995) and the election of an ex-gang member as an alderman in Chicago (Knox, 1994). The conflict of interest that arises in this "exchange" relationship makes enforcement of gang control policies difficult. Self-sufficient political involvement is less common and often fruitless. It is most often experienced during politically charged times, such as the 1960s (Spergel, 1995). **Resistance theory,** as discussed by Moore (1991), views the gangs as "potentially revolutionary organizations of youth that give voice to the frustrations of oppressed minorities" (p. 42). However, this does not seem to be the case in nonpolitical eras, and often "the end result is that the gangs do not change, nor does their resistance have much effect on their life circumstances" (Moore, 1991, p. 42).

There has been a resurgence of gang involvement in social and political mobilization. "[D]uring the last decade a number of 'street gangs' have developed political activities and ambitions among the members, and they have been engaging in a variety of community projects and protest movements" (Brotherton and Barrios, 2004, p. 328). During this time, some gangs have even changed their names to represent their new focus, such as Black P. Stone Nation to Black Peace Stone Nation, and Black Gangster Disciples (BGD) to Black Growth and Development (BGD). It may be that gangs have stable political organizers to mobilize the gang. In some cases, street activists serve this function (Martinez, 2003). The street activists are often recovered gang members, OG street activists, or gang member activists. Street activists are exposed to political activism and learn to organize in the prison setting. As previously discussed, for many gang members, prison is the first time they have been a part of an institution. This experience allows them to redirect street gang activities and move gangs toward social and political activities (Martinez, 2003).

> **BOX 12-2: Focus on Research**
>
> Brotherton and Barrios (2004) offer something different than researchers before them. Their study of New York's Almighty Latin King and Queen Nation (ALKQN) is chronicled in *The Almighty Latin King and Queen Nation: Street Politics and the Transformation of a New York City Gang*. Their study, which was conducted in the mid- to late 1990s, began by using participant observation methodology when Barrios's church was used for ALKQN meetings. The goal of their study was to document the ALKQN during its evolution into a social and political movement. After presenting the ALKQN with preliminary findings, the researchers turned to intensive interviewing as an additional data collection technique, which enabled them to explore in more detail the story of the ALKQN. At each step of the way, the researchers discussed the project with gang members, and they allowed gang members to give feedback about the research process. The members' involvement also included a high-ranking member's work as a research assistant and others working to recruit interviewees. The end result was "sixty-seven individual life history interviews covering a range of the group's membership" (p. 8), including variation in age, gender, and group involvement. Data were also collected from "a large archive of documents relating to the group's practices and history," which "provided a detailed historical and multileveled account of the group's transitional states of development while offering a rare insight into the lives and perspectives of both its rank-and-file and leading members" (p. 9).

There are many examples of the movement of street gangs toward more political and social organization. The New York Latin Kings under King Tone attempted to mobilize the gang toward improving social and economic conditions (Brotherton and Barrios, 2004). However, the Latin Kings were in their early stages of political metamorphosis, and they were still involved in illegal activities, which resulted in the conviction of King Tone and weakened leadership to continue the movement (see Brotherton and Barrios, 2004). This is different than the experiences of the Black Gangster Disciples (BGD). Under the leadership of imprisoned Larry Hoover, the gang attempted to redirect their efforts and become politically involved. Their "Black Growth and Development" era included the previously mentioned 21st Century Vote and political awareness campaigns (Decker, Bynum, and Weisel, 1998; Spergel, 1995).

CHAPTER SUMMARY

In summary, our definition and labeling of gangs has changed over time, although the underlying conditions by which they form have not. Theories that address issues of community disorganization, economic strain, and subculture formation are just as important in understanding gangs today as they were when they first originated. These macro-level dynamics provide a situation in which gangs emerge and some persist.

Over time, a continuum of gang structure has developed, with some gangs loosely structured and others evolving into more cohesive, well-organized entities. The rituals and delinquent behavior of gangs are connected to where the gang falls in the continuum. Just as there is variation in types of gangs, there is variation in gang membership. The difference in gang membership is evident in understanding individual motivations for joining a gang. It is also apparent in how well connected gang members are to the group, with some hard core and others only marginally involved. The world of gangs is further complicated by gender and race experiences and the increasing connections between prison and street gangs.

Understanding the structure of the gang, the distinctions in gang membership, gender and race dynamics, and connectedness to prison gangs is imperative in developing effective local prevention and intervention polices. Without informed policy, gangs will continue to exist and continue to organize. Some may turn their efforts toward social and political mobilization; others may become more enmeshed in a criminal environment.

In the end, the continued evolution of street gangs is only possible because there is a never-ending supply of potential gang members. At very young ages, our nation's children are making the choice to join gangs—a choice that increases the risk of negative lifetime consequences. Imagine an environment where joining a gang is a viable option. Now imagine an environment where it is not.

KEY TERMS

21st Century Vote   resistance theory
exchange relationships

QUESTIONS FOR REVIEW

1. What relationships do gangs have with their communities?

2. What does gang empowerment refer to?

3. Explain exchange relationships between gangs and politics.

4. How does resistance theory explain gang empowerment?

5. Why is it important to distinguish between the gang and the gang member?

DISCUSSION QUESTIONS

1. You have a crystal ball that allows you to see 10 years into the future. What does it tell you about gang activity?

2. What do you think is the most important knowledge about street gangs that everyone should have?

Bibliography

Abadinsky, Howard (2003). *Organized Crime*. Belmont, CA: Thompson-Wadsworth.

Akers, Ronald K. (1973). *Deviant Behavior: A Social Learning Approach*. Belmont, CA: Wadsworth.

Alonso, Alejandro A. (n.d.). Black Street Gangs in Los Angeles: A History. Retrieved February 20, 2006, from: www.streetgangs.com/history/hist01.html.

Alonso, Alejandro A. (1998). Urban Graffiti on the City Landscape. Paper presented at the Western Geography Regional Conference. San Diego State University. Retrieved November 5, 2006, from: www.streetgangs.com/academic/alonsograffiti.pdf.

Amato, Julie M., and Dewey G. Cornell (2003). How do youth claiming gang membership differ from youth who claim membership in another group, such as a crew, clique, posse, or mob? *Journal of Gang Research*, 4: 13–23.

American Correctional Association (1993). *Gangs in Correctional Facilities: A National Assessment, Final Report*. Washington, DC: U.S. Department of Justice, National Institute of Justice.

Anbinder, Taylor (2002). *Five Points: The 19th Century New York City Neighborhood That Invented Tap Dance, Stole Elections, and Became the World's Most Notorious Slum*. New York: Plume.

Anderson, James F., Willie Brooks Jr., Adam Langsam, and Laronistine Dyson (2002). The new female gang member: Anomaly or evolution. *Journal of Gang Research*, 10: 47–65.

Anderson, James F., Nancie J. Mangels, and Laronistine Dyson (2001). A gang by any other name is just a gang: Towards an expanded definition of gangs. *Journal of Gang Research*, 8: 19–34.

Armstrong, Troy L., Philmer Bluehouse, Alfred Dennison, Harmon Mason, Barbara Mendenhall, Daniel Wall, and James W. Zion (editors) (n.d.). Finding and Knowing the Gang *Nayee*. Field Initiated Gang Research Project: The Judicial Branch of the Navaho Nation. Retrieved March 1, 2006, from: www.csus.edu/ssis/cdcps/Zion.pdf.

Asbury, Herbert (1928). *The Gangs of New York: An Informal History of the Underworld*. New York: Thunder's Mouth Press.

Ball, Richard A., and G. David Curry (1995). The logic of definition in criminology: Purposes and methods for defining gangs. *Criminology*, 33: 225–45.

Battin-Pearson, Sara R., Terence P. Thornberry, J. David Hawkins, and Marvin D. Krohn (1998). *Gang Membership, Delinquent Peers, and Delinquent Behavior*. Washington, DC: U.S. Department of Justice, Office of Juvenile Justice and Delinquency Prevention.

Beiser, Vince (2000). Boyz on the Rez. *New Republic*, 223: 15–16.

Bernard, William (1949). *Jailbait*. New York: Greenberg.

Bjerregaard, Beth (2003). Antigang legislation and its potential impact: The promises and the pitfalls. *Criminal Justice Policy Review*, 14: 171–92.

Bjerregaard, Beth, and Alan J. Lizotte (1995). Gun ownership and gang membership. *Journal of Criminal Law and Criminology*, 86: 37–58.

Bjerregaard, Beth, and Carolyn A. Smith (1993). Gender differences in gang participation, delinquency, and substance use. *Journal of Quantitative Criminology*, 9: 329–55.

Bloch, Herbert, and Arthur Niederhoffer (1958). *The Gang: A Study in Adolescent Behavior*. New York: Philosophical Library.

Block, Carolyn R., and Richard Block (1993). *Street Gang Crime in Chicago*. Research in Brief. Washington, DC: U.S. Department of Justice, National Institute of Justice.

Bowker, Lee H., and Malcolm W. Klein (1983). The etiology of female juvenile delinquency and gang membership: A test of psychological and social structural explanations. *Adolescence*, 18: 739–51.

Braga, Anthony A., David M. Kennedy, and George E. Tita (2002). New Approaches to the Strategic Prevention of Gang and Group-Involved Violence. In C. Ronald Huff (Ed.), *Gangs in America III* (pp. 271–85). Newbury Park, CA: Sage.

Briscoe, Daren (May 2005). The new face of witness protection. *Newsweek*. Retrieved November 5, 2006, from: www.msnbc.msn.com/id/7613455/site/newsweek/.

Brotherton, David C., and Luis Barrios (2004). *The Almighty Latin King and Queen Nation: Street Politics and the Transformation of a New York City Gang*. New York: Columbia University Press.

Brotherton, David, and Camila Salazar-Atias (2003). Amor de Reina! The Pushes and Pulls of Group Membership among the Latin Queens. In Louis Kontos, David Brotherton, and Luis Barrios (Eds.), *Gangs and Society: Alternative Perspectives* (pp. 183–209). New York: Columbia University Press.

Brown, Waln K. (1977). Black female gangs in Philadelphia. *International Journal of Offender Therapy and Comparative Criminology*, 21: 221–28.

Bursik, Robert J. Jr., and Harold G. Grasmick (1993). *Neighborhoods and Crime: The Dimensions of Effective Community Control*. Lanham, MD: Lexington.

Bynum, Timothy S., and Sean P. Varano (2003). The Anti-Gang Initiative in Detroit: An Aggressive Enforcement Approach to Gangs. In Scott H. Decker (Ed.), *Policing Gangs and Youth Violence* (pp. 214–38). Belmont, CA: Thompson-Wadsworth.

California Department of Corrections and Rehabilitation (n.d.). Pelican Bay State Prison. Retrieved August 17, 2006, from: www.corr.ca.gov/visitors/fac_prison_pbsp.html.

Camp, George M., and Camille G. Camp (1985). *Prison Gangs: Their Extent, Nature and Impact on Prison*. Washington, DC: U.S. Department of Justice, Office of Legal Policy.

Campbell, Anne (1984). *The Girls in the Gang: A Report from New York City*. New York: B. Blackwell.

Campbell, Anne (1987). Self definition by rejection: The case of gang girls. *Social Problems*, 23: 451–66.

Campbell, Anne (1990). Female Participation in Gangs. In C. Ronald Huff (Ed.), *Gangs in America* (ed. 1, pp. 163–82). Newbury Park, CA: Sage.

Campbell, Anne (1999). Female Gang Members' Social Representation of Aggression. In Meda Chesney-Lind and John M. Hagedorn (Eds.), *Female Gangs in America: Essays on Girls, Gangs and Gender* (pp. 248–55). Chicago: Lakeview.

Campo-Flores, Arian (March 28, 2005). The most dangerous gang in America. *Newsweek*. Retrieved March 11, 2006, from: www.msnbc.msn.com/id/7244879/site/newsweek/.

Carlson, Peter M. (2001). Prison interventions: Evolving strategies to control security threat groups. *Corrections Management Quarterly*, 5: 10–22.

Castro, Alvi J. (2005). Mara Salvatrucha Street Gang: An International Criminal Enterprise with Roots in El Salvador's Civil War. Immigration and Customs Enforcement. Department of Homeland Security. Retrieved March 1, 2006, from: webzoom.freewebs.com/swnmia/ Mara.pdf.

Chesney-Lind, Meda (1993). Girls, gangs, and violence: Reinventing the liberated female crook. *Humanity and Society*, 17: 321–44.

Chesney-Lind, Meda, and John M. Hagedorn (1999). *Female Gangs in America: Essays on Girls, Gangs and Gender*. Chicago: Lakeview.

Chesney-Lind, Meda, Randall G. Sheldon, and Karen A. Joe (1996). Girls, Delinquency, and Gang Membership. In Ronald C. Huff (Ed.), *Gangs in America* (ed. 2, pp. 185–204). Newbury Park, CA: Sage.

Chin, Ko-Lin (1990). Chinese Gangs and Extortion. In C. Ronald Huff (Ed.), *Gangs in America* (ed. 1, pp. 129–45). Newbury Park, CA: Sage.

Chin, Ko-Lin (1996). *Chinatown Gangs: Extortion, Enterprise, and Ethnicity.* New York: Oxford University Press.

Chin, Ko-Lin, Jeffrey Fagan, and Robert J. Kelly (1992). Patterns of Chinese gang extortion. *Justice Quarterly*, 9: 625–46.

Clark, Stephen (August 6, 2006). An echo of gang violence in Highland Park. *Los Angeles Times.*

Cloward, Richard A., and Lloyd E. Ohlin (1960). *Delinquency and Opportunity: A Theory of Delinquent Gangs.* New York: Free Press.

Cohen, Albert K. (1955). *Delinquent Boys: The Culture of the Gang.* Glencoe, IL: Free Press.

Cohen, Albert K. (1990). Foreword and Overview. In C. Ronald Huff (Ed.), *Gangs in America* (ed. 1, pp. 7–21). Newbury Park, CA: Sage.

Cornish, Derek B., and Ronald V. Clarke (Eds.) (1986). *The Reasoning Criminal.* New York: Springer-Verlag.

Curry, G. David (1998). Female gang involvement. *Journal of Research on Crime and Delinquency*, 35: 100–118.

Curry, G. David (1999). Responding to Female Gang Involvement. In Meda Chesney-Lind and John M. Hagedorn (Eds.), *Female Gangs in America: Essays on Girls, Gangs and Gender* (pp. 131–53). Chicago: Lakeview.

Curry, G. David (2000). Self-reported gang involvement and officially recorded delinquency. *Criminology*, 38: 100–118.

Curry, G. David, Richard A. Ball, and Robert J. Fox (1994). *Gang Crime and Law Enforcement Record Keeping.* Research in Brief. Washington, DC: U.S. Department of Justice, National Institute of Justice.

Curry, G. David, and Scott H. Decker (2003). *Confronting Gangs: Crime and Community*, ed. 2. Los Angeles: Roxbury.

Curry, G. David, Scott H. Decker, and Arlen Egley Jr. (2002). Gang involvement and delinquency in a middle school population. *Justice Quarterly*, 19: 275–292.

Curry, G. David, Cheryl L. Maxson, and James C. Howell (2001). *Youth Gang Homicides in the 1990s.* OJJDP Fact Sheet, March 2001 #03. Washington, DC: U.S. Department of Justice, Office of Justice Programs, Office of Juvenile Justice and Delinquency Prevention.

Curry, G. David, and Irving A. Spergel (1988). Gang homicide, delinquency, and community. *Criminology*, 26: 381–405.

Curry, G. David, and Irving A. Spergel (1992). Gang involvement and delinquency among Hispanic and African-American males. *Journal of Research in Crime and Delinquency*, 29: 273–91.

Curtis, Ric (2003). The Negligible Role of Gangs in Drug Distribution in New York City in the 1990s. In Louis Kontos, David Brotherton, and Luis Barrios (Eds.), *Gangs and Society: Alternative Perspectives* (pp. 41–61). New York: Columbia University Press.

Decker, Scott (1996). Gangs and violence: The expressive character of collective involvement. *Justice Quarterly*, 11: 231–50.

Decker, Scott H. (2000). Legitimating drug use: A note on the impact of gang membership and drug sales on the use of illicit drugs. *Justice Quarterly*, 17: 393–410.

Decker, Scott H. (2003). Policing Gangs and Youth Violence: Where Do We Stand, Where Do We Go from Here? In Scott H. Decker (Ed.), *Policing Gangs and Youth Violence* (pp. 287–93). Belmont, CA: Thompson-Wadsworth.

Decker, Scott H., Tim Bynum, and Deborah Weisel (1998). A tale of two cities: Gangs as organized crime groups. *Justice Quarterly*, 15: 395–425.

Decker, Scott H., and Janet L. Lauritsen (2002). Leaving the Gang. In C. Ronald Huff (Ed.), *Gangs in America III* (pp. 51–67). Newbury Park, CA: Sage.

Decker, Scott H., and Barrik Van Winkle (1996). *Life in the Gang: Family, Friends, and Violence.* New York: Cambridge University Press.

Department of Justice (February 15, 2006). Press Release: Initiative to Combat Gangs. Department of Justice. Retrieved on March 2, 2006, from: www.usdoj.gov/opa/pr/2006/February/06_opa_082.html.

Deschenes, Elizabeth Piper, and Finn-Aage Esbensen (1999). Violence and gangs: Gender differences in perceptions and behavior. *Journal of Quantitative Criminology*, 15: 63–96.

DiChiara, Albert, and Russell Chabot (2003). Gangs and the Contemporary Urban Struggle: An Unappreciated Aspect of Gangs. In Louis Kontos, David Brotherton, and Luis Barrios (Eds.), *Gangs and Society: Alternative Perspectives* (pp. 77–94). New York: Columbia University Press.

Dukes, Richard L., Ruben O. Martinez, and Judith A. Stein (1997). Precursors and consequences of membership in youth gangs. *Youth and Society*, 29: 139–65.

Dukes, Richard L., and Jennifer Valentine (1998). Gang membership and bias against young people who break the law. *Social Science Journal*, 35: 347–61.

East Coast Gang Investigators Association (n.d.a.). Almighty Latin King and Queen Nation (a.k.a.: Latin Kings). Retrieved March 2, 2006, from: www.gripe4rkids.org/LKhis.html.

East Coast Gang Investigators Association (n.d.b.). Bloods/United Blood Nation (East Coast Blood Nation). Retrieved March 2, 2006, from: www.gripe4rkids.org/BLhis.html.

Eckhart, Dan (2001). Civil actions related to prison gangs: A survey of federal cases. *Corrections Management Quarterly*, 5: 59–64.

Egley, Arlen Jr. (2005). *Highlights of the 2002–2003 National Youth Gang Surveys.* Washington, DC: U.S. Department of Justice, Office of Juvenile Justice and Delinquency Prevention.

Egley, Arlen Jr., James C. Howell, and Aline K. Major (2006). *National Youth Gang Survey 1999–2001.* Washington, DC: U.S. Department of Justice, Office of Juvenile Justice and Delinquency Prevention.

Egley, Arlen Jr., and Aline K. Major (2004). *Highlights of the 2002 National Youth Gang Survey.* Washington, DC: U.S. Department of Justice, Office of Juvenile Justice and Delinquency Prevention.

Esbensen, Finn-Aage (2001). The National Evaluation of the Gang Resistance Education and Training (G.R.E.A.T.) Program. In Jody Miller, Cheryl L. Maxson, and Malcolm W. Klein (Eds.), *The Modern Gang Reader* (ed. 2, pp. 289–302). Los Angeles: Roxbury.

Esbensen, Finn-Aage, Elizabeth Piper Deschenes, and L. Thomas Winfree Jr. (1999). Differences between gang girls and gang boys: Results from a multisite survey. *Youth and Society*, 31: 27–53.

Esbensen, Finn-Aage, Adrienne Freng, Terrance J. Taylor, Dana Peterson, and D. Wayne Osgood (2002). National Evaluation of the Gang Resistance Education and Training Program (G.R.E.A.T.). In *Responding to Gangs: Evaluation and Research* (pp. 139–67). Washington, DC: U.S. Department of Justice, National Institute of Justice.

Esbensen, Finn-Aage, and David Huizinga (1993). Gangs, drugs, and delinquency in a survey of urban youth. *Criminology*, 31: 565–89.

Esbensen, Finn-Aage, David Huizinga, and Anne W. Weiher (1993). Gang and non-gang youth: Differences in explanatory factors. *Journal of Contemporary Criminal Justice*, 9: 94–116.

Esbensen, Finn-Aage, Dana Peterson, Adrienne Freng, and Terrance J. Taylor (2002). Initiation of Drug Use, Drug Sales, and Violent Offending among a Sample of Gang and Nongang Youth. In C. Ronald Huff (Ed.), *Gangs in America III* (pp. 37–50). Thousand Oaks, CA: Sage.

Esbensen, Finn-Aage, Dana Peterson, Terrance J. Taylor, Adrienne Freng, and D. Wayne Osgood (2004). Gang Prevention: A Case Study of a Preliminary Prevention Program. In Finn-Aage Esbensen, Stephen G. Tibbetts, and Larry Gaines (Eds.), *American Youth Gangs at the Millennium* (pp. 351–74). Long Grove, IL: Waveland.

Esbensen, Finn-Aage, and L. Thomas Winfree Jr. (1998). Race and gender differences between gang and nongang youths: Results from a multisite survey. *Justice Quarterly*, 15: 505–26.

Esbensen, Finn-Aage, L. Thomas Winfree Jr., Ni He, and Terrance J. Taylor (2001). Youth gangs and definitional issues: When is a gang a gang, and why does it matter? *Crime and Delinquency*, 47: 105–30.

Evans, William P., Carla Fitzgerald, Dan Weigel, and Sarah Chvilicek (1999). Are rural gangs similar to their urban peers? Implications for rural communities. *Youth and Society*, 30: 267–282.

Fagan, Jeffrey (1989). The social organization of drug use and drug dealing among urban gangs. *Criminology*, 27: 633–69.

Fagan, Jeffrey (1990). Social Processes of Delinquency and Drug Use among Urban Gangs. In Ronald C. Huff (Ed.), *Gangs in America*, (ed. 1, pp. 183–219). Newbury Park, CA: Sage.

Fang, Irving, and Kristina Ross (1996). The Media History Project. Retrieved August 30, 2005, from: www.mediahistory.umn.edu/time/century.html.

Fearn, Noelle E., Scott H. Decker, and G. David Curry (2001). Public Policy Responses to Gangs: Evaluating the Outcomes. In Jody Miller, Cheryl L. Maxson, and Malcolm W. Klein (Eds.), *The Modern Gang Reader* (ed. 2, pp. 330–43). Los Angeles: Roxbury.

Fishman, Laura T. (1995). The Vice Queens: An Ethnographic Study of Black Female Gang Behavior. In Malcolm W. Klein, Cheryl L. Maxson, and Jody Miller (Eds.), *The Modern Gang Reader* (pp. 83–92). Los Angeles: Roxbury.

Fishman, Laura T. (1999). Black Female Gang Behavior. In Meda Chesney-Lind and John M. Hagedorn (Eds.), *Female Gangs in America: Essays on Girls, Gangs and Gender* (pp. 64–84). Chicago: Lakeview.

Fleisher, Mark S., and Scott H. Decker (2001a). An overview of the challenge of prison gangs. *Corrections Management Quarterly*, 5: 1–9.

Fleisher, Mark S., and Scott H. Decker (2001b). Going home, staying home: Integrating prison gang members into the community. *Corrections Management Quarterly*, 5: 65–77.

Florida Department of Corrections (n.d.). Gang and Security Threat Group Awareness. Retrieved August 17, 2006, from: www.dc.state.fl.us/pub/gangs/index.html.

Fong, Robert S. (1990). The organizational structure of prison gangs: Texas case study. *Federal Probation*, 54: 36–43.

Fong, Robert S., and Salvador Buentello (1991). The detection of prison gang development: An empirical assessment. *Federal Probation*, 55: 66–69.

Fong, Robert S., and Ronald E. Vogel (1995). A comparative analysis of prison gang members, security threat groups inmates and general population prisoners in the Texas Department of Corrections. *Journal of Gang Research*, 2: 1–12.

Fortune, Sandra (2004). Prison gang leadership: Traits identified by prison gangsters. *Journal of Gang Research*, 11: 25–46.

Fremon, Celeste (1995). G-Dog and the Homeboys. In Malcolm W. Klein, Cheryl L. Maxson, and Jody Miller (Eds.), *The Modern Gang Reader* (pp. 276–85). Los Angeles: Roxbury.

Freng, Adrienne, and L. Thomas Winfree Jr. (2004). Exploring Race and Ethnic Differences in a Sample of Middle School Gang Members. In Finn-Aage Esbensen, Stephen G. Tibbetts, and Larry Gaines (Eds.), *American Youth Gangs at the Millennium* (pp. 142–62). Long Grove, IL: Waveland.

Gaes, G. G., Susan Wallace, Evan Gilman, Jody Klein-Saffran, and Sharon Suppa (2002). The influence of prison gang affiliation on violence and other prison misconduct. *The Prison Journal*, 82: 359–85.

Gangresearch.net (n.d.). Crips' and Bloods' Plan for the Reconstruction of Los Angeles. Retrieved March 10, 2006, from: www.gangresearch.net/GangResearch/Policy/cripsbloodsplan.html.

Gaubatz, Derek L. (2005). RLUIPA at four: Evaluating the success and constitutionality of RLUIPA's prisoner provisions. *Harvard Journal of Law and Public Policy*, 28: 501–608.

Geis, Gilbert (2002). Gangs Up on Gangs: Anti-Loitering and Public Nuisance Laws. In C. Ronald Huff (Ed.), *Gangs in America III* (pp. 257–70). Thousand Oaks, CA: Sage.

Geniella, Mike (April 22, 2001). Inside Pelican Bay. *The Santa Rosa Press Democrat*.

Giordano, Peggy (1978). Research note: Girls, guys and gangs: The changing social context of female delinquency. *Journal of Criminal Law and Criminology*, 69: 126.

Goldstein, Arnold P. (1991). *Delinquent Gangs: A Psychological Perspective*. Champaign, IL: Research Press.

Gordon, Rachel A., Benjamin B. Lahey, Eriko Kawai, Rolf Loeber, Magda Stouthamer-Loeber, and David P. Farrington (2004). Antisocial behavior and youth gang membership: Selection and socialization. *Criminology*, 42: 55–87.

Gottfredson, Gary D., and Denise C. Gottfredson (2001). Summary. In Gary D. Gottfredson and Denise C. Gottfredson, *Gang Problems and Gang Programs in a National Sample of Schools* (pp. ii–ix). Elliott City, MD: Gottfredson Associates.

Gottfredson, Michael R., and Travis Hirschi (1990). *A General Theory of Crime*. Stanford, CA: Stanford University Press.

Grascia, Andrew M. (2004). Gang violence: Mara Salvatrucha—forever Salvador. *Journal of Gang Research*, 11: 29–36.

Greene, Jack (2003). Gangs, Community Policing, and Problem-Solving. In Scott H. Decker (Ed.), *Policing Gangs and Violence* (pp. 3–16). Belmont, CA: Thompson-Wadsworth.

Greene, Jack R. (2004). Police Youth Violence Interventions: Lessons to Improve Effectiveness. In Finn-Aage Esbensen, Stephen G. Tibbetts, and Larry Gaines (Eds.), *American Youth Gangs at the Millennium* (pp. 333–50). Long Grove, IL: Waveland.

Grennan, Sean, and Marjie T. Britz (2006). *Organized Crime: A Worldwide Perspective*. Upper Saddle River, NJ: Prentice Hall.

Grogger, Jeffrey (2005). What we know about gang injunctions. *Criminology and Public Policy*, 4: 637–42.

Hagan, John (1993). The social embeddedness of crime and unemployment. *Criminology*, 31: 465–91.

Hagedorn, John M. (1988). *People and Folks: Gangs, Crime and the Underclass in a Rustbelt City*. Chicago: Lakeview.

Hagedorn, John M. (1991). Gangs, neighborhoods, and public policy. *Social Problems*, 38: 529–42.

Hagedorn, John M. (1994). Homeboys, dope fiends, legits, and new jacks. *Criminology*, 32: 197–219.

Hagedorn, John M., and Mary L. Devitt (1999). Fighting Female: The Social Construction of Female Gangs. In Meda Chesney-Lind and John M. Hagedorn (Eds.), *Female Gangs in America: Essays on Girls, Gangs and Gender* (pp. 277–94). Chicago: Lakeview.

Hamm, Mark (1993). *American Skinheads*. Westport, CT: Greenwood.

Harris, Mary G. (1994). Cholas, Mexican-American girls, and gangs. *Sex Roles*, 30: 289–301.

Hart, Steve, and David Brotherton (2003). Snapshots of a Movement: The New York Latin Kings and Queens 1996–99. In Louis Kontos, David Brotherton, and Luis Barrios (Eds.), *Gangs and Society: Alternative Perspectives* (pp. 314–36). New York: Columbia University Press.

Henderson, Eric, Stephen J. Kunitz, and Jerrold E. Levy (1999). The origins of Navajo youth gangs. *The American Indian Culture and Research Journal*, 23: 243–64.

Hill, Karl G., James C. Howell, J. David Hawkins, and Sara R. Battin-Pearson (1999). Childhood risk factors for adolescent gang membership: Results from the Seattle Social Development Project. *Journal of Research in Crime and Delinquency*, 36: 300–322.

Hirschi, Travis (1969). *Causes of Delinquency*. Berkeley: University of California Press.

Homeboy Industries (n.d.). Father Greg Boyle, S.J. Retrieved March 12, 2006, from: www.homeboy-industries.org/father_gregg.php.

Hope, Trina L., and Kelly R. Damphousse (2002). Applying self-control theory to gang membership in a nonurban setting. *Journal of Gang Research*, 9: 41–61.

House of Umoja (n.d.). House of Umoja. Retrieved March 12, 2006, from: www.houseofumoja.org.

Howell, James C. (1998a). *Youth Gangs: An Overview*. Washington, DC: U.S. Department of Justice, Office of Juvenile Justice and Delinquency Prevention.

Howell, James C. (1998b). Promising Programs for Youth Gang Violence Prevention and Intervention. In Rolf Loeber and David P. Farrington (Eds.), *Serious and Violent Juvenile Offenders: Risk Factors and Successful Interventions* (pp. 284–312). Thousand Oaks, CA: Sage.

Howell, James C. (1999). Youth gang homicides: A literature review. *Crime and Delinquency*, 45: 208–41.

Howell, James C. (2000). *Youth Gang Programs and Strategies*. Washington DC: U.S. Department of Justice, Office of Juvenile Justice and Delinquency Prevention.

Howell, James C., and Scott H. Decker (1999). *The Youth Gangs, Drugs, and Violence Connection*. Juvenile Justice Bulletin. Washington DC: U.S. Department of Justice, Office of Juvenile Justice and Delinquency Prevention.

Howell, James C., and Arlen Egley Jr. (n.d.). Frequently Asked Questions Regarding Gangs. National Youth Gang Center. Retrieved February 28, 2006, from: www.iir.com/nygc/faq.htm#q1.

Howell, James C., and Arlen Egley Jr. (2005). *Gangs in Small Towns and Rural Counties*. NYGC Bulletin, No. 1. Washington, DC: U.S. Department of Justice, Office of Juvenile Justice and Delinquency Prevention.

Howell, James C., and Debra K. Gleason (1999). *Youth Gang Drug Trafficking*. Washington, DC: U.S. Department of Justice, Office of Juvenile Justice and Delinquency Prevention.

Horowitz, Ruth (1983). *Honor and the American Dream: Culture and Identity in a Chicano Community*. New Brunswick, NJ: Rutgers University Press.

Horowitz, Ruth (1990). Sociological Perspectives on Gangs: Conflicting Definitions and Concepts. In C. Ronald Huff (Ed.), *Gangs in America* (ed. 1, pp. 37–54). Newbury Park, CA: Sage.

Huff, C. Ronald (1989). Youth gangs and public policy. *Crime and Delinquency*, 35: 524–37.

Huff, C. Ronald (1990). Denial, Overreaction, and Misidentification: A Postscript on Public Policy. In C. Ronald Huff (Ed.), *Gangs in America* (ed. 1, pp. 310–17). Newbury Park, CA: Sage.

Huff, C. Ronald (1998). *Comparing the Criminal Behavior of Youth Gangs and At-Risk Youths*. Research in Brief. Washington, DC: U.S. Department of Justice, National Institute of Justice.

Huff, C. Ronald (2002). Gangs and Public Policy: Prevention, Intervention, and Suppression. In C. Ronald Huff (Ed.), *Gangs in America III* (pp. 287–94). Thousand Oaks, CA: Sage.

Huff, C. Ronald (2004). Youth Violence: Prevention, Intervention, and Social Policy. In Finn-Aage Esbensen, Stephen G. Tibbetts, and Larry Gaines (Eds.), *American Youth Gangs at the Millennium* (pp. 323–32). Long Grove, IL: Waveland.

Hughes, Lorine A., and James F. Short (2005). Disputes involving youth street gang members: Microsocial contexts. *Criminology*, 43: 43–76.

Hunt, Geoffrey, Kathleen MacKenzie, and Karen Joe-Laidler (2000). "I'm Calling My Mom": The meaning of family and kinship among homegirls. *Justice Quarterly*, 17: 1–31.

Hunt, Geoffrey and Karen Joe Laidler (2001). Alcohol and violence in the lives of gang members. *Alcohol Research & Health*, 25: 66–71.

Ice T (1995). The Killing Fields. In Malcolm W. Klein, Cheryl L. Maxson, and Jody Miller (Eds.), *The Modern Gang Reader* (pp. 147–53). Los Angeles: Roxbury.

Ice T (2005). Foreword. In Colton Simpson, *Inside the Crips: Life inside L.A.'s Most Notorious Gang* (pp. xv–xxiii). New York: St. Martin's Press.

Ice T with Heidi Sigmund (1994). *The Ice Opinion*. New York: St. Martin's Press.

Institute for Intergovernmental Research (2000). Analysis of Gang-related Legislation. National Youth Gang Center. Retrieved March 3, 2006, from: www.iir.com/nygc/gang-legis/analysis.htm.

Institute for Intergovernmental Research (2002). Gang-related Legislation by State. National Youth Gang Center. Retrieved February 28, 2006, from: www.iir.com/nygc/gang-legis/.

The Insurgent (2006). White Aryan Resistance. Retrieved August 28, 2006, from www.resist.com.

Jackson, Mary S., and Elizabeth Gail Sharpe (1997). Prison gang research: Preliminary findings in Eastern North Carolina. *Journal of Gang Research*, 5: 1–7.

Jackson, Robert K., and Wesley D. McBride (1992). *Understanding Street Gangs*. Placerville, CA: Copperhouse.

Jacobs, James B. (2001). Focusing on prison gangs. *Corrections Management Quarterly*, 5: vi–vii.

Jankowski, Martin Sanchez (1991). *Islands in the Street: Gangs and American Urban Society*. Berkeley and Los Angeles: University of California Press.

Jensen, Gary F. (1996). Defiance and gang identity: Quantitative tests of qualitative hypotheses. *Journal of Gang Research*, 3: 13–29.

Joe, Karen A. (1994a). The new criminal conspiracy? Asian gangs and organized crime in San Francisco. *Journal of Research in Crime and Delinquency*, 31: 390–415.

Joe, Karen (1994b). Myths and realities of Asian gangs on the West Coast. *Humanity and Society*, 18: 3–18.

Joe, Karen A., and Meda Chesney-Lind (1995). "Just Every Mother's Angel": An analysis of gender and ethnic variations in youth gang membership. *Gender and Society*, 9: 408–31.

Joseph, Janice, and Dorothy Taylor (2003). Native-American youths and gangs. *Journal of Gang Research*, 10: 45–54.

Kassel, Phillip (2003). The Gang Crackdown in the Prisons of Massachusetts: Arbitrary and Harsh Treatment Can Only Make Matters Worse. In Louis Kontos, David Brotherton, and Luis Barrios (Eds.), *Gangs and Society: Alternative Perspectives* (pp. 228–52). New York: Columbia University Press.

Katz, Charles M., Vincent J. Webb, and Todd A. Armstrong (2003). Fear of gangs: A test of alternative theoretical models. *Justice Quarterly*, 20: 95.

Kennedy, David (1998). Pulling levers: Getting deterrence right. *National Institute of Justice Journal*, 236: 2–8.

Kent, Douglas R., and Peggy Smith (2001). The Tri-Agency Resources Gang Enforcement Team: A Selective Approach to Reduce Gang Crime. In Jody Miller, Cheryl L. Maxson, and Malcolm W. Klein (Eds.), *The Modern Gang Reader* (ed. 2, pp. 303–8). Los Angeles: Roxbury.

Khoury, Kathy (1998). Fighting back against Indian gangs. *Christian Science Monitor*, 90: 4.

Kirk, Michael, and Peter J. Boyer (2001). L.A.P.D. Blues. *PBS Frontline*. Retrieved March 12, 2006, from: www.pbs.org/wgbh/pages/frontline/shows/lapd/bare.html.

Klein, Malcolm (1971). *Street Gangs and Street Workers*. Englewood Cliffs, NJ: Prentice-Hall.

Klein, Malcolm W. (1995). *The American Street Gang: Its Nature, Prevalence, and Control*. New York: Oxford University Press.

Klein, Malcolm W. (2002). Street Gangs: A Cross-national Perspective. In C. Ronald Huff (Ed.), *Gangs in America III* (pp. 237–54). Thousand Oaks, CA: Sage.

Klein, Malcolm W. (2005). The value of comparisons in street gang research. *Journal of Contemporary Criminal Justice*, 2: 135–152.

Klein, Malcolm, Cheryl L. Mexson, and Lea C. Cunningham (1991). Crack, street gangs, and violence. *Criminology*, 29: 623–650.

Knowgangs.com (n.d.). Gang Resources. Retrieved March 10, 2006, from www.knowgangs.com/gang_resources/menu_001.htm.

Knox, George W. (1994). *An Introduction to Gangs*. Bristol, IN: Wyndham Hall Press.

Knox, George W. (2000a). Gang Profile: The Latin Kings. Retrieved March 10, 2006, from: www.ngcrc.com/ngcrc/page15.htm.

Knox, George W. (2000b). A national assessment of gangs and security threat groups (STGs) in adult correctional institutions: Results of the 1999 Adult Corrections Survey. *Journal of Gang Research*, 7: 1–45.

Knox, George W. (2001a). Gang profile update: The Black P. Stone Nation. *Journal of Gang Research*, 9: 53–76.

Knox, George W. (2001b). The Gangster Disciples: A Gang Profile. Retrieved March 10, 2006, from: www.ngcrc.com/ngcrc/page13.htm.

Knox, George W. (2001c). Female Gang Members and the Rights of Children. Retrieved November 5, 2006, from: www.ngcrc.com/ngcrc/page16.htm.

Knox, George W. (2004a). Females and gangs: Sexual violence, prostitutions, and exploitation. *Journal of Gang Research*, 11: 1–15.

Knox, George W. (2004b). The problem of gangs and security threat groups (STG's) in American prisons today: A special NGCRC report. *Journal of Gang Research*, 12: 1–76.

Knox, Mike. (1995). *Gangsta in the House*. Troy, MI: Momentum Books.

Korem, Dan (1994). *Suburban Gangs: The Affluent Rebels*. Richardson, TX: International Focus Press.

Kotlowitz, Alex (1991). *There Are No Children Here: The Story of Two Boys Growing Up in the Other America*. New York: Anchor Books.

Kreinert, Jessie L., and Mark S. Fleisher (2001). Gang members as a proxy for social deficiencies: A study of Nebraska inmates. *Corrections Management Quarterly*, 5: 47–58.

Lahey, Benjamin B., Rachel A. Gordon, Rolf Loeber, Magda Stouthamer-Loeber, and David P. Farrington (1999). Boys who join gangs: A prospective study of predictors of first gang entry. *Journal of Abnormal Child Psychology*, 27: 261–76.

Laidler, Karen Joe, and Geoffrey Hunt (2001). Accomplishing femininity among the girls in the gang. *The British Journal of Criminology*, 41: 656–78.

Lane, Jodi (2002). Fear of gang crime: A qualitative examination of the four perspectives. *Journal of Research in Crime and Delinquency*, 39: 437–73.

Lane, Jodi, and James W. Meeker (2000). Subcultural diversity and the fear of crime and gangs. *Crime and Delinquency*, 46: 497–522.

Lane, Jodi, and James W. Meeker (2004). Social disorganization perceptions, fear of gang crime, and behavioral precautions among Whites, Latinos, and Vietnamese. *Journal of Criminal Justice*, 32: 49.

Laskey, John A. (1996). Gang migration: The familial gang transplant phenomenon. *Journal of Gang Research*, 3:1–15.

Lasley, James (1998). *"Designing Out" Gang Homicides and Street Assaults.* Research in Brief. Washington, DC: U.S. Department of Justice, National Institute of Justice.

The Latin Kings Speak (2002, April 1). Retrieved March 6, 2006, from: www.uic.edu/orgs/kbc/latinkings/Reyx.html.

Lauderback, David, Joy Hansen, and Daniel Waldorf (1992). Sisters are doing' it for themselves: A Black female gang in San Francisco. *The Gang Journal*, 1: 57–72.

LeBlanc, Marc and Nadine Lanctot (1998). Social and psychological characteristics of gang members according to the gang structure and its subcultural and ethnic makeup. *Journal of Gang Research*, 5: 15–28.

Lee, Denny (2003, May 11). Years of the dragons. *New York Times.*

Library of Congress (2005). The African Mosaic. Retrieved August 30, 2005, from: www.loc.gov/exhibits/african/afam008.html.

Lizotte, Alan J., Marvin D. Krohn, James C. Howell, Kimberly Tobin, Gregory J. Howard (2000). Factors influencing gun carrying among young urban males over the adolescent-young adult life course. *Criminology*, 38: 811–34.

Loftin, Colin (1984). Assaultive violence as a contagious process. *Bulletin of the New York Academy of Medicine*, 62: 550–55.

Lopez, Robert J., Rich Connell, and Chris Kraul (2005, October 30). MS-13: An international franchise: Gang uses deportation to its advantage to flourish in U.S. *Los Angeles Times.*

L.A. City Attorney Gang Prosecution Section (2001). Civil Gang Abatement: A Community Based Policing Tool of the Office of the Los Angeles City Attorney. In Jody Miller, Cheryl L. Maxson, and Malcolm W. Klein (Eds.), *The Modern Gang Reader* (ed. 2, pp. 320–29). Los Angeles: Roxbury.

Los Angeles Police Department (n.d.). How are gangs identified. Retrieved November 5, 2006, from: www.lapdonline.org/search_results/content_basic_view/23468.

Lurigio, Arthur J., James A. Schwartz, and Jean Chang (1998). A descriptive and comparative analysis of female gang members. *Journal of Gang Research*, 5: 23–33.

Lynskey, Dana Peterson, L. Thomas Winfree Jr., Finn-Aage Esbensen, and Dennis L. Clason (2000). Linking gender, minority group status and family matters to self-control theory: A multivariate analysis of key self-control concepts in youth-gang context. *Juvenile and Family Court Journal*, 51: 1–19.

Major, Aline K., and Arlen Egley Jr. (2002). *2000 Survey of Youth Gangs in Indian Country.* NYGC Fact Sheet. Washington, DC: U.S. Department of Justice, Office of Juvenile Justice and Delinquency Prevention.

Major, Aline K., Arlen Egley Jr., James C. Howell, Barbara Mendenhall, and Troy Armstrong (2004). *Youth Gangs in Indian Country.* Juvenile Justice Bulletin. Washington, DC: U.S. Department of Justice, Office of Juvenile Justice and Delinquency Prevention.

Mara Salvatrucha (n.d.). Retrieved February 10, 2006, from: www.knowgangs.com/gang_resources/ms/.

Mark, Gregory Yee (1997). Oakland Chinatown's first youth gang: The Suey Sing boys. *Free Inquiry in Creative Sociology*, 25: 41–50.

Martinez, Juan Francisco Esteva (2003). Urban Street Activists: Gang and Community Efforts to Bring Peace and Justice to Los Angeles Neighborhoods. In Louis Kontos, David Brotherton, and Luis Barrios (Eds.), *Gangs and Society: Alternative Perspectives* (pp. 95–115). New York: Columbia University Press.

Martinez, Liz (2005). Gangs in Indian country. *Law Enforcement Technology*, 32: 20, 22–27.

Massachusetts Department of Correction (n.d.). Security Threat Group Information. Retrieved February 28, 2006, from: www.mass.gov/?pageID=eopsterminal&&L=4&L0=Home&L1=Law+Enforcement+%26+Criminal+Justice&L2=Prisons&L3=Security+Threat+Group+Information&sid=Eeops&b=terminalcontent&f=doc_securitythreat_stprocess&csid=Eeops.

Mateu-Gelabert, Pedro (2002). Dreams, gangs, and guns: The interplay between adolescent violence and immigration in a New York City neighborhood. Vera Institute of Justice. National Development Research Institute, Inc.

Maxson, Cheryl L. (1995). *Street Gangs and Drug Sales in Two Suburban Cities*. Research in Brief. Washington, DC: U.S. Department of Justice, National Institute of Justice.

Maxson, Cheryl L. (1998). *Gang Membership on the Move*. Juvenile Justice Bulletin. Washington DC: U.S. Department of Justice, Office of Juvenile Justice and Delinquency Prevention.

Maxson, Cheryl L. (2004). Civil Gang Injunctions: The Ambiguous Case of the National Migration of Gang Enforcement Strategy. In Finn-Aage Esbensen, Stephen G. Tibbetts, and Larry Gaines (Eds.), *American Youth Gangs at the Millennium* (pp. 375–89). Long Grove, IL: Waveland.

Maxson, Cheryl L., Karen M. Hennigan, and David C. Sloane (2003). For the Sake of the Neighborhood? In Scott H. Decker (Ed.), *Policing Gangs and Youth Violence* (pp. 239–66). Belmont, CA: Thompson-Wadsworth.

Maxson, Cheryl L., Karen M. Hennigan, and David C. Sloane (2005). "It's getting crazy out there": Can a civil gang injunction change a community? *Criminology and Public Policy*, 4: 577–606.

Maxson, Cheryl L., and Malcolm W. Klein (1990). Street Gang Violence: Twice as Great or Half as Great? In Ronald C. Huff (Ed.), *Gangs in America* (ed. 1, pp. 71–102). Newbury Park, CA: Sage.

Maxson, Cheryl L., and Malcolm W. Klein (1996). Defining Gang Homicide: An Updated Look at Member and Motive Approaches. In Ronald C. Huff (Ed.). *Gangs in America* (ed. 2, pp. 3–20). Newbury Park, CA: Sage.

Maxson, Cheryl L., and Monica L. Whitlock (2002). Joining the Gang: Gender Differences in Risk Factors for Gang Membership. In C. Ronald Huff (Ed.), *Gangs in America III* (pp. 19–35). Thousand Oaks, CA: Sage.

McCorkle, Richard C., and Terance D. Meithe (2002). *Panic: The Social Construction of the Street Gang*. Upper Saddle River, NJ: Prentice Hall.

McCurrie, Thomas F. (1999). Asian gangs: A research note. *Journal of Gang Research*, 6: 47–52.

McDevitt, Jack, Anthony A. Braga, Dana Nurge, and Michael Buerger (2003). Boston's Youth Violence Prevention Program: A Comprehensive Community-wide Approach. In Scott H. Decker (Ed.), *Policing Gangs and Youth Violence* (pp. 53–76). Belmont, CA: Thompson-Wadsworth.

McDonald, Kevin (2003). Marginal Youth, Personal Identity, and the Contemporary Gang: Reconstructing the Social World? In Louis Kontos, David Brotherton, and Luis Barrios (Eds.), *Gangs and Society: Alternative Perspectives* (pp. 63–74). New York: Columbia University Press.

McEwen, Tom (1995). *National Assessment Program: 1994 Survey Results*. NIJ Research in Brief. Washington, DC: U.S. Department of Justice, National Institute of Justice.

McGloin, Jean Marie (2005). Policy and intervention considerations of a network analysis of street gangs. *Criminology and Public Policy*, 4: 607–36.

McNulty, Thomas L., and Paul E. Bellair (2003). Explaining racial and ethnic differences in serious adolescent violent behavior. *Criminology*, 41: 709–49.

McPhee, Michele (2003a, November 30). A reformed thug? Cops skeptical of ex-gangster and his club. *New York Daily News*.

McPhee, Michele (2003b, November 24). Asian Eagles ganging up: Youth thugs stake out Chinatown, Flushing. *New York Daily News.*

McPhee, Michele (2005, January 5). Eastie gang linked to al-Qaeda. *Boston Herald.*

Media Awareness Project (2003). Former cop crossed line, destroyed it. Retrieved March 12, 2006, from: www.mapinc.org/drugnews/v03/n101/a06.html?182.

Merton, Robert K. (1938). Social structure and anomie. *American Sociological Review*, 3: 672–82.

Messerschmidt, James W. (1999). From Patriarchy to Gender: Feminist Theory, Criminology, and the Challenge of Diversity. In Meda Chesney-Lind and John M. Hagedorn (Eds.), *Female Gangs in America: Essays on Girls, Gangs and Gender* (pp. 118–32). Chicago: Lakeview.

Miller, Jody (1998). Gender and victimization risk among young women in gangs. *Journal of Research in Crime and Delinquency*, 35: 429–53.

Miller, Jody (2001). *One of the Guys: Girls, Gangs, and Gender.* New York: Oxford University Press.

Miller, Jody (2002). The Girls in the Gang: What We've Learned from Two Decades of Research. In C. Ronald Huff (Ed.), *Gangs in America III* (pp. 175–197). Thousand Oaks, CA: Sage.

Miller, Jody, and Rod K. Brunson (2000). Gender dynamics in youth gangs: A comparison of male and female accounts. *Justice Quarterly*, 17: 419–48.

Miller, Jody, and Scott H. Decker (2001). Young women and gang violence: Gender, street offending, and violent victimization in gangs. *Justice Quarterly*, 18: 115–40.

Miller, Walter B. (1958). Lower class culture as a generating milieu of gang delinquency. *The Journal of Social Issues*, 14: 5–19.

Miller, Walter B. (1975). Violence by youth gangs as a crime problem in major American cities. Washington, DC: U.S. Government Printing Office.

Miller, Walter B. (1980). Gangs, Groups, and Serious Youth Crime. In David Shichor and Delos H. Kelly (Eds.), *Critical Issues in Juvenile Delinquency* (pp. 115–38). Lexington, MA: Lexington.

Miller, Walter B. (1990). Why the United States Has Failed to Solve Its Youth Gang Problem. In Ronald C. Huff (Ed.), *Gangs in America* (ed. 1, pp. 263–87). Newbury Park, CA: Sage.

Miller, Walter B. (2001). *The Growth of Youth Gang Problems in the United States: 1970–1998.* Office of Juvenile Justice and Delinquency Prevention. Washington, DC: U.S. Department of Justice.

Montgomery, Michael (n.d.). Locked Down: Gangs in Super Max. Retrieved August 17, 2006, from: americanradioworks.publicradio.org/features/prisongangs/index.html.

Moore, Joan W. (1978). *Homeboys: Gangs, Drugs, and Prison in the Barrios of Los Angeles.* Philadelphia: Temple University Press.

Moore, Joan W. (1991). *Going Down in the Barrio: Homeboys and Homegirls in Change.* Philadelphia: Temple University Press.

Moore, Joan W., and John H. Hagedorn (1996). What Happens to Girls in the Gang? In Ronald C. Huff (Ed.), *Gangs in America* (ed. 2, pp. 205–218). Newbury Park, CA: Sage.

Moore, Joan W., and John H. Hagedorn (2001). *Female Gangs: A Focus on Research.* Juvenile Justice Bulletin. Washington, DC: U.S. Department of Justice, Office of Juvenile Justice and Delinquency Prevention.

Moore, Joan W., and James Diego Vigil (1989). Chicano gangs: Group norms and individual factors relating to adult criminality. *Azlan*, 18: 27–43.

Mozingo, Joe (August 2, 2006). 4 Los Angeles Latino gang members convicted of anti-black conspiracy. *Los Angeles Times.*

Murr, Andrew (July 17, 2006). A gang war with a twist: Gangbangers in L.A. on trial for deadly hate crime. *Newsweek.*

National Center for Children in Poverty (January 2006). *Basic Facts about Low-Income Children: Birth to Age 18.* New York: Columbia University, Mailman School of Public Health.

National Gang Crime Research Center (1997). The facts about female gang members. *Journal of Gang Research*, 4: 41–59.

National Institute of Corrections (1991). *Management Strategies in Disturbances and with Gangs/Disruptive Groups*. Washington, DC: U.S. Department of Justice.

National Youth Gang Center (2000). *1998 National Youth Gang Survey*. Washington, DC: U.S. Department of Justice, Office of Juvenile Justice and Delinquency Prevention.

Nurge, Dana M. (2003). Liberating yet limiting: The paradox of female gang membership. In Louis Kontos, David Brotherton, and Luis Barrios (Eds.), *Gangs and Society: Alternative Perspectives* (pp. 161–82). New York: Columbia University Press.

Office of Juvenile Justice and Delinquency Prevention (n.d.). Title V: Community prevention grants program. Retrieved March 14, 2006, from: ojjdp.ncjrs.gov/titlev/index.html.

OJJDP Model Programs Guide (n.d.a.). The Office of Juvenile Justice and Delinquency Prevention model programs guide (MPG). Retrieved March 21, 2006, from: www.dsgonline.com/mpg2.5/mpg_index.htm.

OJJDP Model Programs Guide (n.d.b.). Movimiento Ascendencia. Office of Juvenile Justice and Delinquency Prevention. Retrieved March 21, 2006, from: www.dsgonline.com/mpg2.5//TitleV_MPG_Table_Ind_Rec.asp?id=643.

Orlando-Morningstar, Dennise (1997). *Prison Gangs*. Special Needs Offenders Bulletin. Washington, DC: Federal Judicial Center.

Padilla, Felix M. (1992). *The Gang as an American Enterprise*. New Brunswick, NJ: Rutgers University Press.

Papachristos, Andrew V. (2005a). Gang world. *Foreign Policy*, March/April: 48–55.

Papachristos, Andrew V. (2005b). Interpreting inkblots: Deciphering and doing something about modern street gangs. *Criminology and Public Policy*, 4: 643–52.

Park, Robert E., and Ernest W. Burgess (1925/1984). *The City*. Chicago: University of Chicago Press.

Perkins, Useni Eugene (1987). *Explosion of Chicago's Black Street Gangs: 1900 to Present*. Chicago: Third World Press.

Peterson, Dana, Jody Miller, and Finn-Aage Esbensen (2001). The impact of sex composition on gangs and gang member delinquency. *Criminology*, 2: 411–39.

Peterson, Dana, Terrance J. Taylor, and Finn-Aage Esbensen (2004). Gang membership and violent victimization. *Justice Quarterly*, 21:793–815.

Peterson, Rebecca D. (2000a). Definitions of a gang and impacts on public policy. *Journal of Criminal Justice*, 28: 137–49.

Peterson, Rebecca D. (2000b). Gang subcultures and prison gangs of female youth. *Free Inquiry in Creative Sociology*, 28: 27–42.

Peterson, Rebecca D. (Ed.) (2004). *Understanding Contemporary Gangs in America: An Interdisciplinary Approach*. Upper Saddle River, NJ: Prentice-Hall.

Portillos, Edwardo Luis (1999). Women, Men, and Gangs: The Social Construction of Gender in the Barrio. In Meda Chesney-Lind and John M. Hagedorn (Eds.), *Female Gangs in America: Essays on Girls, Gangs and Gender* (pp. 232–44). Chicago: Lakeview.

Quicker, John C. (1999). The Chicana Gang: A Preliminary Description. In Meda Chesney-Lind and John M. Hagedorn (Eds.), *Female Gangs in America: Essays on Girls, Gangs and Gender* (pp. 48–56). Chicago: Lakeview.

Ralph, Paige, Robert J. Hunter, James W. Marquart, Steven J. Cuvelier, and Dorothy Merianos (1996). Exploring Differences Between Gang and Nongang Prisoners. In Ronald C. Huff (Ed.), *Gangs in America* (ed. 2, pp. 123–36). Newbury Park, CA: Sage.

Regulus, Thomas (1991). *Corrections Model*. Washington, DC: Office of Juvenile Justice and Delinquency Prevention.

Rice, Robert (1963). A reporter at large: The Persian Queens. *The New Yorker*, 39, 153–87.

Rivera, Beverly D., Ernest L. Cowles, and Laura G. Dorman (2003). An exploratory study of institutional change: Personal control and environmental satisfaction in a gang-free prison. *Prison Journal*, 83: 149–70.

RLUIPA.com (n.d.). An Internet Resource on the Religious Land Use and Institutionalized Persons Act. Retrieved February 28, 2006, from: www.rluipa.com/.

Rodriquez, Luis J. (1993). *Always Running: La Vida Loca: Gang Days in L.A.* New York: Touchstone.

Rosenfeld, Richard, Timothy M. Bray, and H. Arlen Egley Jr. (1999). Facilitating violence: A comparison of gang-motivated, gang-affiliated, and nongang youth homicides. *Journal of Quantitative Criminology*, 15, 495–516.

Ross, Edward Alsworth (1919). Socialization. *The American Journal of Sociology*, 24: 652–71.

Sampson, Robert J., Stephen Raudenbush, and Felton Earls (1997). Neighborhoods and violent crime: A multilevel study of collective efficacy. *Science*, 277: 918–24.

Sanday, Peggy (1990). *Fraternity Gang Rape: Sex, Brotherhood, and Privilege on Campus.* New York: New York University Press.

Sanders, W. (1994). *Gangbangs and Drive-Bys: Grounded Culture and Juvenile Gang Violence.* New York: Walter de Gruyter.

Schwartz, Audrey James (1989). Middle-class educational values among Latino gang members in East Los Angeles County high schools. *Urban Education*, 24: 323–42.

Scott, Gregory (2001). Broken windows behind bars: Eradicating prison gangs through ecological hardening and symbol cleansing. *Corrections Management Quarterly*, 5: 23–36.

Shakur, Sanyika (1993). *Monster: The Autobiography of an L.A. Gang Member.* New York: Grove.

Shaw, Clifford R., and Henry D. McKay (1942). *Juvenile Delinquency and Urban Areas.* Chicago: University of Chicago Press.

Sheldon, Randall G. (1991). A comparison of gang members and non-gang members in a prison setting. *The Prison Journal*, 71: 50–60.

Sheldon, Randall G., Ted Snodgrass, and Pam Snodgrass (1992). Comparing gang and non-gang offenders: Some tentative findings. *Gang Journal*, 2: 73–85.

Short, James F. (1989). Exploring Integration of Theoretical Levels of Explanation: Notes on Gang Delinquency. In Allen E. Liska, Marvin D. Krohn, and Steven F. Messner (Eds.), *Theoretical Integration in the Study of Deviance and Crime* (pp. 243–59). Albany: State University of New York Press.

Short, James F. (1990). New Wine in Old Bottles? Change and Continuity in American Gangs. In Ronald C. Huff (Ed.), *Gangs in America* (ed. 1, pp. 223–39). Newbury Park, CA: Sage.

Short, James F. (1996). Personal, Gang, and Community Careers. In Ronald C. Huff (Ed.), *Gangs in America* (ed. 2, pp. 221–40). Newbury Park, CA: Sage.

Short, James F. Jr., and Fred L. Strodtbeck (1965). *Group Process and Gang Delinquency.* Chicago: University of Chicago Press.

Siegel, Loren (2003). Gangs and the Law. In Louis Kontos, David Brotherton, and Luis Barrios (Eds.), *Gangs and Society: Alternative Perspectives* (pp. 213–27). New York: Columbia University Press.

Simpson, Colton (2005). *Inside the Crips: Life inside L.A.'s Most Notorious Gang.* New York: St. Martin's Press.

Spergel, Irving A. (1984). Violent youth gangs in Chicago: In search of social policy. *Social Service Review*, 58: 99–226.

Spergel, Irving A. (1990). Youth gangs: Continuity and change. In N. Morris and M. Tonry (Eds.), *Crime and Justice: An Annual Review of Research* (pp. 171–275). Chicago: University of Chicago Press.

Spergel, Irving A. (1995). *The Youth Gang Problem: A Community Approach*. New York: Oxford University Press.

Spergel, Irving, Ron Chance, Kenneth Ehrensaft, Thomas Regulus, Candice Kane, Robert Laseter, Alba Alexander, and Sandra Oh (1994). *Gang Suppression and Intervention: Community Models Research Summary*. Washington DC: U.S. Department of Justice, Office of Juvenile Justice and Delinquency Prevention.

Spergel, Irving, and G. David Curry (1990). Strategies and Perceived Agency Effectiveness in Dealing with the Youth Gang Problem. In Ronald C. Huff (Ed.), *Gangs in America* (ed. 1, pp. 288–309). Newbury Park, CA: Sage.

Spergel, Irving, and G. David Curry (1993). The National Youth Gang Survey: A Research and Development Process. In Arnold P. Goldstein and C. Ronald Huff (Eds.), *Gang Intervention Handbook* (pp. 359–400). Champaign, IL: Research Press.

Spergel, Irving, Kwai Ming Wa, Sungeun Ellie Choi, Susan Grossman, Ayad Jacob, Annot Spergel, and Elisa M. Barrios (2002). *Evaluation of the Gang Violence Reduction Project in Little Village: Final Report Summary*. School of Social Service Administration, University of Chicago. Retrieved March 12, 2006, from: www.icjia.state.il.us/public/pdf/Research-Reports/GVRP_Eval.pdf.

Starbuck, David, James C. Howell, and Donna J. Lindquist (2001). *Hybrid and Other Modern Gangs*. Juvenile Justice Bulletin. Washington, DC: U.S. Department of Justice, Office of Juvenile Justice and Delinquency Prevention.

Stone, Sandra S. (1999). Risk factors associated with gang joining among youth. *Journal of Gang Research*, 6: 1–18.

Stone, Sandra S., and Jeffrey Wycoff (1996). The extent and dynamics of gang activity in juvenile correctional facilities. *Journal of Gang Research*, 4: 1–8.

Streetgangs.com (n.d.). Media reports connected to the LA corruption scandal. Retrieved March 12, 2006, from: www.streetgangs.com/topics/rampart/.

Sullivan, Mercer L. (1989). *"Getting Paid": Youth Crime and Work in the Inner City*. Ithaca, NY: Cornell University Press.

Sullivan, Mercer L. (2005). Maybe we shouldn't study "gangs": Does reification obscure youth violence? *Journal of Contemporary Criminal Justice*, 21: 170–90.

Sun, Key (1993). The implications of social psychological theories of group dynamics for gang research. *Gang Journal*, 1: 39–44.

Sutherland, Edwin H. (1947). *Principles of Criminology*. Philadelphia: J. B. Lippincott.

Swart, William J. (1991). Female gang delinquency: A search for "acceptable deviant behavior." *Mid-American Review of Sociology*, 15: 43–52.

Taylor, Carl S. (1990). *Dangerous Society*. East Lansing: Michigan State University Press.

Taylor, Carl S. (1993). *Girls, Gangs, Women and Drugs*. East Lansing: Michigan State University Press.

Thomas, Christopher R., Charles E. Holzer III, and Julie A. Wall (2003). Serious delinquency and gang membership. *Adolescent Psychiatry*, 27: 59–81.

Thornberry, Terence P. (1987). Toward an interactional theory of delinquency, *Criminology*, 25: 863–92.

Thornberry, Terence P., and James H. Burch (1997). *Gang Members and Delinquent Behavior*. Juvenile Justice Bulletin. Washington, DC: Office of Juvenile Justice and Delinquency Prevention.

Thornberry, Terence P., Marvin D. Krohn, Alan J. Lizotte, and Deborah Chard-Wierschem (1993). The role of gangs in facilitating delinquent behavior. *Journal of Research in Crime and Delinquency*, 30: 55–87.

Thornberry, Terence P., Marvin D. Krohn, Alan J. Lizotte, Carolyn A. Smith, and Kimberly Tobin (2003). *Gangs and Delinquency in Developmental Perspective.* New York: Cambridge University Press.

Thrasher, Frederic M. (1927/1963). *The Gang: A Study of 1,313 Gangs in Chicago.* Chicago: University of Chicago Press.

Tita, George E., Jacqueline Cohen, and John Engberg (2005). An ecological study of location of gang "set space." *Social Problems*, 52: 272–99.

Tita, George E., K. Jack Riley, and Peter Greenwood (2003). From Boston to Boyle Heights: The Process and Prospects of a "Pulling Levers" Strategy in a Los Angeles Barrio. In Scott H. Decker (Ed.), *Policing Gangs and Youth Violence* (pp. 102–30). Belmont, CA: Thompson-Wadsworth.

Toy, Calvin (1992). A short history of Asian gangs in San Francisco. *Justice Quarterly*, 9: 647–65.

Trump, Kenneth S. (1996). The Community Response to Gangs. Section C: Gang Development and Strategies in Schools and Suburban Communities. In Ronald C. Huff (Ed.), *Gangs in America* (ed. 2, pp. 270–80). Newbury Park, CA: Sage.

Tsunokai, Glenn T., and Augustine J. Kposowa (2002). Asian gangs in the United States: The current stats of the research literature. *Crime, Law, and Social Change*, 37: 37–50.

Turley, Alan C. (2003). Female gangs and patterns of female delinquency in Texas. *Journal of Gang Research*, 10: 1–12.

U.S. Census (2004). Poverty: 2004 Highlights. Retrieved October 30, 2006, from: www.census.gov/hhes/www/poverty/poverty04/pov04hi.html.

U.S. Department of Homeland Security (n.d.a.). Immigration Act of May 26, 1924 (43 Statutes-at-Large 153). Retrieved August 15, 2006, from: www.uscis.gov/graphics/shared/aboutus/statistics/legishist/470.htm.

U.S. Department of Homeland Security (n.d.b.). 2004 Yearbook of Immigration Statistics. Retrieved July 6, 2005, from: uscis.gov/graphics/shared/statistics/yearbook/index.htm.

Valdez, Al (2000). Mara Salvatrucha: A South American Import. National Alliance of Gang Investigators Association. Retrieved February 20, 2006, from: www.nagia.org/Gang%20Articles/Mara%20Salvatrucha.htm.

Valdez, Avelardo (2003). Toward a Typology of Contemporary Mexican American Youth Gangs. In Louis Kontos, David Brotherton, and Luis Barrios (Eds.), *Gangs and Society: Alternative Perspectives* (pp. 12–40). New York: Columbia University Press.

Valentine, Bill, and Robert Shoeber (2000). *Gangs and Their Tattoos: Identifying Gangbangers on the Street and in Prison.* Boulder, CO: Paladin.

Van Ness, Asheley, Robert Fallon, and Sarah Lawrence (2006). *Senator Charles E. Shannon Jr. Community Safety Initiative 2006 Grant Program: Resource Guide: A Systematic Approach to Improving Community Safety.* Boston: Research and Policy Analysis Unit, Massachusetts Executive Office of Public Safety.

Venkatesh, Sudhir (1996). The Gang in the Community. In Ronald C. Huff (Ed.), *Gangs in America* (ed. 2, pp. 241–256). Newbury Park, CA: Sage.

Venkatesh, Sudhir (1999). Community-based interventions into street gang activity. *Journal of Community Psychology*, 27: 551–67.

Venkatesh, Sudhir (2003). A Note on Social Theory and the American Street Gang. In Louis Kontos, David Brotherton, and Luis Barrios (Eds.), *Gangs and Society: Alternative Perspectives* (pp. 3–11). New York: Columbia University Press.

Venkatesh, Sudhir Alladi (2002). *American Project: The Rise and Fall of a Modern Ghetto.* Cambridge, MA: Harvard University Press.

Vigil, James Diego (1988). *Barrio Gangs: Street Life and Identity in Southern California.* Austin: University of Texas Press.

Vigil, James Diego (1996). Street baptism: Chicano gang initiation. *Human Organization,* 55: 149–53.

Vigil, James Diego (2002). *A Rainbow of Gangs: Street Cultures in the Mega-City.* Austin: University of Texas Press.

Walker, Michael L., and Linda M. Schmidt (1996). The Community Response to Gangs. Section B: Gang Reduction Efforts by the Task Force on Violent Crime in Cleveland, Ohio. In C. Ronald Huff (Ed.), *Gangs in America* (ed. 1, pp. 263–369). Newbury Park, CA: Sage.

Walker, Robert (2005). Clothing. Gangs or Us. Retrieved March 10, 2006, from: www.gang-sorus.com/clothing.html.

Wang, Alvin Y. (1994). Pride and prejudice in high school gang members, *Adolescence,* 29: 279–91.

Wang, John Z. (2000). Asian gangs: New challenges in the 21st century. *Journal of Gang Research,* 8: 51–62.

Wang, John Z. (2002). A preliminary profile of Laotian/Hmong gangs: A California perspective. *Journal of Gang Research,* 9: 1–14.

Wang, Zheng (1995). Gang affiliation among Asian-American high school students: A path analysis of social developmental model. *Journal of Gang Research,* 2: 1–13.

Wang, Zheng (1999). An update of Asian gang affiliation: A preliminary analysis of the 1996 survey in 17 states. *Journal of Gang Research,* 5: 53–59.

Webb, Vincent J., and Charles M. Katz (2003). Policing Gangs in an Era of Community Policing. In Scott H. Decker (Ed.), *Policing Gangs and Youth Violence* (pp. 17–49). Belmont, CA: Thompson-Wadsworth.

Weisel, Deborah Lamm (2001). *Graffiti. Problem Oriented Guide for Police Series.* No. 9. Washington, DC: U.S. Department of Justice, Office of Community Oriented Policing Services.

Weisel, Deborah Lamm (2006). The evolution of street gangs: An examination of form and variation. In Arlen Egley, Jr., Cheryl L. Maxson, Jody Miller, and Malcolm W. Klein, (Eds.), *The Modern Gang Reader* (ed. 3, pp. 86–103). Los Angeles: Roxbury.

Wells, L. Edward, and Ralph A. Weisheit (2001). Gang problems in nonmetropolitan areas: A longitudinal assessment. *Justice Quarterly,* 18: 791–824.

Weston, Jim (1993). Community policing: An approach to youth gangs in a medium sized city. *Police Chief,* 60: 80–84.

Whitbeck, Les B., Dan R. Hoyt, Chen Xiaojin, and Jerry D. Stubbin (2002). Predictors of gang involvement among American Indian adolescents. *Journal of Gang Research,* 10: 11–26.

Whyte, William Foote (1943/1981). *Street Corner Society: The Social Structure of an Italian Slum,* ed. 3. Chicago: University of Chicago Press.

Wikipedia (n.d.). Gang. Retrieved March 10, 2006, from: en.wikipedia.org/wiki/Gang.

Williams, Katherine, G. David Curry, and Marcia I. Cohen (2002). Gang Prevention Programs for Female Adolescents: An Evaluation. In *Responding to Gangs: Evaluation and Research* (pp. 225–63). Washington, DC: U.S. Department of Justice, National Institute of Justice.

Williams, Stanley Tookie (2004). *Blue Rage, Black Redemption: A Memoir.* Pleasant Hill, CA: Damamli.

Wilson, John J. (2000). *Second Chances: Giving Kids a Chance to Make a Better Choice.* Juvenile Justice Bulletin. Washington, DC: U.S. Department of Justice, Office of Juvenile Justice and Delinquency Prevention.

Wilson, William Julius (1987). *The Truly Disadvantaged: The Inner City, the Underclass, and Public Policy.* Chicago: University of Chicago Press.

Winfree, L. Thomas Jr., Teresa Vigil Backstrom, and G. Larry Mays (1994). Social learning theory, self-reported delinquency, and youth gangs: A new twist on a general theory of crime and delinquency. *Youth and Society*, 26: 147–77.

Wood, Michelle, Michael J. Furlong, Jennifer A. Rosenblatt, Laurel M. Robertson, Frank Scozzari, and Todd Sosna (1997). Understanding the psychosocial characteristics of gang-involved youths in a system of care: Individual, family, and system correlates. *Education and Treatment of Children*, 20: 281–94.

Wooden, Wayne S., and Randy Blazak (2001). *Renegade Kids, Suburban Outlaws: From Youth Culture to Delinquency*. Belmont, CA: Wadsworth.

Yablonsky, Lewis (1962). *The Violent Gang*. New York: Irvington.

Yablonsky, Lewis (1997). *Gangsters: Fifty Years of Madness, Drugs, and Death on the Streets of America*. New York: New York University Press.

Yearwood, Douglas L., and Richard Hayes (2000). Overcoming problems associated with gang research: A standardized and systematic methodology. *Journal of Gang Research*, 7: 1–36.

Yoko, Baba (2001). Vietnamese gangs, cliques, and delinquents. *Journal of Gang Research*, 8: 1–20.

Zedlewski, Sheila R., Linda Giannerelli, Joyce Morton, and Laura Wheaton (April 2002). *Extreme Poverty Rising, Existing Government Programs Could Do More. New Federalism: National Survey of American Families*. Washington, DC: Urban Institute.

Zhang, Sheldon X. (2002). Chinese Gangs: Familial and Cultural Dynamics. In Ronald C. Huff (Ed.), *Gangs in America III* (pp. 219–36). Newbury Park, CA: Sage.

CASES AND STATUTES CITED

Brown v. Board of Education, 347 U.S. 483 (1954).
Brianna Stephenson v. Davenport Community, 110 F.3d 1303 (1997).
California Penal Code §§ 186.20–27.
Chicago v. Morales, 527 U.S. 41 (1999).
Ruiz v. Estelle, 460 U.S. 1042 (1980).
Haverty v. Commissioner of Correction, 437 Mass. 737 (2002).

INDEX

A

Academic gang research, 7–8
Adjunct gang membership, 76
Adult-dependent gang, 69
African American gangs. *See* Black American gangs
Age
  of females in gangs, 121–22
  of gang members, 12, 63–64
Age-graded gang, 64
Aging out, 82–83
Alcohol use, 91, 114
All-female gangs, rarity of, 119
Alliances of gangs, 107
Almighty Latin Kings and Queens Nation (ALKQN), 70, 102–3, 169
American Indian gangs, 112–14
  experiences of, 113–14
  history of, 112–13
American Notes (Dickens), 4
Anomie, 31
Anomie theory, 31
Aryan Brotherhood, 20, 139
Aryan Youth Movement (AYM), 115
Asbury, Herbert, 3
Asian Bloods, 111
Asian Crips, 111
Asian Eagles, 112
Asian Empire, 112
Asian gangs, 11, 99, 108–12
  contemporary, 111–12
  experiences of, 109–11
  history of, 108–9
Attachment, 51
Authority patterns in gangs, 65–66
Auxiliary gangs, 76, 122

B

Baby Avenues, 105
Barksdale, David, 106
Barrio gangs, 69–70
  in East Los Angeles, 39
Baton Rouge Partnership for Prevention of Juvenile Gun Violence, 155
Beating in, 75

Behavior. *See also* Criminal behavior
  organized criminal gangs and, 2
  rules of prohibited, 67
Behavioral typologies, 62–63
Black American gangs, 11, 99, 104–8
  Black experience, 107–8
  Chicago Black, 106–7
  history, 104–5
  Los Angeles Black, 105–6
Black Disciples, 107
Black Gangster Disciples (BGD), 107, 168, 169
Black Guerilla Family, 138, 139
Black migration, 36
Black P. Stone Nation, 106, 107, 168
Black P. Stone Rangers, 106, 135
Black Power Revolution, 105
"Blood in, blood out" oath, 138
"Blood oath" prison gangs, 141
The Bloods, 105, 106, 107
Body language, 79
Boston
  gangs in, 3, 4
  Mid-City Project in, 152
  Operation Ceasefire in, 160–61
Boyle, Gregory, 154
Boys and Girls Club of America's Gang Prevention through Targeted Outreach (GPTTP) program, 153
Brainstorming, 7
Brims, 105
Brown, Charlie, and his Peanuts pals, 1
Brown v. *Board of Education*, 6
Building Resources for the Intervention and Deterrence of Gang Engagement (BRIDGE), 154
Bush, George W., 159

C

Cabrini-Green Homes, 36
Cafeteria style offending, 91
Catch-22 of gang membership, 83

Caucasian gangs. *See* White gangs
Ceasefire strategies, 161
Changing urban centers as theme is gang history, 8
Chicago
  antigang ordinance in, 157
  black gangs in, 106–7
  gangs in, 3, 4, 5, 6, 7, 90
  Gang Violence Reduction Project in, 159–60
  Henry Horner Homes in, 33
  Latin Kings in, 102–3
  Robert Taylor Homes in, 6
Chicago Area Project (CAP), 152
Chicago School, 29–31
Chicago v. *Morales*, 157
Chicano gangs, 75
Chicano Pinto Research Project, 39
Cholo subculture, 101
Chronic gang cities, 7
  gangs in, 7
Civil gang injunctions in gang suppression, 155–56
Civil Rights Movement, 6
Classical school, 53–55
Clique structure, 63–65, 68
Coed gangs, 122
Coercive recruitment, 74
Cognitive purification, 120
Cohesion and group development, 71
Collective efficacy, 31
Colors, efforts to eliminate in prisons, 144
Commitment, 52
Community
  assessing, in prevention and intervention, 149–58
  mobilization of, in Spergel model, 151–52
  support in, 166–67
Community Prevention Grants Program, Title V of, 159
Community Resources against Street Hoodlum (CRASH) (Los Angeles), 155
Community risk, 46
Conditioning

189